BRUNEL'S
'Great Western'

BRUNEL'S
'Great Western'

DENIS GRIFFITHS

PSL

Patrick Stephens, Wellingborough

Dedication
This book is dedicated to the memory of James and May
Molyneux, my grand parents

First published 1985

British Library Cataloguing in Publication Data

Griffiths, Denis
   Brunel's 'Great Western'.
   1. Great Western (*Ship*)
   I. Title
   623.8′204   VM383.G7/

   ISBN 0-85059-743-9

*Patrick Stephens Limited is part of the
Thorsons Publishing Group.*

Text photoset in 10 on 11 Garamond by MJL Typesetting,
Hitchin, Herts. Printed in Great Britain on 115 gsm
Fineblade coated cartridge, and bound, by The Garden
City Press, Letchworth, Herts, for the publishers, Patrick
Stephens Limited, Denington Estate, Wellingborough,
Northants, NN8 2QD, England.

Contents

Author's acknowledgements

Any historical work requires considerable documentary research and this work is no exception. The author is indebted to many people at a number of museums and libraries who so freely gave of their time to offer help. Most are unknown by name and so my thanks must be expressed through the establishment in which they work. If I omit any individual or establishment it is not deliberate and I offer sincere apologies.

Acknowledgements are due to the staff members of the Science Museum Library, the Public Record Office, Kew, Bristol Record Office, the National Maritime Museum, University College Library, the British Library, Liverpool City Library, the Central Library Southampton, New York City Library, the City of New York Municipal Archives and Merseyside County Museum.

Individuals who have helped in my research: Mr Maby of Bristol University Library, Mr G. Langley of the Central Library in Bristol, Paul Elkin of Bristol City Museums, Miss C.A. Parker the Librarian at the Royal Academy of Arts, Mr R. Broughton of The Mersey Dock & Harbour Company, Mr J. Watson at the Local History Library in Greenwich and Mr Grahame Farr. My colleagues in the Mechanical, Marine and Production Engineering Department at Liverpool Polytechnic have offered advice, and criticism, whenever it has been sought.

Finally, but by no means least, I am extremely grateful to my wife, Patricia, and children, Sarah and Patrick, for the consideration they have shown over the years whilst I 'got the *Great Western* out of my system'.

Chapter 1
Prelude

The idea of using a steam engine to power a ship probably goes back to the infancy of the steam engine itself. It is known that Denis Papin, a Frenchman, considered the use of a steam pumping engine to propel a model boat, sometime towards the end of the 17th century. About 50 years later Jonathan Hulls patented an arrangement for a steam propelled tug-boat; however, no vessel was built. Later in the 18th century operational steam boats were demonstrated by a number of people. Amongst the more notable designers were John Fitch, an American, and Patrick Miller, a Scotsman. One of Miller's successful boats was engined by William Symington in 1788 and it was Symington who later engined the first reliable steamer to operate in Britain, *Charlotte Dundas* (1801). This vessel had a single cylinder engine of 22 inches bore driving a stern paddle wheel and she successfully towed barges on the Forth and Clyde canal. Meanwhile, in America, Robert Fulton was developing his own ideas on steam propulsion. Following trials with a number of smaller craft, in 1807, he built the paddle driven *Clermont* and demonstrated the advantages of steam driven ships to the Americans. *Clermont* operated on the Hudson River between New York and Albany and on her first trip averaged 4.7 miles per hour. After a refit at the end of her initial season *Clermont* returned to the Hudson River and operated without trouble for many years.[1]

During the second decade of the 19th century steam propulsion gradually found favour amongst shipowners, but the early growth was painfully slow. The year 1812 found the steamer *Comet* in service on the Clyde and later on the Forth. Of only four nominal horse-power, compared with the 20 horse-power of *Clermont*, *Comet* is considered to be the first commercial steamship to operate in European waters. She steamed between Glasgow and the Western Highlands on a regular schedule until wrecked in December 1820. The steamers which followed *Comet* operated only in coastal waters, but size and engine power gradually increased. In 1818 the steamer *Rob Roy* inaugurated the first regular sea-going steamship service when she carried mails and passengers on the Glasgow and Belfast route. Of 90 tons burthern, *Rob Roy* was propelled by a 30 horse-power engine. The first Royal Navy steam vessel followed a year later when the Admiralty introduced their 40 horse-power craft, also called *Comet*.[2]

One factor holding back the rapid growth of steam navigation was the not unnatural fear of fire and explosion. Accidents did occur and people were injured, but the increasing use of steam engines led to greater experience in their building and operation. Gradually, amongst people connected with ships and shipping the steamer became accepted, though not all were so readily convinced. Increased reliability and safety gave the prospective passenger and shipper more confidence in the ability of the steamship to transport him, or his cargo to a chosen destination in one piece. The seal of approval for the steamship would be its acceptance for the transport of mails deep sea. Such acceptance was not forthcoming until 1830.

Between 1820 and 1830 marine steam engines of higher powers were developed and placed in ships of greater and greater tonnage, which in turn were required to operate on longer and longer voyages. Marine engine builders prospered throughout this period, but none more so than the company owned and run by Henry Maudslay, later to become Maudslay, Sons and Field. Henry Maudslay was a brilliant and skilled engineer who designed and made some of the earliest machine tools. In 1830 he constructed, to the design of Marc Isambard Brunel, the block making machine for the Portsmouth Dockyard. Although he had previously manufactured many steam engines for stationary sites, his first marine steam engine is considered to have been that of ten horse-power made in 1814 for the 50 ton Thames steamer *Richmond*. Maudslay's reputation for high quality, reliable workmanship obtained for him many of the early Admiralty contracts for steam engines. In 1824 he supplied the 137 horse-power machinery for the second Royal Navy steamer HMS *Lightning*. Two years later Maudslay's firm manufactured a pair of side lever engines, with a combined output of 160 horse-power, for the steamer *Enterprise*, the first steam powered vessel to make the voyage to India[3].

Enterprise took 113 days to complete the journey from London to Calcutta, effectively destroying her owners' hopes of competing with the sailing ships belonging to the East India Company. The idea of, and hoped for, longer sea passages by steam vessels had, however, taken root. Following the success of HMS *Lightning*, the Navy constructed further steamships and by 1830 The Fleet included HMS *Meteor*, HMS *Messenger* and HMS *Echo*. These vessels replaced ageing sailing packets on the Falmouth to Mediterranean mail service when the Admiralty inaugurated the world's first deep-sea steam ship mail service in February 1830. This was not achieved without considerable opposition from some very influential people. When, in 1828, a request was made for the use of steamers to convey the mails between Malta and Corfu, it was rejected. In reply to the request, Lord Melville, then First Lord of the Admiralty, echoed the thoughts of many people connected with the shipping industry when he gave the official view: '. . . my Lord's Commissioners were unable to comply with the request of the Colonial Department, as they felt it their bounden duty, upon national and professional grounds, to discourage, to their utmost ability, the employment of steam vessels, as they consider that the introduction of steam was calculated to strike a fatal blow at the Naval supremacy of the Empire. . . '[4] At that time Britain

possessed an extensive sailing ship fleet and such protectionist sentiments carried much weight, not only amongst those with power but also amongst those who feared for their livelihoods. With a little foresight they, and others, would have realised that the development of a steam fleet could only increase trade, employment prospects and profits.

Fortunately by 1830 that realisation had dawned on 'my Lord's Commissioners' and the idea of utilising steam to power warships quickly found favour. During the first three years of that decade five 800 ton, 200 horse-power steam frigates were built; HMS *Dee*, HMS *Rhadamanthus*, HMS *Phoenix*, HMS *Salamander* and HMS *Medea*. These were amongst the largest and most powerful steamships then afloat and they represented the best in naval construction and marine engineering. Responsibility for the ship construction lay in the hands of Robert Seppings, who retired from his position as Surveyor to the Navy in 1832. Seppings had developed a system of ship construction which produced extremely strong and sound hulls, the same principles being employed until iron replaced wood as the major shipbuilding material. Maudslay, Sons and Field constructed the side lever engines which were considered to be amongst the finest marine engines of their time.

The growth of steam navigation during the early years of the 1830s was dramatic and extensive. Such growth may be ascribed to three main factors. The increase in trade demanded a greater tonnage of shipping. Steamships actually helped increase trade due to the greater reliability of the service that they offered. Secondly, comparisons between steam and sailing vessels illustrated the superiority of steam and encouraged owners to update their tonnage or lose business. Steamer services developed because, in many cases, steamships could transport goods faster, and more cheaply, than land or canal transport. Thirdly the improvement in the efficiency and reliability of marine steam engines encouraged growth.

These factors had an influence upon each other. For instance, the demand for marine engines resulted in more competition between the growing number of engine builders which, in turn, resulted in each builder improving his product so that he might remain competitive. Only one steamship exceeding 69 tons was in commercial service in Britain during the year 1814. Ten years later this had risen to 116 with a total tonnage of

11,947, and during the next decade the figures almost quadrupled with 430 steamships being in service, the tonnage reaching 44,090. (The two latter sets of figures also include vessels built for the Admiralty.)[5] Thus it can be seen that, by 1835, the steamship had improved its position considerably; it had actually replaced the sailing ship on many more important services. Such services were, however, basically coastal and the commercial steamship was still tied to the continental shelf. Fortunately, some men had other ideas and wanted to free the steamer from its confined waters to trail black threads of smoke across the oceans of the world. The first, and biggest, prize was the Atlantic.

It must be appreciated that passengers and goods had crossed the Atlantic for hundreds of years in ships of one form or another. The usual routine was for a ship to be advertised as available for the transportation of passengers and goods between particular ports. When cargo space and/or berths were full the vessel would depart, earlier if the master had been able to offer suitable inducement. Such a situation was not ideal as it might take weeks before the ship was ready to sail. For the passenger or cargo shipper in a hurry there had to be something better. In 1816 an enterprising American shiping company decided to provide that better service. The Black Ball Line built a number of fast sailing ships to operate a regular scheduled service between New York and Liverpool. On the first day of every month a ship would leave Liverpool for New York, with a similar operation in the opposite direction. Sailings actually commenced in January 1818 and the ships were destined to make money as well as history. The first ships were not large, about 430 tons with two decks and three masts, but they offered convenience, regularity of sailing (though not of arrival), reasonably good food and acceptable accommodation. Naturally, the service prospered and the enterprise attracted competition. The Black Ball Line soon offered a twice monthly service.

By 1836 regular sailings were provided by the Black Ball, Red Star, Black X, Swallow-Tail and Dramatic lines with a number of smaller concerns also offering passages. All sailing ships on these liner services were worked very hard and they were well loaded, if cargoes happened to be available. Each ship's master received a percentage of the freight, passenger and mail receipts, thus giving every inducement to ensure a well loaded

ship. Because of the exacting operating conditions the service life of a vessel on that Atlantic run was comparatively short. In fact, one in six of the earlier packet liners was wrecked, presumably due to being pressed so hard.[6] In spite of this the packet liners thrived.

Fares were set at 35 guineas for saloon passengers and, although this represented a considerable sum of money at that time, there was always a steady stream of willing takers. The majority of vessels operated on the New York run, with weekly sailing to, and from, Liverpool by various companies. A similar arrangement existed for London. On the American side of the Atlantic, Boston and Philadelphia acted as home ports for other services. Although the sailing date was fixed and well advertised, no such guarantee could be offered regarding the day of arrival. Prevailing winds and currents assisted the eastbound crossings and passage times in this direction were, generally, less than for the return. In 1839 the average crossing time from New York to Liverpool was 22 days 1 hour. The fastest passage that year was 17 days whilst the slowest, a staggering 36 days. Running to the west that year the packet liners averaged 34 days 1¼ hours between the same ports. The fastest time, in that direction, was 22 days with the slowest lasting some 26 days longer[7] In 1838 the sailing packet *Cambridge* took over 42 days to complete the crossing from Liverpool to New York. Her chart shows that she had covered upwards of 5,000 miles, nearly 2,000 miles more than the normal distance between these ports. For all their organisation and planning the packet ship owners were very much at the mercy of the weather and they had no way to combat it. Having spent, in 1832, 54 days on the packet ship *St Leonard* heading west, and a further 32 days in *Westminster* returning to Plymouth, Junius Smith wrote to his nephew: 'Thirty-two days from New York to Plymouth and forty to London is no trifle. Any ordinary steamer would have run it, the weather we had, in fifteen days with ease.'[8] At the time Junius Smith, an American businessman with interests on both sides of the Atlantic, was trying to attract backers for a scheme to run steamers between the old and new worlds. In the same letter he added, 'I shall not relinquish this project until I find it absolutely impracticable.'

That early scheme of Smith's called for four steamers operating between England and America, these, he summised, would replace twelve of the sailing packets. His ideas were not well received in either country, but he doggedly persisted. It took a number of years of earnest meetings with bankers, merchants and ship-owners before, in October 1835, he issued his first prospectus. Throughout those years he faced constant ridicule and opposition, particularly from people with a vested interested in the sailing ship. His initial prospectus did not attract the support it needed and was soon followed by a second. It took a third prospectus before sufficient capital had been pledged to bring, in 1836, the British and American Steam Navigation Company into existence. Although he was unaware of it at the time, Junius Smith, through his persistence, had spurred other like minded people into action and Atlantic steam navigation schemes increased in number. His perseverence and eventual success, short lived though it was to be, have surely earned for Junius Smith the honour and title of 'Father of Atlantic Steam Navigation'.

Before Smith advocated his Atlantic plan steam powered vessels had crossed that water, the first of these being *Savannah*, if she can be classed as a steamship. Little more than a square rigged sailing ship with a small steam engine driving paddle wheels, she made the trip from Savannah to Liverpool during May and June 1819. That crossing took 29½ days but the paddles were only in use for a total of 84 hours during that period. The paddles, when not in operation, could be folded and stowed clear of the water. She carried neither passengers nor cargo and, despite being the first vessel with a steam propulsion unit to make a crossing of the Atlantic she was not a serious attempt at Atlantic steam navigation.

It was another fourteen years before the next black thread of smoke from a steamship's funnel threaded its way from America to Britain. This time a Canadian vessel *Royal William* provided the air pollution. She made the crossing between Quebec and London but, again, it was not a serious attempt to institute a trans-atlantic steamship service but a simple business manoeuvre to obtain a better price for the vessel. *Royal William* was built at Quebec in 1831 for a consortium of businessmen going under the title of the Quebec and Halifax Steam Navigation Company. Amongst the registered shareholders were three Cunard brothers from Halifax, Nova Scotia, one of whom was called Samuel. The service between Quebec and Halifax was not a success and *Royal William* was sold to a small group of the company's shareholders. Their new venture to Boston was no more successful and the group decided to dispose of the ship. Considering that a better price might be had in Europe they had *Royal William* made ready for an Atlantic crossing. With seven saloon passengers and two more in steerage, as well as a small amount of cargo the 363 ton *Royal William* left Quebec on August 4 1833. Following a stop for coal, at Pictou, Nova Scotia, the little ship arrived off Cowes, Isle of Wight, three weeks later. Eventually, *Royal William* arrived at Gravesend on September 11. The complete trip had taken longer than the packet ships were averaging and could not be classed as a success in steam navigation terms. A week after arrival in London *Royal William* was sold, at a profit, and had no further connection with any Atlantic crossing.

The first steam engined vessel to cross the Atlantic the hard way, east to west, was reputedly the Dutch ship *Curacao*. She made a 28 day crossing between Holland and Surinam in April and May 1827. For twelve of those days her small steam engine was driving the paddle wheels. During the next two years *Curacao* made two further round trips before she was converted into a warship. The Atlantic crossings of *Curacao*, though not entirely under steam, are significant as she was the first steam powered ship actually laid down and built for service across the Atlantic. However, it was to have been the North Atlantic not South Atlantic and her original owners were not Dutch.

In 1824 Maurice Fitzgerald and a group of business friends decided that there was money to be made in sending steamships on regular voyages to America. Calling themselves The American and Colonial Steam Navigation Company, they issued a prospectus requesting funds for the operation of these services. The prospectus outlined a plan for regular steamship crossings between Valentia, on the south-west coast of Ireland, and Halifax with the route extended to New York. Small steamers were to pick up passengers at ports on the English and Irish coasts and transfer them to the larger Atlantic vessels. A similar service between Valentia and Jamaica was also contemplated. Money was not forthcoming but, nonetheless, the company went ahead and ordered its first ship, which was named *Calpe* when launched at Dover in September 1825. With the realisation that it could not operate the intended service, the company laid aside its plans and disposed it its only asset. Purchased by the Dutch Government *Calpe* became the *Curacao* and eventually steamed on the Atlantic, though a little to the south of its originally intended track.[9]

Some years later, actually in 1836, the title of The American and Colonial Steam Navigation Company appeared again. This time the organisation concerned planned to operate steamships between Liverpool and New York; a service between the west coast of Ireland and New York would also be provided, if found to be desirable. This new company was to be managed by the City of Dublin Steam Packet Company and its prospectus called for a capital of £600,000 in £50 shares.[10] Needless to say the plan failed, but the same City of Dublin Steam Packet Company, a little late, formed the Transatlantic Steam Ship Company with the same objective, a steamship service between Liverpool and New York.

The Valentia scheme did have a champion, namely Dr Dionysius Lardner, renowned authority on the steam engine and many other things. Lardner was a leading member of The British Association for the Advancement of Science and lectured widely on many aspects of steam power, including railways and steam navigation. On a number of occasions, one of the first being at Liverpool during December 1835, he ventured to express his opinions upon the subject of 'Steam Communications with America'. During the course of the lectures he outlined the reasoning behind the choice of Valentia as the most suitable port from which to begin an Atlantic steam passage. His ideas were based upon the coal consumption figures for steamers then in service and upon the faulty premises that to increase the size of a ship, to allow the carriage of more coal for a longer voyage, would require a proportionate increase in the power of the machinery. In short, he considered that doubling the size of the ship necessitated a doubling of the engine power. (This matter was raised by Isambard Kingdom Brunel at Lardner's lecture in Bristol the following year. Brunel had different ideas on the subject.)

Lardner's figures were based upon the fuel consumptions of a number of steamships, mainly engaged in the coastal trade but also including those for HMS *Medea* and HMS *Dee*. HMS *Medea* was considered to be the most economical steamship afloat at that time and so any argument based upon statistics provided by her carried considerable weight. Lardner concluded that the best adapted vessel for a voyage to the United States would be one of 800 tons and powered by an engine of 200 horse-power. Such a ship would be able to stow 400 tons of coal, but a 200 horse-power engine would require 20 tons of coal daily which, allowing 100 tons of coal for contingencies, resulted in a steaming period of 15 days. Given the daily distance steamed by the Mediterranean steam packets to be 170 miles the distance which could be steamed in 15 days was 2,550 miles. Not enough to get from Liverpool to New York, or even Bristol to New York, direct.

In advocating the Valentia scheme he went on to make the following comment: 'As to the project, however, which was announced in the newspapers of making the voyage directly from New York to Liverpool, it was, he had no hesitation in saying, perfectly chimerical, and they might as well talk of making a voyage from New York or Liverpool to the moon'.[11] It is for this metaphorical statement that Dr Dionysius Lardner is best known, at least in terms of maritime history. The statement attracted much comment, most of it hostile, and the doctor later attempted to modify his views or, as he saw it, correct the misinterpretations. At a meeting in Bristol during 1836 he offered an amended view in that he '. . . considered such a voyage practicable, but he wished to point out that which would remove the possibility of a doubt, because if the first attempt failed it would cast a damp upon the enterprise and prevent a repetition of the attempt.'[12] Perhaps then, Lardner would have been better served if he had adhered to the figures and reasoning, no matter how speculative, rather than resorting to the imprudent use of metaphors. In fairness to the good doctor, it should be added that he made many contributions to engineering in general and the steam engine in particular. One such offering was a device to automatically measure and record marine engine operating details including boiler and condenser pressure, boiler water level and rotational speed of the paddle wheels. This work was performed under the patronage of The British Association for the Advancement of Science which was desirous of investigating the performance and operation of steam vessels. Although not a complete success when fitted in the steamer *Tagus*, belonging to the Peninsular Steam

Navigation Company, it was the precursor of the electronic data logger used today to record the operating details of a ship's machinery[13]

Notwithstanding the opposition to a direct steamship service between England and America, in 1835 two sparks lit the tinderbox which was to set alight fires in the boilers of numerous magnificent liners later to ply the Western Ocean. Junius Smith provided one of those sparks, the other came from Isambard Kingdom Brunel.

Isambard Kingdom Brunel by J.C. Horsley (Courtesy City of Bristol Museum and Art Gallery).

Chapter 2
Birth of a ship

Credit for the initial idea of steam navigation between Bristol and New York is, through legend, given to Isambard Kingdom Brunel principally because of the biography written by his son. The story goes that, during October 1835, Brunel was meeting with a group of directors of the Great Western Railway Company at Radley's Hotel in Bridge Street, Blackfriars, when the comment was made that the proposed line between London and Bristol exceeded in length any railway line then contemplated. Brunel countered with the remark, 'Why not make it longer, and have a steamboat go from Bristol to New York?'[1] Apparently, this suggestion was treated as a joke by those present with the exception of Thomas Guppy, who found the idea interesting. The two men discussed the proposition long into the night becoming more enthusiastic as time moved on. Like Brunel, 38 year old Guppy was an engineer but he also had considerable business experience and was, therefore, well able to consider the financial implications of the scheme — a matter Brunel frequently neglected in many of his propositions.

Whether, or not, such a suggestion was actually made in those terms is not known, nor does it matter, although it would make a story-book beginning to the project. The certainty is that it was Brunel and Guppy who initiated the discussions which brought about the Great Western Steam Ship Company. Having agreed upon the feasibility of an Atlantic steamship line between Bristol and New York, the two men set about canvassing support from fellow members of the railway company and other associates. Three board members took an interest as soon as they realised that Brunel's proposition was serious, they were Mr Robert Scott, Mr Thomas Pycroft and Mr Robert Bright. These were closely followed by Captain Christopher Claxton, a half-pay naval officer who held the public post of Quay Warden at Bristol. Brunel and Claxton had been firm friends since 1832 when Brunel was invited, by the Bristol Dock Company, to survey the Floating Harbour with a view to its operational improvement.[2]

These men formed a provisional committee whose first task was to draw-up and issue a prospectus. Because of the prevalent mania for steamship project speculation and for fear of being copied by another concern, the prospectus was neither printed nor advertised. Six handwritten copies were made and held by as many interested gentlemen. Considering that their scheme was a very good one, the committee felt that there would be no difficulty in attracting subscribers from amongst those 'who had an interest in the well-doing of Bristol, and were likely to be earnest in following up the measure properly'.[3] Many shares were taken up but, apart from Brunel's large holding, they were generally taken by residents of Bristol and Bath. This rather parochial interest emanated from the failure to widely advertise the prospectus and was, perhaps, one of the reasons for the company not fulfilling its initial promise. Certainly the clandestine circulation of the prospectus had the result of limiting the number of shares actually taken up. By the time the list closed and the first general meeting of the subscribers convened, on March 3 1836, only about 1,500 of the 2,500 £100 shares had been allocated. A £5 deposit needed to be paid on each share with calls of £5 or £10 being made, up to the full £100 value of the shares, whenever capital demands necessitated it.

Although not realised at the time, the limit on maximum capital from the 2,500 £100 shares was to play an important part in the affairs of the company.

The handwritten prospectus called for two ships of about 1,200 tons burthen and 400 horse-power each. It also precluded the convening of a meeting of subscribers until at least half of the 2,500 shares had been taken. Some people were, understandably, loath to commit their money until certain questions as to the practicality of the venture had been answered. Claxton, by means of a letter published in the *Bristol Mirror* of December 19 1835, hoped to satisfy some of the queries being raised in the commercial quarter of Bristol. Concern had been expressed about the availability and cost of coal at New York. Claxton supplied figures which indicated that prices fell within the limits expressed in the prospectus. However, events were not to prove so straight-forward and most coal had to be shipped in by the company itself. A main anxiety was that regarding the beam of the proposed vessels, as this exceeded the width of the locks to the Bristol Floating Harbour. Optimistically, Claxton expressed the belief that the lock gates would be widened before the first ship was ready, or failing this, that there would be no difficulty in replacing the paddle wheels outside the Floating Harbour. Things were not to prove as easy as Claxton imagined.

Whilst copies of the handwritten prospectus circulated amongst the merchants and gentlemen of Bristol and Bath, Claxton, Guppy and William Patterson, a Bristol shipbuilder of repute, made a tour of British steamship ports, including Glasgow and Liverpool. They had been given the brief to investigate steamship operations and to gather sufficient facts as might be useful in formulating a more accurate prospectus. Claxton, through his naval contacts, was able to gain access to the drawings of Oliver Lang, then Chief Shipwright at the Royal Naval Dockyard, Woolwich. The assistance given by Lang and Sir William Symons, Surveyor to the Navy, proved to be extremely valuable in the building of the first ship.[4]

Upon conclusion of the tour the group presented a report, dated January 1 1836, incorporated in which were the results of their investigation together with the recommendation that consideration be given to the construction of larger vessels as these would prove to be more advantageous than smaller ones.[5] This recommendation came from Brunel[6] and the reasoning behind it had great significance for Atlantic and other oceanic steam navigation. Brunel stated: 'It is well known that the proportionate consumption of fuel decreases as the dimensions and power of the engines are increased, and consequently that a large engine can be worked more economically than a small one. The resistance of vessels on the water does not increase in proportion to their tonnage. This is easily explained — the tonnage is increased as the cube of their dimensions, whilst the resistance increases about as their squares; so that a vessel of double the tonnage of another, capable of containing an engine of twice the power, does not really meet with double the resistance. Speed, therefore, will be greater with the large vessel, or the proportionate power of the engine and consumption of fuel may be reduced. This accounts for the success of large vessels over small ones.'[7] That fundamental statement was in opposition to the arguments put forward by Lardner and showed, conclusively and simply, that a steamship service across the Atlantic was a practical proposition.

Perhaps because of Brunel's reasoning, the power plant for the planned vessels was reduced from 400 horse-power to 300 horse-power. At that time, steamships belonging to the Royal Navy had a tonnage to power ratio of four tons to one horse-power and the proposed vessels would thus have the same ratio. Following the report came a new prospectus which was circulated to subscribers prior to the first general meeting held on March 3 1836. Two steamships of 1,200 tons and 300 horse-power, costing in the region of £35,000 each, would be required to perform twelve round trips each year between Bristol and New York; space for 100 first class passengers, at 35 guineas per crossing, and 80 second class passengers, at 20 guineas per crossing, would be provided. The revenue from this and the small quantity of freight which could be carried would provide an income likely to yield a dividend of 15 per cent on the cost. Further ships for the Bristol line, or for additionally formed lines, were not precluded and, if necessary, the issue of new shares could be made to increase the capital of the company.

The first official business of the company took place at that initial general meeting. Having dispensed with queries regarding the prospectus and committee report, the meeting set about appointing the company officers.

Directors were to be Peter Maze, Thomas Kington, William Edward Acraman, Robert Bright, Henry Bush, Thomas Richard Guppy, Robert Scott, Thomas Bonville Were and Christopher Claxton; all, with the exception of Claxton, local businessmen. The trustees, who became the 'subscribing owners' as far as ship registration purposes were concerned, were John Harford, Joseph Cookson, John Vining and Thomas Kingsbury. The first three were consequently named as 'subscribing owners' of the first ship. The Great Western Steam Ship Company, as the organisation was to be called, had been formed as a joint stock company and that first meeting resolved, unanimously, to make the concern a 'large partnership' for the term of 31 years, rather than a public company.[8] By classifying themselves as such, the company was not required to hold public meetings. This privilege they exercised on a number of occasions in order to avoid public debate on contentious issues which might have resulted in financial damage.

Although, from the time of that first general meeting, the company was known by its full title of the Great Western Steam Ship Company, it did not officially come into being until established by the deed of settlement on June 2 1836. The deed embodied the 'rules' for the operation of the company and amongst its clauses were those concerned with the extension of the partnership and capital, as well as the transfer of shares. In some respects the deed turned out to be too restrictive, particularly when, at a later date, the company considered it desirable to increase its share capital.

Between the first general meeting and the establishment of the company its officials were not idle. They determined not to build their first vessel by contract as a contract would have limited their ability to incorporate any modifications found to be necessary during construction. As it turned out, additional hull strengthening was found to be desirable and this had to be incorporated whilst the frames were in the course of erection.[9] At Brunel's suggestion, a 'building committee' was selected to guide the construction, whilst William Patterson superintended the building. This committee consisted of Brunel, Guppy and Claxton and, together with Paterson, would meet at least once every week in order to discuss the design details of the unique ship they were in the process of creating. The

'building committee' appears to have been well balanced including as it did an engineer, a businessman/engineer and a seafarer, these men together with Patterson, the practical shipbuilder, were admirably suited to the challenging task in hand; the designing and construction of the first, true ocean going steamship.

William Patterson, in whose abilities Claxton had the utmost confidence and who had an open mind when it came to the introduction of new ideas[10], ran a shipbuilding business at Wapping, Bristol. Actually he was in partnership with John Mercer, but Mercer appears to have been less involved than Patterson. Understandably, the 'building committee' turned to Patterson for the use of his yard in which to construct the first ship. The yard, situated by the Princes Street bridge, allowed the slipway to be positioned so as to take advantage of the additional width of water resulting from the confluence of the River Frome and the Floating Harbour. (A plaque on a warehouse wall marks the position of the slipway.) Without ceremony, the keel of the first ship was laid during the early part of June 1836, shortly after the deed of settlement established the company. Brunel desired that the ship be larger than he had originally intended but, influenced by Patterson's concern regarding her stability, the directors decided, at first, to leave any increase in size to the second vessel. (The tonnage was increased when it was considered advantageous to instal an engine of increased power.)[11] Before the keel laying actually took place the directors had also decided to build only one vessel initially, leaving the construction of subsequent ships to be decided upon when the practicability of the line had been established. Though a sensible step in view of the originality of the project the unforseen consequences worked to the detriment of the company.

Brunel, who gave his services free, undertook responsibility for selection of the engine builders and this matter occupied him for some considerable time. Tenders were invited, for a steam plant of about 400 horse-power, from a number of the most eminent marine engine builders of the day. Three tenders were received, from Messrs Winwood, a local firm; Messrs Fawcett and Company; and from Messrs Maudslay, Sons and Field. Brunel carefully considered each tender with regard to price, the reputation and workmanship of the firm and, primarily, the record of that firm in the production of large marine engines. The latter factor became of critical importance as the machinery required would be the largest and most powerful yet built for a ship. This factor swayed Brunel and his recommendation to the Board of Directors was that Maudslay, Sons and Field should be awarded the contract.[12] Maudslay's had built the largest marine engines in service at that time and Brunel also knew that they had built more large engines than any other firm. In a letter to the board, after scrutinising the tenders, Brunel wrote: 'In considering the three tenders for the supply of marine engines for your first vessel, which you have submitted to me for my opinion, I have assumed that the interests of the company are paramount, and that all feelings of partiality towards any particular manufacturer or any local interest must yield to the absolute necessity, in this the first and the boldest attempt of the kind yet made, of not merely satisfying yourselves that you will obtain a good engine, but also of taking all those means of securing the best which in the eyes of the public may be unquestionable. In this view of the case, if you agree with me, I think you will

consider that, provided the prices are fair individually, the relative amount of the tender is of secondary consideration.' Showing his concern that the first voyage must be a success he went on to add, 'You will remember, also, that it will be the longest voyage yet run; that in the event of unfavourable weather a total failure might be the result of the engine not working to its full power, or consuming too great a quantity of coals — a very common occurrence with engines apparently well made, after six or seven day's constant work; and, lastly, that the future success of the boat as a passenger ship — nay, even of the company's boats generally, and, to a great extent, and for some time, the reputation of Bristol as a steamboat station, may depend upon the success of this first voyage. It is indispensible, therefore, to secure as far as possible a machine that shall be perfection in all its detail from the moment of its completion.'

Nobody could accuse Brunel of not having the best interests of the Great Western Steam Ship Company at the forefront of this thinking. His concern that the first voyage must progress smooothly and be a success is very much apparent. The letter concludes with Brunel's

Fig 1: Map of Bristol Harbour and River Avon, 1838.

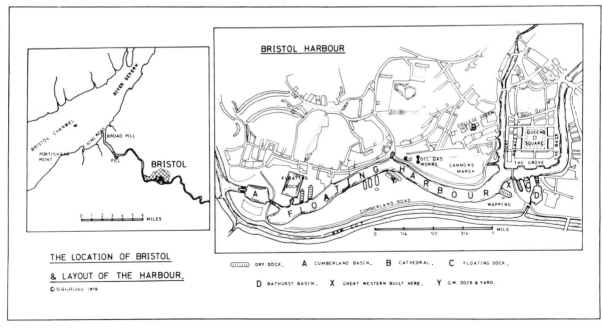

recommendation: '. . . With these facts before you, it remains only for you to consider how far you agree with me in the conclusions that I have come to, and which I have no hesitation in expressing — that I think you will be safest, in the peculiar case of the first ship, in the hands of the parties who have had most experience, and that Messrs Maudslay are those persons. Their price is, I think, moderate.' The board did agree and Maudslay, Sons and Field were awarded the contract for the machinery. (The specification for the engines is given in Appendix 1.)

Having laid the, then, largest keel in the world without attendant ceremony, the company was not about to be deprived a second time of ritual and consequential publicity. The afternoon of Thursday, July 28, 1836, saw the raising of the stern frame at the yard of Patterson and Mercer. On that day vessels in the immediate vicinity of the building yard were gaily decorated wtih flags and bunting, one particularly so as she accommodated the directors and their friends. At half past three o'clock, a signal from Claxton started the proceedings and, amidst the sound of cannons discharging and loud cheering from the assembled throng, the stern frame was raised and fixed in its final position. Following the ceremony, which lasted no more than half an hour, the directors and their friends repaired to a loft within the shipyard wherein a cold collation had been laid out for their refreshment. Many speeches followed, all praising the enterprise and those connected with it; with some casting disparaging remarks at similar ventures afoot in London and Liverpool.

Prior to this event many people had expressed amazement at the size of the projected ship, there having been nothing of comparable magnitude built before. To construct such a vessel in the Floating Harbour at Bristol was considered, by many, to be the height of folly due to the tortuous and narrow path of the Avon from Bristol to the sea. Answering these critics, in a speech after the ceremony, Claxton said: '. . . There are people — and among them, some who have pretentions of scientific information — who are sadly puzzled to discover how we are to get the ship into the river, and then again how we are to get our ship round its corners. Their enquiries, it seems, have reached the builder's yard and there the wags — for there are wags among shipwrights as well as among other people — have solved their doubts by informing them that the ship is to be made with a joint in the middle [laughter][7]; and again that she is to be constructed on the principle of a collapsing apparatus, so that she may be lengthened, or shortened, at pleasure, and when asked how it could be done, I believe they have been told that the beams were to be hollowed out so as to act like the tubes of a telescope [increased laughter][7]; and strange to say this had been believed.'[13] This says a lot for Claxton's sense of humour, for he would have been well aware that some of the people around the table with him had little, or no, technical knowledge and were as bemused as others when it came to solving the problem of river passage. Another aspect of Claxton's character is illustrated by the fact that he, and he alone of all the assembled mass, left the soiree, then being entertained by three Italian musicians, and went to the Bathurst Hotel where a large body of the shipwrights were regaling themselves. Always a popular man he received three hearty cheers on arrival, but was cheered the more when he ordered an extra allowance of strong beer for the men.

A month later The British Association for the Advancement of Science held its sixth meeting at a venue in Bristol. The fact that Doctor Dionysius Lardner was to lecture on the subject of 'Steam Navigation' added interest to the proceedings and ensured that at least one session would be well attended. Lardner presented the same case he had offered at previous lectures and, using the same statistics, reached the identical conclusion. He did, however, avoid repeating his earlier assertion that Atlantic steam navigation was 'chimerical'. *The Times* of August 27 1836 reported the meeting and printed some of the comments made by Brunel and Joshua Field, the Field of Maudslay, Sons and Field. Both pointed out that his (Lardner's) conclusion was based on information gathered from old vessels, not information which was more up to date and scientific. Unfortunately, no detailed report of the discussion between the opposing factions appears to have survived.

It has been postulated that Lardner's Bristol lecture actually harmed the Great Western Steam Ship Company by deterring potential investors from taking shares in the enterprise. This is not so. The company had, just prior to its first general meeting in March 1836, closed

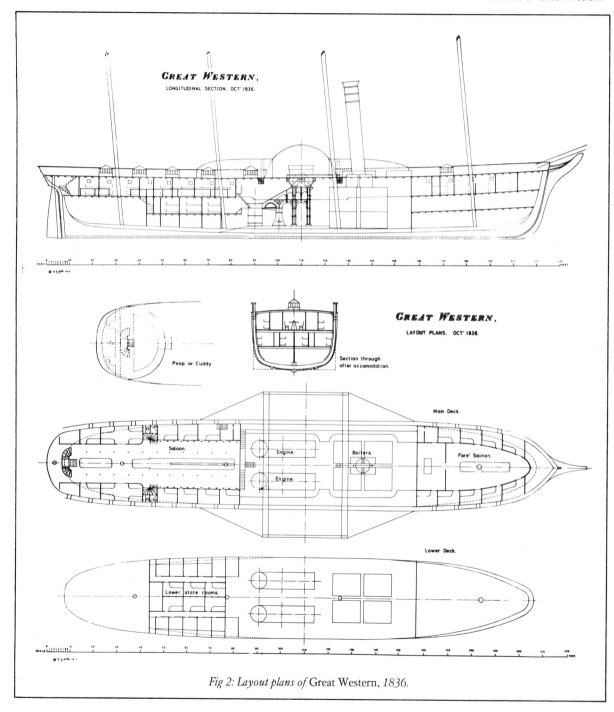

Fig 2: Layout plans of Great Western, *1836.*

the share list with some 1,700 of the 2,500 shares allocated, and so that Bristol meeting can have had no effect upon the share capital of the company. Possibly Lardner's earlier tirades at Dublin and Liverpool, during the latter part of 1835, influenced some people to question the feasibility of the scheme, but not so the Bristol lecture. By time it took place, the die had been cast, the share list was closed.

Whilst the hull of the ship rose on the stocks at Wapping, construction of the machinery progressed at the Lambeth works of Maudslay, Sons and Field. Brunel made regular visits to the works in order to see for himself the progress being made. This was necessary, not only from a professional point of view, but also for financial reasons as payment for the machinery had been arranged in instalments; each instalment becoming due at a particular stage in the construction. In a letter to Claxton, dated April 4 1837, Brunel reported that the work was in such a forward state as to justify payment of the second instalment.[14] The original intention had been for the ship to make its first voyage in the autumn of 1837 and, in the same letter, Brunel expressed his optimism that the voyage could still be made despite the increase in engine size and power which had been requested in order to match the increase in tonnage of the ship. The engines were of unprecedented size and must have presented many problems in the casting and machining of the large components involved. However, as will be seen, when completed, they operated to perfection.

During the early stages of hull construction a decision had been made to enlarge the vessel by over one hundred tons, and also to change the nature of the accommodation offered. Only a single class of berth would be available, with the charge levied being dependent upon the part of the ship occupied. A layout plan, dated October 1836, is shown in figs 2a and 2b, — the original from which these are redrawn is in the Science Museum Library, London. The drawings illustrate the earliest proposed layout for the ship. Although the overall dimensions remained unchanged the cabin arrangements were altered during construction with a poop, or cuddy, and a fo'c'sle also being added before the ship entered service. A number of additional strengthening measures had to be incorporated so as to ensure that the hull could withstand the battering of the Atlantic gales and Brunel, with Pat-terson's assistance, had the responsibility for the planning and implementation of them.

Eventually, the hull advanced to completion and launch day grew near. This was arranged for the morning of Wednesday July 19 1837. On the appointed day vast crowds gathered along the banks of the Floating Harbour, in the vicinity of the shipyard, in order to witness the scene as the future 'Queen of the Atlantic' took to her natural element. A large stage, to accommodate the directors and their friends, had been erected in the yard of Patterson and Mercer, whilst the adjacent yard, belonging to Beeston and Wooley, provided additional viewing space for ticket holders only. On the harbour itself many vessels were crowded with spectators as the citizens of Bristol sought the best positions from which to see the spectacle. *The Bristol Mirror,* for Saturday July 22 1837, carried the following description of the launch: 'At five minutes past ten, the dog shores having been struck away, the screw was applied, and a general shout arose — ''She moves'' — which indeed she did, in the most majestic and graceful manner. For the moment all was hushed, whilst the beautiful and magnificent vessel glided into the water; not the least wavering or irregular motion occurred. As she left the shore, Lieutenant Claxton performed the usual ceremony of dashing a demijohn of Madeira upon the figurehead of Neptune at the bows, and she was named by Mrs Miles, who also cracked her bottle against the side, the *Great Western.* At the calculated distance she was checked by a chain cable, and brought up within a few feet of the opposite shore, without the smallest accident. The launch being concluded, loud, spontaneous and continued cheers took place, and the immense crowd began to disperse.'

The Bristolians must have enjoyed the auspicious and historic occasion they had just witnessed although for some it would have been tinged with sadness. Those employed on construction work, and their families, had observed their source of income slide away from them into the water. Construction of the hull had occupied 180 workmen for over a year, with more than £8,000 being paid to them in wages during that period.[15] The launch itself occasioned no accidents but prior to it two shipyard employees were injured by a falling timber; one of them had to have a leg amputated due to the injuries he received and, unfortunately, died a few days later.[16]

GREAT WESTERN

Fig 3: Lines plan.

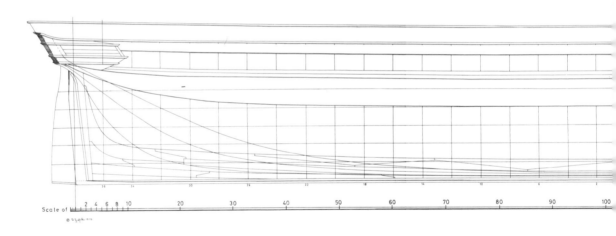

Scale of

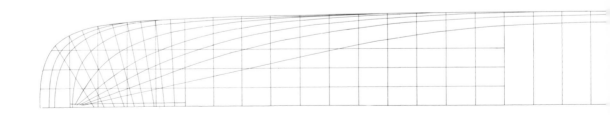

GREAT WESTERN STEAM SHIP COMPANY, BRISTOL.

P.S. GREAT WESTERN.

First registered at Bristol 2nd September 1837.

Length b.p.   212 ft.

Length keel.   205 ft.

Breadth of hull. 35 ft. 4 in.

Breadth over paddle boxes. 59 ft. 8 in.

Depth of hold.   23 ft. 2 in.

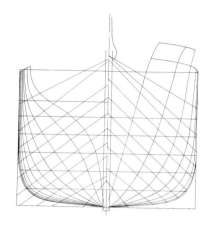

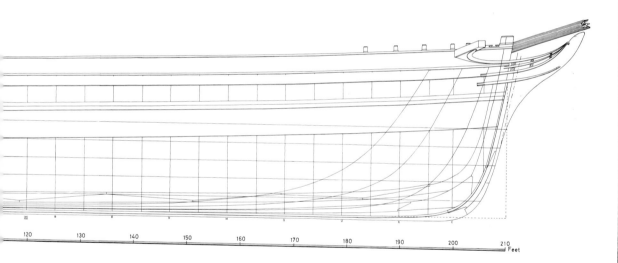

| 120 | 130 | 140 | 150 | 160 | 170 | 180 | 190 | 200 | 210 Feet |

GREAT WESTERN.

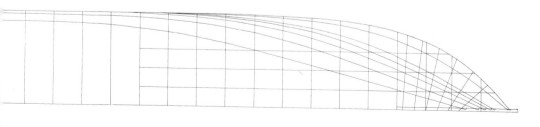

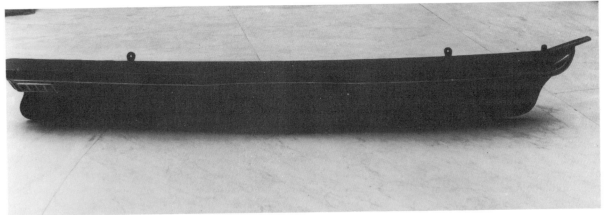

Above *Fig 4: Builder's model of* Great Western*'s hull* (Courtesy City of Bristol Museum and Art Gallery).

Below *Fig 5: The launch of the steamship* Great Western, *by W. Parsons, (c 1920)* (Courtesy City of Bristol Museum and Art Gallery).

An hour after the launch saw 300 citizens, including directors and local dignitaries, sit down to a banquet in the main cabin of the ship, now known to all as *Great Western*, which had, by that time, been brought alongside a berth. A plentiful supply of delicacies adorned the tables and, for those whose taste did not prompt them to take champagne, tea and coffee were available. At the conclusion of the feasting Peter Maze, chairman of the Great Western Steam Ship Company, presided over the toasts and speeches. The first three toasts were to The Queen, Victoria having ascended the throne but a few weeks previously, The President of the United States and Mrs Miles, wife of William Miles the MP for Somerset. Many of the speeches made it clear that Christopher Claxton had been the guiding hand behind the project and only through his unstinting efforts had the ship reached the launching stage on time. Typically, in reply, Claxton gave much credit to his fellow members of the building committee, particularly Patterson who had drafted the lines for the ship and monitored the whole construction of the hull fabric. He also added that his task on the committee had been to bring some nautical experience into the discussions and, through such, maintain the practicability of the plans. That nautical knowledge and experience was essential on one occasion in particular when Brunel and Guppy wished to have the cabin windows made like drawing-room windows. Claxton, aided by Patterson, took the liberty of reminding the two 'land-lubbers' that there would be water outside which could get very uneven in appearance. The message was not lost on the two engineers and the stern windows of the cabin adopted appropriate nautical proportions.[17]

It had been decided to send *Great Western* to London in order to have her machinery fitted, presumably on cost grounds. The relative costs for the fitting of the engines at Bristol and London are not known but, in 1839, Brunel estimated a difference in cost, for larger engines to be fitted in the second ship, of £3,150 in favour of London. The extra cost would be entailed in shipping the machinery to Bristol and insurance en route.[18] Obviously, the additional cost would have been somewhat less in the case of the machinery being installed aboard *Great Western* but it would have still been a significant amount. Due to the novel dimensions of the engines, installation as close as possible to the manufacturing workshop would also have been advantageous. Before the ship could leave for London a little work still remained to be done, with special attention being paid to the rigging.

In the early stages of the company's development it had been planned that the paddles would be disconnected during periods of favourable wind allowing the ship to proceed under sail alone. This idea was, however, abandoned before the ship reached the launching stage.[19] The engines of *Great Western* were to provide the main, continuous, means of propulsion with auxiliary canvas being employed, advantageously, whenever wind permitted. To this end the company adopted a four masted topsail schooner rig. All masts carried spencer sails with provision for trysails and staysails, whilst the foremast also carried three square sails, topgallent, topsail and foresail; studding sails could also be fitted whenever necessary. The jib provided connection for three triangular sails. Naturally, the number and type of sails employed at

Fig 6: Great Western *leaving Bristol Docks for London to be engined, August 18 1837* (Courtesy City of Bristol Museum and Art Gallery).

any time depended upon the wind conditions and, as the surviving log books indicate, would be changed frequently if the strength or direction altered. The after-most or jigger mast, together with its attendant sails was given the prefix Claxton, in appreciation of that man's efforts in the services of the company.

On August 18, less than a month after being launched, *Great Western* left Bristol for the Thames. Departing from the locks at the river end of Cumberland Basin she entered the Avon for the first time. Here the steam tug *Lion* took her in tow for the tricky passage to the sea. Nothing of the size had navigated that meandering stretch of water before and so the journey was anxiously watched. However, *Lion* brought its

charge safely to the sea. A coastal steamer *Benledi* had been chartered to accompany *Great Western* on the run to London, providing towage when required. The lines of the Atlantic vessel were so good, however, that she frequently left *Benledi* far behind. Under sail for four-fifths of the passage her steering exceeded expectation and she was reported to be very easy to handle. The evening of August 22 saw her off Gravesend from where it was but a short tow to the booked berth in the East India Dock. There she would have her accommodation completed and receive her machinery, eventually emerging, the metamorphosis complete, as the first true Atlantic steamship.

Chapter 3

Preparations

By the time *Great Western* arrived in London it was patently obvious that the first voyage could not be made before the Atlantic winter weather set in. Cognisant of the fact that a first voyage across the Atlantic during the winter would not be under conditions favourable to success, the directors decided that the spring of 1838 offered the better prospects. This later date allowed more time for installations and testing of the engines as well as for the completion and decoration of the passenger accommodation. Relaxation of the departure

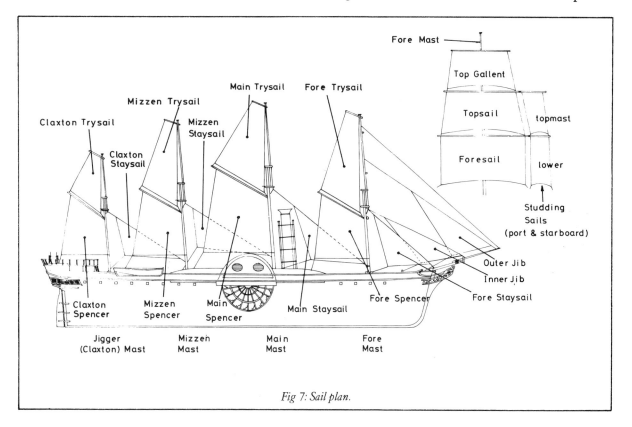

Fig 7: Sail plan.

schedule presented the opportunity to another interested party, one only too willing to steal some of *Great Western's* thunder.

Within the East India Dock, Maudslay, Sons and Field had berthed an old hulk to serve as a floating workshop for the fitting out of steamships.[1] It was close to this hulk that *Great Western* berthed. Casting and machining of the engine components took place at Maudslay's works in Lambeth, the parts being transported, on horse drawn carts, through the streets of London to Blackwall. A small army of craftsmen and labourers were employed on the installation work, which entailed not only final assembly in the ship but the manufacture of many small items only found to be necessary as installation proceeded. Although the

engines would have been assembled at the Lambeth works, actual fitting in the ship required other parts such as bolts, brackets, pipes, etc, and the use of the floating workshop and stores, on site, allowed the work to continue without undue delay. No large dockside cranes existed at the time but most items could be lifted aboard by using derricks erected on deck. Heavy and bulky boilers could not be dealt with in this manner but, fortunately, the East India Dock Company possessed a masting machine, a very large derrick like rig which was used for the removal and replacement of sailing ship masts. At a charge of four shillings per ton Maudslays hired this to place the boilers on board.[2]

Accommodation installation progressed alongside that of the machinery, but changes had been made in

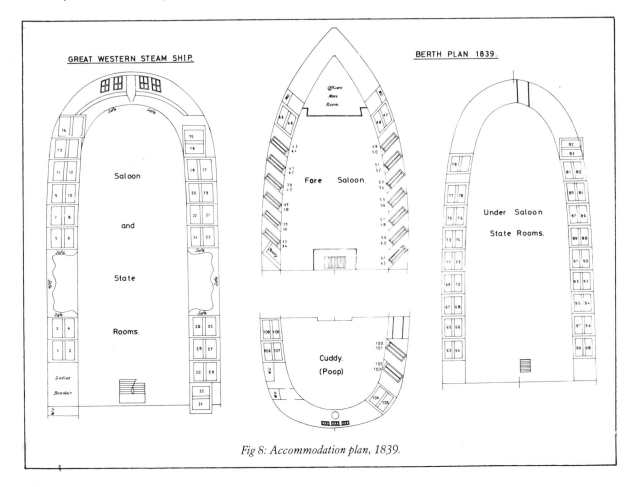

Fig 8: Accommodation plan, 1839.

the planned layout. The alterations came about in order to maximise the number of berths available. Essentially the cabins were formed, in the saloon area, by the erection of light wooden partitions, thus providing some privacy but little sound insulation. Three areas of the ship were set aside for passenger cabins, the main saloon, the under cabin and the fore saloon. A fourth area, the poop or cuddy, was fitted with cabins following the first voyage. Though small and containing two or three berths the cabins were considered adequate for their purpose.

Style and grandeur attracted comment, and passengers, during the early Victorian years and the Great Western Steam Ship Company spared no expense to ensure that their first vessel lacked either. All who viewed the ship were impressed. Messrs Jackson, of Rathbone Place, London, were responsible for the main ornamental work whilst Mr Edward Thomas Parris, historical painter to the Queen, was engaged to decorate the panels in the main saloon. Mr Grace, of Wigmore Street, undertook the painting and decoration of the remaining passenger accommodation.[3] Newspapers and journals of the day occupied much space with descriptions of the main saloon and its furnishings. *The Civil Engineer's and Architect's Journal* for March 1838 contained the following, typical, description:

'The Saloon, which for size and splendour exceeds any that we have seen afloat, is seventy-five feet in length and twenty-one feet in breadth, exclusive of the recesses on each side, where the breadth is thirty-four feet, and nine feet high in clear of the beam, which is increased by the lantern lights; each side, excepting where the recesses intervene, are occupied with ''state cabins''. The ornamental work is very judiciously arranged, there being neither a profusion nor paucity of decoration. The front of the two recesses is divided into three compartments by small columns, formed in imitation of palm trees, with branches of leaves entwined over the openings, which have a neat and pleasing effect. At each end of these two recesses are large pier glasses, fitted in richly ornamental frames, in imitation of Dresden china. The fronts of the small cabins are divided into compartments, with panels about five feet high, and one foot-six to two feet wide, tastefully decorated by no less an artist than Edward Thomas Parris, RA, and historical painter to Her Majesty. Each panel contains an admirable painting in the Wateau style, representing rural scenery, agriculture, music, the arts and sciences, interior views and landscapes. Above the doors are small panels, containing (by the same artist) beautifully pencilled paintings of Cupid, Psyche, and aerial-like figures, which considerable heighten the appearance of the saloon. The ceiling and such parts of the saloon not occupied with the paintings are painted by Mr Grace, of Wigmore Street, of a warm and delicate tint with the mouldings and enrichments, picked in a light colour, and relieved in gold, not too much so as to give a gaudy appearance, but just sufficient to produce a richness of effect, without encroaching or detracting from the principal features of the saloon (Mr Parris' paintings). Small cabins on each side and communicating with the saloon, each contain two sleeping berths, so arranged that in the day time they may be turned up against the side of the vessel, and conceal the bedding, thereby forming a small sitting room, seven feet by eight feet. At the end of the state cabin is the ladies' saloon, tastefull fitted by the upholsterer, and on the opposite side is the steward's room, containing every convenience to render this important department (to the passengers) complete. It is furnished with an ample supply of salt and fresh water, and one of Stirling's filters . . . Between the steward's room and the ladies' cabin, in the midship, is a spacious staircase with handsome ornamental railing bronzed and gilded, the wood work painted in imitation Pollard oak.' (Note: Edward Thomas Parris was not a Royal Academician, RA, although he did exhibit at the Royal Academy.[4] The 'Grace', of Wigmore Street, evidently refers to the famous decorating firm of Frederick Crace.)[5]

At the after end of the saloon sofas were arranged against the windows and the recesses were fitted with settees, carved in oak and upholstered in imitation silk. It was not until *Great Western* returned to Bristol, prior to her first voyage, that the majority of furniture was put on board. In the main saloon this consisted of two rows of benches and tables to allow for dining and recreation. *The Mirror of Literature, Amusement and Instruction*, No 889, for May 6 1838, gives the only contemporary engraving of the main saloon area, at least the only one to, apparently, survive. It shows the tables displaced across the saloon rather than lengthwise, indicating that the drawing was made

Fig 9: Drawing of the main saloon, 1838 (Courtesy Liverpool City Library).

before the ship left London. A certain degree of artistic licence is obvious from the scale of the figures which give the illusion of a saloon much higher than nine feet. The rather generous proportions were probably deliberate, in order to foster a favourable impression, a ruse still perpetrated today.

The staircase, between the steward's room and the ladies' cabin, led down to the lower cabin which was entirely fitted out with first class sleeping berths for gentlemen. Forward of the engine room was the fore-cabin, some 46 feet long. It contained a number of side cabins similar to those situated next to the main saloon but the forward cabins were of irregular shape due to the curvature of the ship towards the bow. Although not as ornate as the main saloon, the decoration of the forward saloon was as good as anything then afloat, the mouldings being painted gold and the doors coloured to resemble ornamental wood. In total 128 berths could

be provided for first class passengers with an additional number being available for servants, though not first class.[6] If necessary, the recesses in the main saloon could be partitioned off in order to provide extra saloon cabins, three cabins coming from each recess.[7]

Sometime during mid-March 1838 *Great Western* left the East India Dock for a river berth at Brunswick Wharf, near the dock entrance. At this river berth preparations continued for the engine trials which were to test machinery and ship down the Thames. Slow turning of the engines and steam tests on the boilers were carried out whilst at the wharf, but the real tests had to be against the tide. For two days prior to the first test, on Saturday March 24, the boilers had been under steam confirming that the ship was ready. At 11 o'clock that morning *Great Western* left the wharf at Blackwall and began her career as a steamship. Throngs of people crowded the shore as she made her triumphant passage downstream towards Gravesend. At first *Great Western* steered wildly until the pilot, Mr Grundy, had another man put on the wheel; following this she manoeuvred with ease. Shortly after setting out the big steamer was involved in an accident. A large sailing barge crossed the bows of *Great Western* and, to avoid ramming it, the pilot had the engines put to reverse; this, however, resulted in *Great Western* fouling a ship lying at anchor, causing her serious damage. Uninjured the Bristol steamer proceeded on its way down river.

Not long after, a race developed with the popular Gravesend steamer *Comet* but, despite her machinery being new, the larger ship showed her power and class and soon left her little rival far behind. At Gravesend it seemed that the whole town had turned out to witness the passage of this 'sea monster', for people crowded every vantage point and cheered as she went by. The turn, three miles below Gravesend, was accomplished with ease and *Great Western* returned to Blackwall shortly before 4.00 pm. Without doubt the trial was a complete success and the shipbuilder, engineers and other men of science who had made the trip all expressed themselves exceedingly satisfied. Needless to say so were Brunel, Guppy and Claxton. Upon her return many more people were waiting to cast their eyes over the giant, now come to life. Amongst the crowd was Lord Sandon, MP for Liverpool, probably a little concerned about the efforts of the merchants from his own city to produce a competitor. It had been the practice to insert the names of all visitors in a book but so great was the number that the clerk gave up.[8] Such a popular sight was *Great Western* that a constant stream of visitors walked her decks, no doubt to the considerable annoyance of the craftsmen trying to complete their tasks.

A second trial followed four days later, on March 28, and, again, was not without incident. Shortly after leaving her berth at noon *Great Western* stranded on a mud bank, the tide being rather lower than expected. This resulted in a considerable delay before the trial could proceed. Little vibration could be observed during the trip and, following adjustments to the paddle wheels, the swell set up by the passage through the water was minimal. A remarkable average speed of 11 knots was achieved for the return run to Gravesend and Maudslay's expressed complete satisfaction with the machinery. All was now ready for the maiden voyage, first to Bristol and then on to the ultimate goal of New York.

Lieutenant James Hosken had been appointed to the command of *Great Western*, before the ship left Bristol and so, presumably, Hosken had taken her round to London. During December 1837 Hosken sailed for New York aboard the sailing packet *Garrick* his instructions being to arrange an agency to handle the American affairs of the company and also to organise a berth for *Great Western*.[9] With Hosken in New York responsibility for the ship lay in the hands of the mate, Mr Barnard Matthews, who had formerly been in comman of the steamer *Benledi*. Whilst the Great Western Steam Ship Company appointed its own deck officers it left to the engine builders the nomination of personnel for the engine department. It was considered prudent to carry, for the first few voyages at least, a special pilot experienced in the waters of the Bristol Channel and Irish Sea. Also carried, primarily for the benefit of the passengers, was a surgeon.[10] The early steamship owners always emphasised the presence of such a person in their advertisement, no doubt to ease the mind of any prospective traveller concerned about his own ability to combat sea-sickness. Early in 1838 there appeared, in a number of shipping publications, advertisements offering four cadetships aboard *Great Western*, a premium of £200 being required for the four year indenture. As well as gaining practical seamanship skills these young men were also to be instructed in arithmetic, navigation, mathematics and steam engineering, the Chief Engineer having the responsibility for the latter subject and the practical engineering training. The same advertisement also offered the post of Ship's Accountant, the successful applicant also being expected to act as tutor to the cadets in the subjects of arithmetic, navigation and mathematics.[11] Obviously, the company was intent on having well trained officers for its future ships.

It may appear that *Great Western* was to have the Atlantic to itself but this was not so as, for some time, other interested parties had been making ground. Conspicuous amongst them was Junius Smith's British and American Steam Navigation Company. Fortune did not, however, smile on that organisation and its first steamer, *British Queen*, suffered many delays during construction. More seriously, the engine builders, Claude Girdwood and Company, found it impossible to fulfill the contract and another had to be made with Robert Napier, on the Clyde. Desirous of the honours afforded to that concern making the first scheduled Atlantic steamer crossing and *British Queen* still being on the stocks, Smiths company decided to charter a vessel for the service. *Sirius*, of 703 tons and 320 horsepower, belonging to the St George Steam Packet Company was prepared and advertised to make a voyage from Cork to New York. With *Great Western* at Blackwall preparing for her second trial trip *Sirius*. carrying 22 passengers, sailed down the Thames enroute for New York, via Cork.[12] After taking coals and embarking further passengers, on April 4 1838, the little *Sirius*, deeply laden with her bunkers, headed into the Atlantic and history.

Meanwhile, *Great Western* lay at Brunswick Wharf completing her engine adjustments and decoration, at the same time allowing the London gentry a final view of her splendid interior. Coal bunkers had been taken at Bristol and unloaded upon arrival in London, this coal provided necessary ballast for the passage under sail and was reloaded, together with local coal, filling all available bunker spaces. Departure for Bristol had been arranged for the morning of Saturday March 31. Just before 4.00 am that day the boiler fires were lit and, in calm misty weather, *Great Western* left her berth at ten minutes past six. On board were a number of distinguished visitors including Sir Marc Isambard Brunel, the ageing father of Isambard Kingdom Brunel. Following a brief stop at Gravesend, to disembark the visitors, the voyage to Bristol continued. About half an hour later, as the vessel approached the Nore, a strong smell of heated oil attracted attention but the source was not immediately obvious. It soon became so when flame and dense smoke appeared from the region of the funnel base. The vividness of the flame and abundance of the smoke must have caused considerable alarm amongst those on board. Fearing that his ship might be lost Hosken put her aground on the soft mud off Leigh. During the confusion a number of stokers quickly decided that the seafaring life was not for them and made their departure over the side.

Immediately upon seeing the flames George Pearne, the Chief Engineer, took action and endeavoured to save the ship and its engines, of which he was so proud. Details of these actions and his personal observations were later written up in his log: '. . . the fore stoke-hole

and engine room soon became enveloped in dense smoke, and the upper part in flame. Thinking it possible the ship might be saved, and that it was important to save the boilers, I crawled down, after a strong inhalation of fresh air, and succeeded in putting on a feed plunger and opening all the boiler feed cocks, suffering the engines to work to pump them up, as steam was generating fast from the flames round the upper part of the boilers. A small fire engine was got to work on deck; C. Claxton, Esq, and the Chief Officer, descending with the hose, at great risk. We shortly after got the engines and hand pumps to work and all hands baling, pumping, etc, succeeded in extinguishing the fire. The most melancholy part of the catastrophe was that I. K. Brunel, Esq, in attempting to go down the fore stoke-hole ladder, stepped on a burnt rung, several of which, in this state, giving way, precipitated him down to the bottom about 20 feet, falling on Mr Claxton. He was taken up, apparently seriously injured, and ultimately sent ashore.'[13]

Fortunately, Brunel's injuries were not as serious as first thought but they did confine him to bed for a number of days. This, however, did not prevent him from dictating a letter, concerning the state of the ship and her engines, to the man on whom he had fallen. Undoubtedly Claxton had saved the engineer's life for the unconscious Brunel had fallen face downwards in a pool of water and only Claxton's swift action had retrieved him from a watery death.[14] The steps taken by Pearne had certainly saved the boilers from damage or, possibly, destruction. Had he not forced extra feed water into them, the heat from the fire in generating additional steam could have resulted in overpressure and probable explosion. The cold feed would have had a cooling effect and kept the boiler pressure within safe limits. Safety valves were fitted to the boilers but, as Pearne would have been aware, the fire could have caused them to seize and become inoperative. The 'small fire-engine' mentioned in Pearne's log book had, fortunately, been placed on board shortly before *Great Western* sailed from London. Claxton, ever aware of dangers which others seemed to have ignored, obtained a Merryweather hand-operated, portable fire-engine, which was only delivered late on the Friday night before the ship departed.[15] Without that piece of equipment the fire may well have spread, as it was some time before the engine operated and manual pumps, situated in the engine room, were made to bring water to bear on the seat of the fire.

Ignition of the insulation around the boiler top turned out to be the cause of the fire. This insulation consisted of felt held in place by oil and red lead, a mixture which was satisfactory for moderate temperatures but highly combustible under high temperature conditions. Injudicious application of the felt too close to the funnel uptakes resulted, after a period of time, in overheating and ignition. After the fire had been extinguished Joseph Maudslay and Joshua Field, who were making the trip to Bristol in order to check the operation of the machinery over a prolonged period, inspected the damage and reported that all was safe and sound. Following the raising of steam and refloating on the next tide, *Great Western* proceeded on her way to Bristol without further problem. Except that is, for the shortage of stokers in the engine room. The remaining hands worked hard but had difficulty in maintaining steam, the life-blood of the ship. *Great Western* arrived off the mouth of the Avon at 6.00 am on Monday April 2, after accomplishing the 670 mile passage in 58½ hours, 6½ hours of which she was detained by the fire. This produced an average speed of almost 13 knots, exceeding all expectations.[16] News of the accident had, however, preceeded her to Bristol and, as with all bad news, it suffered distortion en-route. Many Bristolians, having been confidently informed that she was lost, were extremely surprised to see her at all. Understandably, a number of passengers, who had booked berths on that first voyage, suffered renewed doubts about the safety of steamers and transferred their patronage to the tried and tested, but slower, sailing packets. Some 50 people cancelled their bookings and had their money refunded.[17]

Due to the width across her paddle boxes being nearly 60 feet, Great Western could not enter the Floating Harbour, at Bristol, but had to lie at a mooring downstream, a mooring laid down by the Great Western Steam Ship Company at a cost in excess of £300.[18] Mooring the ship off Broad Pill, some seven miles downstream from Bristol, necessitated the employment of barges for the loading and discharging of cargo as well as for bunkering. Berthing within the Floating Harbour would have cost little more than at Broad Pill. The Bristol Dock Company levied charges though it did not provide full facilities, a matter which caused subsequent, acrimonious, dispute — though greater security and convenience would have resulted. The Floating Harbour had been formed by building lock gates at each end of a section of the River Avon, where it flowed through Bristol, thereby maintaining a constant water level in that section. A 'New Cut' had to be excavated in order to carry the tidal waters of the Avon and to allow the river flow access to the sea without rushing through the harbour section. Devised by William Jessop and carried out between 1804 and 1809, the Floating Harbour scheme greatly improved the standing of Bristol as a port.[19] Locks at the Cumberland Basin afforded passage to and from the Avon for sea going craft. The locks, however, only had a width of 45 feet whilst those between the Floating Harbour and the Cumberland Basin were one foot narrower. Unless the lower portion of her paddle wheels were removed the locks barred *Great Western* from the Floating Harbour.

Departure on the maiden voyage was advertised for Saturday April 7, and the intervening period saw a flotilla of boats commuting between Bristol and Broad Pill with coal, stores, cargo and the remaining furniture. Small items could be carried aboard but the heavy or bulky packages required the assistance of one of the two derricks erected at the main and mizzen masts. Loading from barges was slower than from a berth due to the inherent difficulties in such an arrangement and also due to the fact that the state of the tide and wind often prevented the barges from lying alongside. Aware of the considerable interest in their vessel the Great Western Steam Ship Company allowed visitors to inspect her as she lay off Broad Pill, no doubt occasioning discomfort to the visitors and considerable annoyance to those endeavouring to complete their allotted tasks. During the Wednesday, prior to sailing, some one thousand proprietors and their friends toured *Great Western*, whilst on the succeeding two days nearly three thousand members of the public viewed the lavishly decorated apartments and inspected the engine room. When the intending passengers arrived, later on Saturday afternoon, they found the ship in a state of confusion with loading and stowing still going on. Last minute activities could not be attributed solely to the delays caused by the visitors as gales on the Friday and Saturday had prevented, for long periods, the barges coming alongside.

Chapter 4
The first voyage

The maiden voyage of any ship has always been an occasion for celebration and hope for the future; in that respect the first voyage of *Great Western* was no exception but the hopes it carried were more than those of its owners, they were for a new chapter in maritime history. Throughout the days preceeding departure a certain amount of apprehension must have filled those connected with the ship and her voyage, whilst more Bristolians not directly involved in the venture would have still registered excitement and curiosity. Some, however, persisted with the belief that the project was foolhardy and a waste of money. It should be remembered that once the ship left British waters little, if anything, would be heard of her until she returned, hopefully, some six weeks later. Until the advent of transatlantic telegraphy news of a vessel's arrival at New York often reached England by that same ship when she made her return passage. Only with the introduction of ship to shore radio communication, many years later, was a ship able to maintain contact with its home port. These then were the circumstances under which *Great Western* prepared to set upon her 'great' adventure.

As already mentioned, conditions on board were rather chaotic immediately prior to departure with bunkering and the loading of stores, cargo and baggage still in progress late on Saturday, April 7, the day appointed for departure. However, the weather had other ideas and the wind, which had hindered loading on the previous days, blew up a full gale by Saturday afternoon with the result that Captain Hosken resolved to lie at the moorings until next morning. A significant decision as it turned out, for the hours lost almost certainly lost *Great Western* her 'race' with the

Fig 10: Hand-bill advertising first voyage (Courtesy City of Bristol Museum and Art Gallery).

STEAM TO NEW YORK.

THE

Great Western,

Of 1340 *Tons Regis'er, and* 450 *Horse Power,*

Strongly built, Coppered and Copper-fastened, with Engines of the very best construction, by Maudslay, Sons, and Field, AND EXPRESSLY ADAPTED FOR THE BRISTOL AND NEW YORK STATION,

Lieut. JAMES HOSKEN, R.N., Commander,

Will Sail DIRECT *from Bristol*

On the 7th APRIL, 1838,

AT TWO O'CLOCK IN THE AFTERNOON.

The rate of Cabin Passage is 35 Guineas, to be paid on securing State Rooms, for which please to apply at

The GREAT WESTERN RAILWAY OFFICE,
· Prince's-Street, Bank, London.

Messrs GIBBS, BRIGHT, & CO., Liverpool.

Messrs HAMILTON, BROTHERS & CO., Glasgow.

Mr ROBERT HALL, Cork.

Mr C. CLAXTON, Managing Director, Great Western Steam Ship Office, 19, Trinity-Street, Bristol.

To Officers on duty in her Majesty's Service, and their Families, some allowance will be made for their travelling expenses to Bristol; and those from the Depot at Cork will have their passage money, by the regular Steamers to Bristol, allowed. For Families, a reduction will be made in proportion to their numbers and the berths they require. Children under 13 years and Servants half-price. No Letters will be taken except on payment of 1s. the single sheet each. Newspapers and Slips, 3d. each. Parcels in proportion to size and weight, and a small quantity of Light Goods at £5 per ton. Specie and Valuables, one-half per cent.

This Ship has Coal Storage for 25 Days' constant Steaming, and therefore will not require to touch at Cork for Coal.

Printed at the Bristol Mirror Office by John Taylor.

Fig 11: Statement of dimensions (Courtesy Bristol Reference Library).

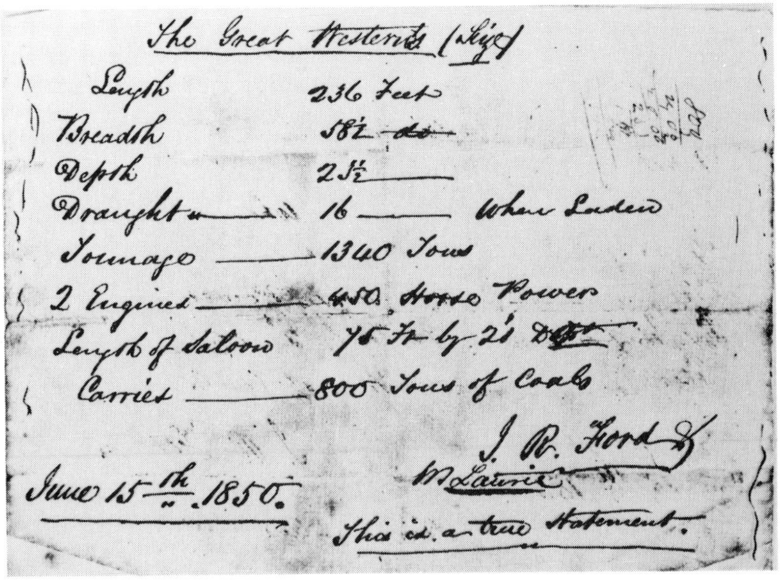

The Great Western's [Ship]

Length	236 Feet
Breadth	58½ do
Depth	23½
Draught	16 — When Laden
Tonnage	1340 Tons
2 Engines	450 Horse Power
Length of Saloon	75 Ft by 21 do
Carries	800 Tons of Coals

J. R. Ford
W. Lewis

June 15th 1850.

This is a true Statement.

diminutive *Sirius*. Following the accidents during the two trial trips and the outbreak of fire whilst on passage back to Bristol the prophets of doom were, no doubt, signalling that the further delay was fate's final warning on the folly of the venture. The delay did, however, allow time for the clearing away of cargo, stores and coal from the deck, twelve labourers being employed to assist the crew in the task, which was not completed until early on Sunday morning.[1] By that time, the weather having abated somewhat, Hosken decided that it was safe to commence the voyage and instructions were passed to the engineers for steam to be raised.

The first voyage of *Great Western* has, fortunately, been well documented. Extensive coverage was given by the national and local press at the time and a few months later Claxton published a small volume containing the deck and engine room logs. Though small in size the publication bore the rather lengthy title, *The Logs of the First Voyage made with the Unceasing Aid of Steam between England and America by the* Great Western *of Bristol,* and not only contained the logs but also other relevant information including a journal, kept during the outward passage by a passenger, Mr Foster, of Philadelphia. Extracts from the journal appeared in many of the contemporary newspapers on both sides of the Atlantic, such was the interest in the

voyage. Upon the return of *Great Western* the *Bristol Mercury,* for May 26 1838, issued a supplement which contained the full version of Foster's journal, Claxton's having been slightly abbreviated. The supplement also included extracts from the American newspapers concerning the arrival and stay at New York. It is interesting to relate that *Sirius* did not rate the same extensive coverage by the British national press, although she arrived back home some days earlier than her Bristol rival.

Consequent upon the fire, only seven intrepid passengers retained their bookings, these being James Willer, Charles Maitland Tate, Cornelius Birch Bagster, Colonel Vernon Graham, W. A. Foster, John Gordon and Miss Eliza Cross.[2] According to Foster's journal the passengers boarded a 'twaddling little steamer' at the foot of Cumberland Basin just after 2.00 pm on Saturday April 7. After a spectacular, if uneventful, trip down the Avon, during which they passed beneath the partially constructed abutments of Brunel's Clifton Suspension Bridge, they arrived at the moorings, off Broad Pill, at about 5.00 pm. The journey took nearly three hours due to the fact that the tide was in flood and acting against their little steamer. Looming before them the shining black hull of *Great Western* must have been an impressive sight dwarfing, as it did, the attendant barges and visiting steamers. Having threaded their respective ways amongst the assortment of packages which littered the deck, the 'magnificent seven' passengers located the cabins assigned and set about making themselves at home, at least as well as they were able. Although the main saloon cabins measured only some eight feet by seven feet, each passenger would have had sole occupancy of one thus making conditions rather more tolerable. Certainly those first passengers were to receive better treatment than any others the ship ever carried for, undoubtedly, the stewards and waiters outnumbered them. The only female on board for the first crossing, Miss Eliza Cross, owner of a stay, straw and millinery wareroom in Bristol, must have been well served by the single stewardess.

Unfortunately the crew agreement for that historic first voyage appears to be lost but, from the log books and other sources, it is possible to piece together a partial crew list; this is given in Appendix 2. At the time it was only necessary for persons directly concerned with operating the vessel to sign the articles of agreement and so no hotel staff would have appeared on the crew list. Such hotel staff would have included stewards, waiters, a stewardess, a baker, a butcher and, at least

one cook. Although there were but seven outward passengers sufficient stewards and waiters would have been carried to cater for, hopefully as far as the company was concerned, a much larger complement on the return. Crew members and hotel staff could have been engaged at New York, a practice frequently adopted during later voyages, but, in order to minimise the possible risk of any shortfall, it is likely that a larger number of stewards and waiters were carried than the seven passengers would justify.

At 9.00 am on Sunday, April 8, steam being up, raising of the anchor commenced. This task was not completed, however, until well past 10.00 am due to the length of cable laid out, the newness of the equipment and the inexperience of the crew members. With the anchor weighed the engines were started ahead and *Great Western* set off in pursuit of the interloping *Sirius*. To assist the engines sails were set and soon a rate of nine knots had been achieved against a north-westerly swell, which caused the ship to pitch heavily. Having stowed the anchor cable and cleared the decks, the seamen divided into watches and, for them, shipboard life quickly settled into the normal routine of setting, trimming and stowing sails. In the engine room, however, conditions were much more arduous.

Fig 12: Great Western *off Portishead on first voyage to New York* (Courtesy City of Bristol Museum and Art Gallery).

The engineers' constant preoccupation was the efficient operation of the machinery and all which that entailed. Bearings in particular, had to be regularly checked as, being new, they had a predisposition to work hot. Regular adjustments to the steam expansion valve, by means of the expansion cam, allowed the engine power to be altered so that coal consumption could be reduced whenever the wind provided assistance. Because the wind strength and direction could change many times during a period of duty such adjustments became routine. In order to estimate the operating efficiency of the plant, coal consumption had to be measured at intervals of about three days. This entailed counting the total number of barrow loads of coal consumed during a period of time, the steam throttle and expansion cam setting having to remain constant throughout the period. Intermittently, cylinder indicator diagrams would also be taken so that the engineers could gauge the actual horse-power being developed by each cylinder. (See chapter on machinery.) Engine room temperatures were high, frequently above 90°F, making working conditions extremely difficult. Small skylights at the top of the engine room provided some ventilation, but temperatures would rise rapidly unless a cooling draft of air could be obtained from the canvass scoops, known as wind sails, set above the ventilators.

Though engine room temperatures might be considered high, the presence of boilers caused the stokehold temperatures to rise to even higher values. There the firemen (stokers) toiled in hellish conditions to keep some semblance of a steam supply, with only the flickering flames of the oil lamps and the sudden orange glow from an opened furnace door to supplement any daylight which might creep in through the skylights. In their dark, grimy and oppressive world the firemen constantly fed coal to the voracious furnaces in the almost futile attempt to satisfy the seemingly insatiable appetite of the boilers. For the coal trimmers the situation was no better, particularly when they were required to fetch the coal from the farthest ends of the ship. As *Great Western* pitched in the heavy Atlantic swell the coal trimmers would one instant be pushing their laden wheel-barrows up hill and the next fighting to prevent them from running away. It is no wonder, therefore, that difficulties were experienced in maintaining a steam supply.

On the fifth day out George Pearne, the Chief Engineer, decided that the stokers and trimmers would have to work for twelve hours each day instead of the eight hours originally intended. They were organised into two watches of eight men each, a sailor being drafted in to make up the numbers. Understandably, they protested at the increase but, following explicit instructions from the captain, they reluctantly set about their task.[3] Conditions for the unfortunate stokers and trimmers did not improve when they finished duty because their sleeping berths, being placed close to the boiler space, became too hot for effective sleep resulting in considerable fatigue of the men.[4] As the trip progressed it became increasingly difficult to maintain steam for want of a coal supply at the boilers, the coal having to be fetched from the bunkers at the extreme ends of the ship. On a number of occasions the coal supply rate was so low that two out of the four boilers had to be shut down. The coal supply situation became so acute that, on April 19, Pearne had to turn all engine room hands out, with the promise of an extra half dollar pay, in order to move coal from the extreme end bunkers. Seamen, on a number of days, were also required to assist with coal trimming operations as well as with the hauling on deck of the ashes for disposal overboard. The imposition of such tasks caused, 'much murmuring amongst the seamen.'[5]

One of the stokers, by the name of Crooks and described by Pearne as a lazy shuffling fellow, decided that it was all too much for him and took to the bottle. As a result he did not turn to for his duty the next day, April 20, and became abusive to both Pearne and the Captain, who then had him restrained on the poop. A little later Crooks managed to free himself and attempted to throw Hosken overboard but was prevented and subsequently more securely restrained. That action provoked retaliation from the remaining engine room hands who 'knocked-off' until Crooks was released. The incident petered out when the miscreant, Crooks, a little while later, complained of being ill and, after being given some medicine, retired to his bed.[6] Not surprisingly the mutinous incident did not find its way into Claxton's publication of the logs where the only comment covering the occurrence was, '10.00 am, scarcely any steam produced.'

There were only fifteen stokers and coal trimmers on board and as the voyage progressed it became patently obvious that the number was totally inadequate to

maintain steam and keep the stokeholds clear of ashes, even in the most favourable of circumstances. Pearne, more than anyone, became quickly aware of the situation as the entries in his log book show. An entry for April 17 includes the following statement: '. . . difficulty in maintaining steam, by reason that coal cannot be got from the ends of the ship and brought to the furnaces fast enough for consumption; stokers and trimmers becoming languid from continued work; number of men not being adequate to the duty'. It is surprising that the possibility of such a shortages of hands was not forseen, particularly as difficulty in maintaining steam had been experienced during the passage between London and Bristol. Perhaps if Brunel had been able to complete the trip and had seen, at first hand, the problems involved in working a ship of such unprecedented size and power, he would have considered that additional men were essential. Certainly, in the light of experience, the number of stokers and trimmers carried on subsequent voyages was increased.

The machinery itself worked effectively and well although there were some teething troubles. Loose paddle boards required tightening and, on April 14, the engines were stopped in order to facilitate the task. Both connecting rod and plummer block (main) bearings worked hot during the voyage and the use of

cooling water, played on the overheated section, had to be resorted to on more than one occasion. A second engine stoppage took place three days later when adjustments to plummer block and connecting rod bearings was required. The log book indicates that the stoppage was also made in order to get a 'cast of lead' (depth of water sounding) and so engine malfunction cannot be held solely responsible. Apart from the difficulties experienced in maintaining steam the boilers functioned well with but two minor inconveniences. Brine pumps, which reduced the saltiness of the water in the boilers by continuously removing some of that water, were connected to the boilers by means of cocks and two of these became blocked early in the voyage. The result was that boilers had to be blown down directly to the sea and, hence, they operated less efficiently. Upon inspection at New York, the cock on the forward, starboard boiler was found to be obstructed by an old pair of canvas trousers, whilst the forward port boiler had its brine pump cock partially chocked with wood shavings.[7] The defects were probably a result of uncharacteristic sloppy workmanship on the part of Maudslay's installation team, as the boilers were not completely blown down at Bristol[8] and would not, therefore, have been opened up.

Although no sightings of *Sirius* took place, *Great*

Western did not have a lonely journey for, on a number of occasions, fellow ocean venturers came in view. Flag signals were exchanged with some but with others verbal communication actually took place. This maritime tradition, still carried on today by means of radio, was no mere courtesy as it enabled shipowners, and other interested parties, to obtain news of a vessel which might have had no direct contact with its home port for many months. Newspapers of the period, whenever reporting the arrival of a sailing or steam packet ship, would also give a list of ships, including dates and positions, with which contact was made. Perhaps the most emotive encounter on the outward crossing occurred during the morning of April 10 when *Great Western* came upon the Black Ball liner *South American*, outward bound from Liverpool to New York. That meeting of the old and new must have stirred, within members of both crews, certain feelings on the significance of the event and their own irrevocably changing world. The death knell of the sailing packets had been sounded, but it would be many a long year before the corpse finally disappeared. At the time of meeting *Great Western* had completed two days of her passage whilst *South American* was into the seventh of hers, proof, if anyone needed it, of the superiority of the steam ship. With the two masters having exchanged messages and amidst cheering from the decks of both ships, *Great Western* pulled away from her fellow traveller which, within a few hours, was left far out of sight behind.

Typically, the Atlantic weather did not make the crossing easy. Although the early days were completed with fair winds and moderate weather the ever present heavy Atlantic swell resulted in deep and uncomfortable pitching which, during the second day out, caused the trident to be washed from the Neptune figurehead. Perhaps, a reminder from the deep as to the identity of the real master of the seas. The wind's unremitting change in direction and force necessitated constant attention to the sails. A heavy squall on April 15 carried away part of the fore topmast as well as the top-gallant mast, yard and cross trees. Fortunately, nobody suffered any injury as the debris fell, but all hands had to be turned out in order to clear the wreckage and set the spare mast section together with its rigging. A day later the gaff on the main mast carried away in similar conditions, whilst two days later a wave breaking into the gig, a small boat kept in davits at the ship's side, caused severe damage. Apart from the indignity suffered by Neptune through the loss of his trident, the damage caused by the weather was rectified by the crew, spare parts and materials being carried for such eventualities as a matter of course.

The motion of the ship resulted in some inconvenience to the passengers for, as Foster's journal for Tuesday April 10 records: '. . . sea sickness stalks in stifling horror among us . . .' However, they soon recovered from their 'mal de mer' to take an increasing interest in the events about them. Notwithstanding, the sea still tried its best, or worst, to make the voyage

Fig 14: Track of Great Western's *first voyage across the Atlantic.*

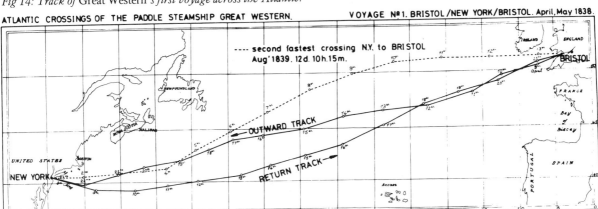

unforgettable with water from the main deck leaking, by any available aperture. into the saloon and cabins. Until 'sea legs' were found, rolling and pitching of the ship required tenacious exertion in order to retain a reasonable posture, whilst 'to take to ones berth may be likened to seeking refuge within the arms of a demented sentry box.'[9] The cacophony caused by the clatter of pans and plates, the creaking of the hull, the crashing of water on deck and the howling of wind in the rigging provided continuous entertainment until ears became accustomed to the din and automatically filtered out the normal shipboard sounds. Mysteriously, on the morning of Wednesday April 11 there appeared on one of the main saloon tables a bouquet of flowers. In such an unnatural environment the flowers became the focus of cossetting attention. Three days later, following a particularly rough night, the passengers awoke to find their floral charge lying damaged upon the carpet. A trivial incident ashore but one which occupied much conversation at sea. Even the creatures of the Atlantic waters endeavoured to amuse, with porpoise performing a ballet in front of the bow wake and a dance of death with the paddle wheels.

Certainly the passengers can have had no complaints about the value of their 35 guinea passages. Not only did they receive a swift crossing to New York but they also obtained, unintentionally, spacious accommodation and individual attention, together with the best food and wine available aboard any ship then afloat. With only seven passengers to grace the saloon entertainment had to be limited as it would all have been down to self help. At least one of the passengers was regularly occupied with his journal and it is probable that most of the others kept some form of diary, a popular Victorian pastime. Having famliarised themselves with the ship and its machinery the travellers are likely to have spent most of their time, when not eating, by reading, talking or watching the sea. Evenings would be spent in similar pursuits with the playing of card games a favourite source of amusement. Naturally, all entertainment was subject to the vagaries of the weather. A much needed diversion came during the afternoon of Saturday April 21 when a snow storm lasted long enough to produce a two inch layer on the deck and drape the masts and rigging in fleecy white. That much welcomed interlude allowed the 'idlers of

Fig 15: Arrival at New York, April 23 1838 (Courtesy Bristol Reference Library).

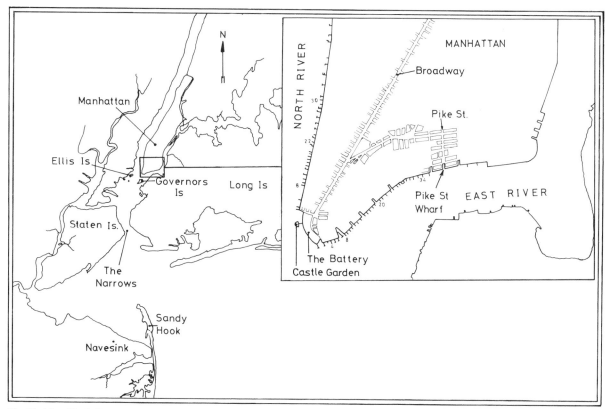

Fig 16: New York Harbor, 1838.

the cabin' to indulge in the universal treat of a snowball fight.[10]

Arrival at New York had, for some days, been expected to be on Monday April 23 and at 10.00 am that day the New York pilot boarded *Great Western*, although it was to be another two hours before land came in sight. The passengers had arranged two of the saloon skylights as tables, one christened 'Victoria' and the other 'President', decking them with an extravagant array of wine and fruit in order that their safe arrival might be ceremoniously proclaimed. At 2.00 pm *Great Western*, with no sails set, steamed through the Narrows into the Port of New York and an hour later the cannons on the fort at Ellis Island boomed out their enthusiastic welcome. With the city in better view there, for all on board to see, was *Sirius*, lying proudly at anchor near the mouth of the North River. *Great*

Western had, after all, lost its race with the little interloper. That is if there had ever been any race. The Great Western Steam Ship Company made no effort to put its ship to sea from Bristol any earlier than the advertised sailing date, of April 7, even though their rivals planned to put a ship on the route ahead of *Great Western*. Certainly Hosken did not attempt to push his ship but contented himself with letting her settle in smoothly. The aim of the company, from the outset, was the accomplishment of a safe, not necessarily a fast, crossing.

Sirius, having failed to obtain a pilot off New York, had attempted to run in without guidance and had grounded off Sandy Hook late in the evening of April 22. She was forced to await the high tide during the following morning in order to lift clear.[11] Aroused by the arrival of *Sirius* the citizens of New York made for the Battery in order to satisfy their curiosity as the little ocean wonder lay at anchor. Whilst they gazed in amazement, there appeared above Governor's Island a dense cloud of black smoke. A short while later the source of pollution manifested itself, *Great Western* had arrived. By the time she reached the city shores many thousands of New Yorkers crowded onto the battery so as to witness the black 'sea-monster', almost contemptuously, circle the little *Sirius* before heading up the East River to her berth at the foot of Pike Street. For those on deck there was excitement and euphoria but this was later to give way to tragedy.

George Pearne, the Chief Engineer, held the trust and confidence of the engine builders and the ship-owners as well as the respect of his fellow officers and subordinates. Not only was he a good engineer but he also possessed the ability to record details of events accurately and logically, thus enabling him to produce, if only in part, a valuable chronicle of that first voyage. Prior to or shortly after arrival at New York, Pearne had pencilled a note, probably to the directors and to Maudslay, Sons and Field, giving performance facts and his own observations. A number of spaces were left blank for the insertion of figures, such as coal consumption, when the full data was available. The note, given in Claxton's *Logs of the First Voyage . . .* contained the following: I beg to announce to you by the first ship leaving after our arrival here that we reach this port in no worse condition than when we left Bristol, excepting that all hands are much fatigued . . . The engines, I am proud to say, have performed even beyond my expectations, which was set at all times sanguine. Some of the little usual difficulties of hot bearings, occasional loss of vacuum, loose joints, etc, were met, and enabled the engines to work as intended . . . In summing up, the engines are a piece of magnificent perfection. I believe, Gentlemen, you are aware of the mental depression I experienced from anxiety to have the engines and all   '. At that point the copy abruptly ended and Pearne never had chance to complete it or make a final draft.[12]

Shortly after arrival, as the log book records, 'The Chief Engineer, Mr George Pearne, was severely scalded in the act of blowing off the boilers; Roberts (an assistant engineer) slightly.'[13] Exactly what happened is not recorded but Pearne, with the assistance of Roberts, was, obviously, trying to remove residual water from one of the boilers. Upon completion of such a prolonged passage it would have been standard practice to completely empty the boilers in order to allow a thorough internal inspection. Inspection of the two forward boilers was essential in order to ascertain the nature of the blockage in the brine pump cocks. As the boilers were below the water-line it is unlikely that the residual steam pressure would have been sufficient to blow the water directly out to sea. The most expedient method of removing the water from the boilers, the brine pumps not operating when the engines were stopped (anyhow, the brine pump cocks were choked), would be to drain it into the bilge and then pump it overboard by hand. A cock fitted to the heat exchanger on the change water apparatus (see chapter on the machinery) allowed the boilers to be emptied without using the brine pumps and without an additional connection to the engine. However, the heat exchanger came after the brine pump cock and, on the forward two boilers, the cocks were blocked. The only option left was to slacken off one of the pipe connections or an inspection door low down on the boiler shell. It is probable, therefore, that Pearne or Roberts attempted to perform such a task and in the process fractured some component or, unwittingly, loosened a connection by too great an amount releasing scalding water, Pearne taking most of the force.

It has been presumed that the accident occurred during the day of arrival but this is not so as the report of the coroner's court states, '. . . the said George Pearne came by his death by being accidentally scalded by steam from the ship *Great Western* on the 24 April'.[14] A doctor attended as soon as he could be procurred. The injuries to Roberts were not serious and Pearne did not appear to be in any danger. He was, however, a man of delicate health[15] and his condition deteriorated so much that he was removed to the New York City Hospital two days later. Following treatment, '. . . he appeared to be getting better until late evening when he was taken by a fit of vomiting which would not check and he died about quarter past 12 o'clock'.[16] Dr C. Rogers, giving evidence before the coroner's court, indicated that death had been occasioned more by utter exhaustion, brought on by excessive vomiting, than as a result of the injuries; the jury gave a verdict to that effect.[17] In modern terms the delicate engineer probably died as a result of shock. With the demise of

Pearne the Great Western Steam Ship Company had lost a valuable and capable servant, whilst the marine industry was deprived of the skills of an exceptional engineer.

The inhabitants of New York took as much, if not more, interest in the two ships as their British counterparts, flocking to the dockside in order to view them or, if fortunate enough, be allowed on board. Throughout the entire period of her stay *Great Western* attracted countless numbers of people to her wharf making cargo handling and bunkering the most difficult of tasks. Such became the demand to see on board that Hosken had to introduce an admission by ticket system. Bunkering occupied the first few days in port with some 410 tons of coal being taken on board. (The log book indicates that 445 tons of coal were consumed during the outward passage.) Cargo shippers appear to have been as reluctant as the passengers to test the qualities of *Great Western* during her first crossing, the outward cargo comprising one goat's hair shawl, 228 gallons of bottled beer, 25 gallons of cider, 668 cases of sheet copper, one case of thread lace, 868 oz of silver plate and 40 cases of brass manufactured goods. The homeward cargo consisted of one trunk of clothes, 90 bales of cotton, six seroons of cochineal, 13 cases of indigo, two barrels of apples and 26 bales or cases of unknown contents.[18]

The New York City Council, well aware of the benefits which Atlantic steam navigation could bring to the city, paid visits to both ships. In honour of the visiting councillors a reception was held aboard the Bristol ship on Friday April 27 with Captain Hosken and Richard Irvin, the agent, acting as hosts. A small flotilla of boats from the Naval Yard conveyed the dignitaries down the East River from a wharf near the Battery to the Pike Street berth, Pike Street being in a rather disreputable part of the city and not a fit area in which some of the 'gentlemen' should be seen.[19] In addition to the mayor and council the distinguished assembly included the British Consul, the Hon Daniel Webster, the Governor of Michigan, Mr Luther Braddish, formerly speaker of the New York State Assembly and Captain Roberts of *Sirius*. The usual multitude of congratulatory toasts were drunk with praise being heaped upon those most responsible for the venture. One political incident entered the proceedings and subdued, for a while, the merriment. John Ridge, a proud Cherokee Indian, had

been invited and when called upon to speak decided to ignore the maritime nature of the occasion and vent his feelings as to the treatment and fate of the original Americans. He pointed out the injustice perpetrated on the red man in forcing him from his home causing him to retreat to the highest peaks of the Rocky Mountains, adding that the Indian asked only for peace. At the conclusions of his speech Ridge restored the conviviality of the occasion by offering the following sentiments: 'The Queen of England: All ladies reign in the hearts of brave men.'[20]

Such had been the demand for tickets to see over *Great Western* that Saturday April 28 was set aside as a special 'Ladies Day'. From early morning a myriad of ladies, with and without escorts, the disreputable nature of the Pike Street area apparently not worrying them as much as it worried some 'gentlemen', made their respective ways, on foot and by coach, to the quayside. For ladies only the ship would be open between the hours of 11.00 am and 4.00 pm. During that period nearly 11,000 people ventured aboard, though a number were male escorts to the ladies. Only the females, however, had access to the saloon, into which they squeezed for entertainment, and entertained they were, for at least one report indicates that they ate all that was put before them and consumed 346 bottles of wine. Cramped like sardines in a can, few people can have seen much of the ship but one person evidently enjoyed himself. A young officer, by the name of Phillips, had been assigned the duty of assisting the visitors down onto the deck. At the end of the day he observed that he had had the handling of more American girls than any man since the world began.[21]

Whilst on shore officers and crew of both ships received attention and treatment usually reserved for dignitaries but, in many ways they were special, for their ventures had reduced the separation of the old and new worlds. One note of discord did, however, sour the otherwise merry proceedings when totally unfounded accusations were made regarding crew misconduct and ship mishandling. Two of the New York daily papers appear to have been at the centre of the dispute. The papers concerned were James Watson Webb's *Courier and Enquirer* and *The Morning Herald* belonging to James Gordon Bennett. Webb had hired a boat to intercept *Sirius* whilst she was off Sandy Hook and thus procurred the British newspapers, thereby scooping the European news from under Bennett's nose. With the imminent arrival of *Great Western*, Webb placed one of his servants on the pilot boat with orders to obtain all European newspapers from the Bristol steamer. Not only did the lackey lay hands upon the papers he also managed, perhaps unwittingly, to remove the mailbags, resulting in fierce protests from the authorities. However, Bennett had been scooped again and suspected that there had been a certain amount of collusion with those on board *Great Western*. Having taken umbrage at the incident Bennett proceeded to castigate not only Webb but also those involved with *Great Western*, circulating unfounded tales about the ship and its crew. Those who favoured the Bristol ship set about casting similar disparaging remarks about *Sirius*. Amongst the tales were the often repeated stories regarding the burning of furniture and even a child's doll when the fuel ran low and of a near mutiny during the crossing. None of the imagined events were actually true but the tales lived on and became part of the legend of the crossing by *Sirius*. The press antagonism did not extend to the officers and crew who, for the entire period in New York, remained on the best of terms.[22] Interest in the ships extended beyond their American terminus and many letters were received from Philadelphia requesting that they visit that city. Such a request could not, however, be acceded to without disrupting service schedules and causing problems with the insurance policies.[23]

At 2.00 pm on May 1 *Sirius,* with 26 first class passengers, including James G. Bennett and Colonel Vernon Graham, who had made the outward passage aboard *Great Western*, headed home for England. A further 21 steerage passengers were also on board.[24] As on the outward passage no cargo could be carried as all available space was occupied by coal bunkers. Not until Monday May 7 did the larger steamer take her leave of New York. At 11.30 am she moved from her Pike Street berth to No 1 berth on the North River, just beside the Battery, in order to take on board her passengers and their luggage. Multitudes crammed onto the Battery and other vantage points, including the roof tops of nearby houses, whilst afloat an armada of craft brought normal river traffic to a standstill. In answer to the continued cheering of the assembled throng a regular cannon salute rang out from the deck of *Great Western*.

Having received her 66 passengers (only first class) and their friends, the steamship cast off at 2.20 pm and steamed nobly up the North River for a while, displaying her graceful lines, before turning to head for the Narrows and the open sea. On shore and aboard the thirteen accompanying steamers cheering and the waving of handkerchiefs persisted for the whole of the harbour passage. A number of the attendant steamers came perilously close to capsizing as their human freight crowded the rails on one side in order to gain a better view.[25]

Abreast of the Narrows, Hosken ordered the engines to be stopped and the steamer *Providence* came alongside to take off the returning friends and dignitaries. With that task safely accomplished the steamers separated and, trailing a ribbon of black smoke, *Great Western* headed for Sandy Hook with five small steamships still shadowing. At 5.00 pm the pilot disembarked and, with a final salute, the accompanying ships also headed back for New York harbour. An hour later the first of a number of unscheduled stops took place when letters were received on board from the packet ship *Wellington*, then 26 days out from Portsmouth. The letters would inform the British agents of the *Wellington's* safe arrival at New York. That five minute delay acted as a prelude to a much more serious stoppage later that evening. No sooner had full sea speed been achieved than a crank bearing on the port engine began to overheat. The usual practice of cooling the offending part with water only served to fracture the upper of the two bearing brasses necessitating the disconnection of that engine. Following a three and a half hour delay, during which disconnection of the port engine took place, the ship proceeded on its course powered only by the starboard engine.[26]

Working under difficult conditions, the engineers had to reassemble the jigsaw of bearing brass pieces and construct straps with which to hold them together. The task occupied sixteen hours on the following day and a further three hours the next morning; throughout the same period the remaining operational engine and the boilers had to receive attention and so, with no chief engineer to assist them, the engineers must have been sorely tried. Eventually, at 10.00 am on Wednesday May 9 the engines were recoupled but had to be stopped fifteen minutes later in order to cool and slacken off the troublesome bearing.[27] Throughout the next week the engines were stopped periodically so that adjustments might be made and the bearings cooled; stoppages also took place to allow communication with other vessels and, no doubt, the engineers used the time effectively to give further attention to the engines. During the early morning of Thursday May 10 the lower brass of the damaged bearing began to break up requiring that the port engine again be disconnected. A little over 26 hours later[28] normal steam power from both engines resumed and no further trouble occurred that voyage. Had Pearne been present things might have been a little easier but it is highly unlikely that the bearing failure would have been avoided. Certainly Pearne's ability to keep accurate records was missed as the engine room log book for the return crossing is but sparsely entered, a fact commented upon by Claxton in his published version of the logs of the first voyage. The nature of the task facing the engineers should not be underestimated for they repaired the damaged parts and still kept the ship operational.

Generally, the weather throughout the return crossing did not reach the severity of that encountered going out, making life a little easier for the passengers and crew; apart from the engineers who were probably too involved in their tasks to be much concerned about the weather. With a much larger complement of passengers entertainment must have been a little easier to find, one person in particular noticing the difference. Miss Eliza Cross, of Bristol, had also made the outward crossing giving her claim to the title of the first female passenger to cross the Atlantic by steam in both directions. The first male to do so was Colonel Vernon Graham who made the outward passage aboard *Great Western* and return aboard *Sirius*. Despite the lack of power caused by the bearing failure, the port engine being disconnected for over 60 hours in total, and despite other stoppages, *Great Western* dropped anchor at the mouth of the Avon during the morning of Tuesday May 22 after a passage of just over fourteen days. *Sirius* took eighteen days for the crossing from New York to Falmouth.

Fig 17: Great Western *passing* Clevedon *on return from New York* (Courtesy City of Bristol Museum and Art Gallery).

THE GREAT WESTERN STEAM SHIP OF BRISTOL.

Fig 18: Newspaper page announcing return from first voyage (Courtesy City of Bristol Museum and Art Gallery).

The enthusiastic scenes which greeted the arrival of *Great Western* at New York were re-enacted upon her arrival at Kingroad, with the salute from cannon and the peal of bells echoing across the water as she made her triumphant way to the anchorage. The arrival drew comment from many national and local newspapers with *The Times* determined not to be outdone. A correspondent from that newspaper had stationed himself at Kingroad some time before the ship became due in order to ensure first hand coverage of the event. Having obtained his story he despatched it by express coach to Maidenhead and from there, via the recently opened section of the Great Western Railway, to London. *The Times* for May 23 1838 reported the words of their correspondent; 'It is with great satisfaction that

I communicate to you the safe arrival of the *Great Western* Steam Ship from New York at half past 10 o'clock this morning. Having lain in the Roads in expectation of her, I had a full view of the majestic vessel immediately after her passing the Holmes (about 21 miles down the channel), and nothing could exceed the beauty of her appearance as she gallantly breasted the waves; and although a smart breeze was blowing from the north west she sailed triumphantly along without rolling in the slightest degree, or appearing to be at all affected by them.'

Great Western had thus completed the task assigned to her, namely to accomplish the voyage with a discreet use of fuel and within the time normally taken by the sailing packets under similar conditions of wind and weather.[29] Although *Sirius* had also safely made the double crossing her voyage could not be considered a practical test of Atlantic steam navigation as she was unable to carry any cargo and could barely carry sufficient coal for a crossing in reasonably favourable conditions. *Great Western*, on the other hand, had coal to spare having used but 411 tons during the return crossing to Bristol. She also offered large passenger and cargo potential. The Bristol owners made a loss of some £3,826 on the first voyage, the receipts being £2,615 and disbursements of £6,441. Realising that the first voyage would make a loss the directors had decided to class it as an experiment and write down the loss to the formation of the company. An accounting measure which made the first year's trading figures seem better than they, in fact, were.[30] Notwithstanding the financial loss *Great Western* had proved the economic feasibility of Atlantic steam navigation and because of that must be considered as the real winner of the 'race' with *Sirius*. As indicated earlier no race as such actually took place, for to have a race competitors are required and the Great Western Steam Ship Company made no effort to compete with the little *Sirius*. Unfortunately, over the years, historians have insisted upon calling the event a 'race' and so the classification has remained. No matter how the voyages are labelled there is no doubt that *Great Western* succeeded in proving that steamships could operate a regular commercial service on the North Atlantic.

Chapter 5

Early years

The success of the first voyage created an infectious enthusiasm, drawing to Kingroad crowds of people desirous of viewing the ship and, in the process, making a small fortune for the operators of the small river steamers. Certainly, confidence in the sailing abilities of the vessel increased as she drew 57 passenger bookings for her second westward crossing. The total would have been greater had not two families withdrawn the morning of sailing due to bereavements. An almost full cargo, considerable specie (gold and silver coin), numerous parcels and letters as well as an extensive array of newspapers all added to the profitability of the voyage. With her decks again littered by luggage, etc, *Great Western* departed from Kingroad late in the afternoon of Saturday June 2. A number of well crowded steamers ensured a lively send-off, with the cheering almost drowning out the band playing aboard *Great Western*. Guests of the passengers were allowed to set out with the ship and that evening all sat down to dinner in the main saloon, entertainment being provided by the band. At 8.00 pm, off Minehead, Captain Claxton, the guests and band reluctantly transferred to a waiting steamer for the trip back to Bristol, whilst *Great Western* proceeded westward leaving behind nothing but a column of smoke and a white trail in the water.[1] The uneventful crossing to New York took 14 days 16 hours whilst the return, which attracted 91 passengers and a fair cargo, occupied a remarkable 12 days 14 hours — an average speed of a little over 10 knots. Obviously things were looking up.

Whilst the ship was away on her second voyage bookings for the third westward crossing poured in, as did reservations for cargo space, prompting the Board of Directors to make two important decisions. Firstly the number of berths available on the ship would be increased and, secondly, a consort, or rather consorts, would be constructed. To provide a large number of additional cabins would require major work involving a considerable amount of revenue earning time. That, after only two voyages the directors were, sensibly, not willing to contemplate. The only practical proposition was the erection of substantial, but temporary, cabins on the after deck as an extension to the poop. Work on the two berth rooms occupied most of the twelve day stay at Kingroad between the second and third voyages and increased the nominal first class accommodation from 128 berths to 140 berths. In order to avoid any passenger discomfort which might arise from new paint, the cabins were lined with chintz. As a measure to maximise the income from the ship, due to her obvious attraction to would-be passengers, the fare scales were amended. Berths in the main saloon and new cuddy (poop) staterooms were to cost 40 guineas whilst those in the fore-cabin and under the main saloon remained at 35 guineas, the same fare charged for first class accommodation aboard the sailing packets.

Having satisfied themselves that an Atlantic steamship service offered lucrative possibilities the directors determined upon increasing the maximum share capital of the company from £250,000 to £1,000,000, a step which required an alteration to the deed of settlement. Through the increased capital it was decided, as a first step, to build two ships with similar dimensions to *Great Western*. Both would operate an Atlantic service to New York, one from a base at Bristol but the other would use Liverpool as its British terminal.[2] Obviously, the directors had recognised, even at this stage of their project, the possibilities and potential of Liverpool as a home port for Atlantic steamships. Discussions regarding the alterations to the deed of settlement resulted in friction between groups of proprietors from Bristol and Bath, those from Bath considering that the concern required no extension. A number of Bath based proprietors actually sold their shares in the company rather than be party to any change.[3] Eventually the far sighted notion had to be abandoned as it proved difficult, in such a short period of time, to satisfy all conditions necessary for the amendment to the deed to be completed. The company did, however, determine to build a single running mate for *Great Western* and, for that purpose, went so far as to purchase a shipment of African oak. This timber was destined never to be used by the company as, in a matter of months, wood gave

way to iron and *City of New York,* as the sister ship was to have been called, became *Great Britain.* But that is another story.

Passenger numbers, both outward and homewards, showed a considerable improvement, at least until 1840, thus confirming the directors' confidence in the drawing power of their ship. Cargo, however, presented a different picture. Freight rates had been set at £5 per ton of measured goods, increased in 1844 to £7 per ton, and there appeared to be little difficulty in attracting sufficient cargo for carriage to New York. Some manufacturers were prepared to pay an even higher rate in order to ensure that their goods did not suffer delay on the Atlantic and reached American markets quickly. Freight from America to Britain did not offer the same lucrative possibilities. In the easterly direction the sailing packets provided much sterner competition as their passage times to Europe were shorter than when going the other way. As a consequence *Great Western*

Fig 19: Great Western *at her moorings at Broad Pill in the River Avon.* (Courtesy City of Bristol Museum and Art Gallery).

was forced to take cargo, if available, at whatever rate happened to be in force at the time, usually £1 10s or £2 per ton.[4] As a crossing progressed coal consumption caused a gradual reduction in draft with the result that the paddle wheels would lose about three feet of immersion over a crossing. For the final few days, therefore, propulsive efficiency would be adversely influenced. Experience soon showed that *Great Western* required between 60 and 100 tons of cargo in her holds in order to ensure the necessary paddle wheel dip at the end of a crossing. At times, such an amount of cargo could not be obtained and Claxton, in an attempt to alleviate the problem, made a costly error of judgement.

Expensive and time consuming shipping of ballast had to be avoided as did the taking of too much coal at New York; coal cost a third as much again at New York as at Bristol. The solution proposed by Claxton was the purchase of apples at New York for, hopefully profitable, resale at Bristol. The trade would be seasonable but it was a long season. A trial shipment, carried home on the fourth voyage, indicated a handsome profit potential as barrels of apples were purchased in New York for ten shillings and sold in Bristol for twenty eight shillings. Claxton instructed the New York agent to lay in apples, for the company's account, if sufficient freight was not forthcoming on the next (the fifth) voyage. In the event some 500 barrels of apples were purchased and put aboard *Great Western* for shipment to Bristol. Unfortunately, a very large consignment of apples arrived, by sailing packet, shortly before those aboard *Great Western* resulting in a slump in apple prices.[5] The exercise was never repeated.

The fifth voyage seems to have been fated to illustrate the overwhelming uncertainties of any commercial venture, for cargo losses were also suffered on the outward crossing. Only six days were available at

Fig 20: Great Western *in a storm during her fifth crossing to New York. From a contemporary painting by J Walters* (Courtesy City of Bristol Museum and Art Gallery).

Kingroad between the fourth and fifth voyages and during this time all movement of coal, stores and cargo had to be accomplished. In spite of bad weather the work continued throughout each day of that period and also for the two nights prior to sailing. Although the company took steps to regulate the cargo in accordance with the space available, the situation was aggravated because a larger than normal amount of cargo was offered during the final few days, much of it being urgent single packages and these the company felt obliged to take. Needless to say, the cargo had not all been stowed away by the time the passengers arrived on the afternoon of sailing day. In fact, many of the packages could not have been stowed below as they were too large to pass through the hatches. Rather than contemplate a delay, Claxton ordered that sailing take place at the appointed time, although the decks were still littered with cargo, stores and baggage. Passengers actually made matters worse by bringing on board additional luggage. Under normal circumstances the decks would have been cleared within two days of sailing and all but the largest packages stowed below. During the second day out *Great Western* encountered a hurricane which resulted in damage to the goods still on deck. Meeting all of the claims cost some £1,500.[6] In order to minimise the risk of such an incident happening again the company quickly took action. Passenger baggage was strictly controlled and any in excess of fifteen cubic feet per person had to be booked as cargo. Merchants were informed that all outward cargo had to be on the quay at Bristol five days before sailing.[7]

A contributing factor to the cargo problem was the lack of a suitable berth at the dockside. Had *Great Western* lain at a berth, excess cargo could have been easily removed before she sailed or not put on board in the first place. Lying at anchor meant that ships had to be recalled in order to take off excess freight, this together with difficulties involved in the unloading would result in considerable delay. Notwithstanding the fact that they did not provide a berth, the Bristol Dock Company still levied dues on both ship and cargo. The cargo charges were fair as the cargo did, ultimately, pass through Bristol docks by way of the smaller steamers. However, the tonnage levy does seem unreasonable at over £100 per trip. For each of the first two voyages the actual charge was £101 17s, with increases for the later voyages to take account of the tonnage increase due to the alterations. The Great Western Steam Ship Company was also faced with the additional costs of servicing a ship down river at Kingroad; voyages No 1 and No 2 each cost an additional £255 8s 10d, representing, over six voyages annually, upwards of £1,500 dead loss.[8] Initially, in response to requests from the owners of *Great Western*, the dock company returned the tonnage levy but, after much legal wrangling, the steamship company had no option but to pay the charges. Throughout the prolonged discussions between the parties many suggestions were postulated as to ways in which the situation might be relieved. One was the widening of the locks at the Cumberland Basin, thus providing a means of access for *Great Western* without the inconvenience of removing the lower part of her paddle wheels. Another was to build a floating pier near Portishead, at the mouth of the Avon. Indecision and intransigence on the part of the dock company board members not only cost the Great Western Steam Ship Company a great deal of money and put them to considerable inconvenience, but it also lost for Bristol the chance of taking a major share in the growing oceanic steamship traffic. Not all in Bristol were blind to the consequences of the dock company's action, or rather inaction. Many merchants opposed, voiciferously, the stand taken by the dock company, but to no avail. It was only years later, after the city had taken control of the docks, that the locks at the Cumberland Basin were widened, unfortunately too late for *Great Western* and her owners.

At the end of the first season the company decided to drydock their vessel in order to facilitate an overhaul of hull and machinery. Whilst at Kingroad *Great Western* was left high and dry at each low tide but that did not allow sufficient time to carry out more than trivial repairs. Rather than bring the ship up to Bristol Docks, relations with the dock company still being strained, the owners of the ship sought, and obtained, permission from the Admiralty to use the dockyard at Pater, Pembroke. Little in the way of repair work had to be carried out as the vessel showed herself to be in the very best of condition, however, major new deck works were to be put in hand. The temporary cabins on the poop and the poop itself had to be removed in order to make way for an entirely new quarter deck which extended from the stern to the mizzen mast. That addition contained a number of cabins, a promenade area and a greatly enlarged cooking and stewarding facility. Alterations to the cabin below and the main saloon reduced the number of berths available to 109, although extra beds could be provided whenever necessary. Cargo capacity increased by some 50 tons as a result of the changes.[9]

The winter overhaul at the end of the 1839 season did, however, take place within the Bristol Docks, the lower portion of the paddle wheels being removed in order to facilitate entry. The dock company actually displaced some bridges so as to assist the operation. Throughout the preceeding two seasons a certain amount of passenger discomfort had been experienced due to officer and crew accommodation being positioned below the fore saloon. The company decided to alleviate the annoyance caused by the crew as watches changes by repositioning the officer and crew accommodation on the fore deck. The space below the fore saloon was then thrown open to cargo. On the after deck a sixteen foot long section, added to the poop, increased the number of first class berths available. (A more detailed account of the accommodation can be found in a later chapter.) Aware of the need to maintain their ship in the very best of condition and also to be seen to be doing so, the company had her surveyed by the local Lloyds' Surveyor of Shipping, Mr George Bayley. There was no obligation for such a survey as *Great Western* did not come under a *Lloyds' Register* classification.[10] The survey report indicated that the ship was in perfectly good condition, free from any defect inside and with a smooth unstrained copper outside. Bayley wrote in the report: 'My attention was particularly directed to the Trusses immediately before and abaft the Engine Room, where the first indication of straining and movement in Steam Vessels are invariably given, and I found even less straining than is commonly seen in much smaller vessels at the same age and after so much service; in fact I found the Abutments there to be in the same state as when I examined them whilst receiving her machinery on board in London.' Not at all a bad report for a prototype Atlantic steamship after 75,000 miles of service. Bayley concluded his report with the comment, '. . . I heartily congratulate you on the successful result of this magnificent experiment in Steam Navigation.'[11]

The only drydock within the Bristol dock system capable of accommodating *Great Western* was Merchant's Drydock, situated close to the Floating Dock. Whilst afloat for repairs *Great Western* would lay in the spacious confines of Cumberland Basin. Situated alongside the quay wall she did not obstruct normal traffic through the basin and the uncluttered quayside allowed for easy movement of equipment and materials. Drydock inspections were not carried out every year but only when repairs to the copper sheathing, hull or ship's side valves dictated. Whilst at Kingroad the ship would rest on the mud at each low tide allowing visual inspection of the copper to take place whenever required. Under normal circumstances most of the drydock work involved renewing sections of the copper sheathing which had been rubbed away by coal barges and other small craft moored alongside. Expensive drydocking did not take place during the winter of 1842/43 and it is highly improbable that any drydocking was carried out at the end of the 1844 season. Certainly the author has been unable to find any evidence of such action. The extensive overhaul lasting until the middle of 1844 would have dealt with any major defects. Whenever *Great Western* visited the Bristol docks she became the focus of attention with many people eager to visit her. The company charged six pence for a tour of the ship, the proceeds being donated to the General Hospital and Bristol Infirmary. During the winter of 1839/40 upwards of 5,000 visitors were attracted to the ship producing donations to each medical institution of £53 13s.[12] Contributions of such an amount were extremely welcome and put to good use. Claxton felt concerned when, at the end of 1842, the company's ship did not make the trip up river and so he suggested to the master of the Royal Mail steamer *Severn,* then fitting out in the Floating Harbour, that he make his ship available for the same purpose. The result is, unfortunately, unknown.[13]

The benevolent attitude adopted by the company seemed to permeate through to the passengers for whenever the need arose they were always willing to offer the hand of charity to those who served them. During the course of the first voyage of 1839 a young seaman sustained serious injury when he fell from a topsail yard. The wounds were such that he had to be left in hospital at New York. Although the company would have arranged certain of the medical expenses, the westbound passengers took up a collection which realised £20; a considerable amount for him when his wages came to no more than £2 per month.[14] Two voyages later a similar collection raised nearly £70 for an unfortunate crew member whose heel was torn off by a piece of machinery whilst going about his duty. At the termination of each crossing it appears to have been traditional for the satisfied passengers to present an item of silverware to the master as a testimonial to his attention and seamanship. No doubt Hosken, and later Matthews, had amassed an admirable collection of silver plate by the time he retired.

Selection of suitable crew members always presented problems as there were but few available who possessed previous steamship experience. Those who had were generally only familiar with coastal steamships and not large ocean going vessels. Navigators and engineers tended to serve on board for a number of voyages, as did the craftsmen, ie, carpenter and joiner, but sailors and, to a lesser extent, firemen and coal trimmers were more difficult to retain, thus necessitating frequent replacement. Behaviour on board was, generally good with few disciplinary problems revealing themselves. The main difficulty appears to have been in encouraging reasonably well qualified men to sign articles and then to ensure that they actually joined the ship. The latter requirement was not always fulfilled. A typical incident was outlined in *The Times* for March 25 1839, which reported that *Great Western* '. . . was unexpectedly detained by some of her hands refusing to go in her after having signed articles.' The *Bristol Mirror,* for March 30 1839, gave more details; '. . . four seamen and three firemen did not report on board at the appointed time; . . . three of them arrived aboard the steamer bringing down the mails, but the remaining four were too drunk to be allowed on board.' As replacements were not brought to the ship until past 10.00 pm that Saturday, *Great Western* did not finally depart until 2.00 am on Sunday, nearly twelve hours late'. According to the *Bristol Mirror* a number of ships had been similarly delayed at Kingroad and, no doubt, throughout the succeeding years *Great Western* suffered other crewing difficulties but none appear to have resulted in much delay.

During the first four years of service passage times between Bristol and New York remained remarkably good; westbound crossings averaged just over sixteen days whilst those eastbound just under thirteen and a half days. Weather obviously influenced the times to a considerable extent, little action being possible to combat head winds and rough seas apart from keeping the engines running in order to make as much progress as possible. Although severe gales mainly occur during the winter months on the North Atlantic, extremely dangerous storms can, and do, blow up at any time of the year. In her eight years of North Atlantic service *Great Western* showed that she was capable of withstanding any ravages which the elements could produce. Heavy weather resulted in the loss of spars, rigging and sails, but items of that nature could be readily repaired, spares and materials being carried. A different and, perhaps, more serious hazard emanated from the icebergs and pack-ice which littered the North Atlantic during the months of April, May and June. In the days before radar and radio warnings a ship's master had to be very wary or risk his vessel and all on board. Accompanying the ice would often be fog, making the situation much worse. A dramatic fall in sea water temperature is associated with ice nearby and that provided the only indication during foggy conditions or on dark nights. Frequent checks on the water temperature were always carried out at times when ice might be in the vicinity.[15] A first encounter with ice came during April 1840 whilst the ship was just off the Newfoundland Bank. Until that time *Great Western* had always run many miles to the south so as to avoid the ice during the danger months. Although the ice field extended for some thirty or forty miles the Bristol steamer ploughed her way steadily through it. One day, the following April, a much denser field was encountered. From early evening *Great Western* forced a passage through the thickening ice but at 10.00 pm Hosken was compelled to turn back and experienced considerable difficulty in getting clear. After two hours the edge of the ice field was found and a southward track made in order to coast the ice. Next morning showed an ice field extending northwards as far as the eye could see.[16]

Coal quality had a considerable influence upon steaming capability and hence upon speed. The first year of operation saw numerous experiments undertaken using coals from a variety of sources. Coals supplied at Bristol generally came from Tredegar and proved to be extremely good. At New York the company had erected a coal yard for the purpose of supplying its ships for the homeward passage. Setting up the yard with its storage facilities and crane cost some £200.[17] American coal was expensive and to be avoided whenever possible, but good quality and reasonably priced supplies of coal had to be obtained. Inexpensive Canadian coals, from the mines at Pictou, Nova Scotia, could be readily procurred. When tried, during the homeward passage in July 1838, the Canadian coal proved completely unsuitable. In a letter to *Mechanics Magazine,* Claxton corrected their previously printed erroneous statement regarding the suitability of Pictou coal and gave the following extracts from the engine room log for that voyage: 'Monday July 2. Picton (sic) coals are very soft and will not bear the bars pricking, but burn freely.' 'Thursday July 5. Picton (sic) coals used forward, the consumption larger than before, and more difficulty in keeping steam up; a great deal of dirt from them, the clinker soft, and not injurious to the bars. Of the four descriptions of coals used this voyage, the Tredegar is the best for our purposes.' Claxton went on to add that *Great Western* had never shipped a second lot of Pictou coal and that, including the voyage in question, nine types of coals had been tried on the ship, the best being that from Tredegar.[18] All coal for the return passage had, therefore, to be shipped, at considerable cost, to New York where it attracted an import levy of two pence per bushel. Nearly five shillings per ton on upwards of 1,000 tons shipped to that port during the year 1838.[19] Coal prices varied, as did transportation coasts, but the 830 tons of coal in stock at the New York yard were, in December 1838, valued at £1,464 18s, representing a cost per ton of £1 15s. During the return passage of the fourth voyage coal shipped from Liverpool was used; that coal probably originated from one of the Lancashire coal fields and its performance illustrates the problems faced by steamship owners. In use it burned so poorly that difficulty was experienced in maintaining steam. The log book for the voyage indicated that the *Great Western* would have arrived home one day earlier had the coals not been so bad. Less steam was produced with 35 to 40 tons of the Liverpool coals than with 25 tons of that from Tredegar.[20]

Early steamships were frequently delayed on their voyage for one of a variety of reasons, many already outlined above, and in that respect *Great Western* was no exception. Without modern ship to shore communication techniques a delay of one or two days on an Atlantic crossing attracted little comment or concern. As the delay ran into a third or fourth day, however, anxiety would manifest itself and speculation would begin as to the fate of the vessel, often serving only to increase the anxiety. Throughout those early years, in all cases but one, prophesies of disaster proved to be premature; that single tragedy, the loss of the steamship *President,* will be dealt with later. To such speculation the *Great Western* was not immune. A catalogue of incidents would be pointless and unnecessary, but two cases should illustrate the problem. The second crossing to New York during the year 1839 occupied no less than 22 days due to extremely adverse weather and the arrival was awaited with considerable uneasiness; business houses were said to be apprehensive. The loss of a ship such as *Great Western* would, certainly, have affected trade, the financial markets (steamships carried considerable quantities of specie as well as bankers drafts) and the cause of Atlantic steam navigation. The families of friends and passengers had more tangible reasons for fear. Newspapers of the time mirrored the concern felt by people, directly involved or not, but the majority tended to remain optimistic offering comfort to the uneasy. Some journals, however, gave less creditable performances. The day before *Great Western* departed on her fifth voyage from Bristol there appeared, in the *Dublin Evening Mail* an article reporting her loss. With no press agencies in existence, newspapers frequently extracted interesting stories from sister journals. The *Lancashire Herald,* without checking the facts, copied the report from the Dublin paper; unfortunately it also displayed an advertising placard, informing of the loss, near the Stock Exchange in Manchester. Needless to say, considerable apprehension resulted. The *Manchester Guardian* decided to investigate the source before it became party to the transmission of any rumour; its investigations revealed a rather unsavoury tale.

The original Dublin report turned out to be a stupid and pointless paragraph intended as a joke against Lord Durham. Durham had, at the time, only recently resigned as Governor General to Canada and Judge Crane was making the outward passage in the Bristol steamer with despatches for him. Judge Crane had brought over despatches from Durham when he made the previous eastbound crossing aboard the *Great Western*. The 'joke' was, apparently, aimed at making Lord Durham believe that his despatches had gone astray. All it did was to cause alarm to those having family or friends on the ship.[21] Regrettably, there was no way in which the company could counteract the rumours apart from the issue of a denial and to re-emphasise the sea keeping qualities of its ship.

Following the successful completion of the first voyage insurance underwriters looked upon steamships with greater favour. Initially the rates of premium had been set at £12 per cent upon a value of £50,000, but later during the first year the insurance premium fell to £10 per cent,[22] obviously as a result of the safe completion of the early voyages. Regarded as a much better risk, premiums on the fabric of *Great Western* reduced to eight per cent for the year 1839. The following year saw the premiums fall by two guineas per cent with a reduction of ten shillings per cent for each month that the ship lay unemployed.[23] During those first three years of operation the insurance charges totalled £13,606 16s,[24] a considerable sum for a company trying to establish itself. Such costs were not borne by steamship companies coming later into the field, for, by then, the steamship *Great Western* had shown, by its robust and expensive construction, that steam navigation on the Atlantic could be accomplished safely and consistently. Throughout the years which followed the insurance premiums on the fabric of *Great Western* reduced still further. For the year 1844 the insurance bill was only £1,000, although the figure is misleading as the vessel only performed three round voyages. However, the charges do reflect the gradual reduction in insurance premiums which took place annually from the first year of operation. That fact indicates the growing acceptance amongst the underwriters that a soundly built, well maintained and efficiently managed steamship was a very good risk.

Important though low insurance premiums were, maximum revenue from its single ship was vital to the well being and survival of the company, only a well filled passenger list could ensure that. Fortunately, following the first voyage passenger confidence increased and, more importantly, so did their numbers. Throughout the first three years of operations passenger numbers showed a steady upward trend. Early and late season books were always lower than those at other

times due to the reluctance of people to venture onto the Atlantic during the bad winter weather; despite that fact, *Great Western* regularly carried more passengers than her rivals. As already indicated, fares were initially set at 35 guineas for all berths but the cost of a main saloon berth soon rose to 40 guineas. When *British Queen* entered service, in 1839, her berths cost more than the equivalent aboard the Bristol steamer and so, for a short period the Great Western Steam Ship Company raised its fares by five guineas. Competition quickly ensured a return to former levels.[25] Following the improvements to the forward cabin accommodation a uniform fare structure came into force from February 1840, with all berths to cost 40 guineas.[26] Fares remained at that level until September 1841 when a reduction of five guineas took place.[27] With the Cunard steamers on the Atlantic, intense rivalry resulted in a lowering of fares to 30 guineas for all berths. That fare structure remained in force from April 1843 until *Great Western* ceased service on the North Atlantic at the end of 1846. Evidently, competition worked to the advantage of the passenger.

It is unnecessary to give the respective eastbound passage rates for the various westbound fares but the cost of a passage from America to England was always less than one in the opposite direction. A single example should serve to illustrate the differentials. Compared with a 30 guinea fare to New York the passage from that port cost 100 dollars;[28] with the exchange rate then standing at five dollars to one pound the eastbound cost was only £20, less then two thirds of the westbound fare. The large differential may be accounted for by two factors. Firstly, eastbound crossings took two or three days less than those towards New York and hence operating costs, such as coal, wages and provisions, would have been correspondingly lower. Secondly, and perhaps more significantly, the sailing packets offered greater competition due to their swifter passages in that direction. Passage rates quoted always concerned the occupancy of a single berth in a multi-berth cabin. The company, always eager to attract additional business, indicated a willingness to negotiate charges for family occupancy of a number of cabins. An advertising poster for the first voyage stated; 'For families, a reduction will be made in proportion to their number and the berths they require.' The secretary's letter book for 1843 gives an example of such an arrangement. A letter to a Mr Orville Devcy confirms that the company would allow his family sole occupancy of cabins No 43 to 47 upon payment of four full fares.[29] All fares, children and servants had passage at half the standard rate, included were normal provisions but wines and spirits had to be purchased separately. An additional stewards fee of one guinea (five dollars at New York) provided the funds for the hiring of the requisite number of stewards in order to obtain reasonably efficient service during any particular voyage.

In November 1838 there appeared, in various sections of the press, an advertisement calling for tenders for the operation of a mail carrying steamship service across the Atlantic. The government advertisement indicated two possible services, between England and Halifax, Nova Scotia, and also between England and New York, calling at Halifax. Steam vessels of not less than 300 horse power had to be employed. This is not the place for a complete discussion of that mail contract but some account must be given in order to illustrate the part played by the owners of the *Great Western*. The service contract, to commence on April 1 1839, called for twelve round voyages annually and was to run, initially for a period of one year. The choice of starting date was, perhaps, appropriate in the light of the conditions laid down. At that time no company had sufficient ships of the required power nor would any company contemplate building such ships for a one year contract. It would, in any case, have been impossible to construct enough vessels to commence the contract by the required date. Some official at the Admiralty was optimistic, had a weird sense of humour or, most probably, was just trying to test the reaction.

Only two tenders were received by the closing date of December 15 1838, one from the Great Western Steam Ship Company and the other from the St George Steam Packet Company, owners of the *Sirius*. The latter concern could have commenced operating the service on the appointed date but only had two vessels of the necessary power and more were, certainly, needed. They offered to perform the service for £45,000, or for £60,000 if New York was included. The government turned the offer down. The Bristol concern found it impossible to comply with the contract terms but tendered nevertheless. Its letter not only offered to perform a service from a later date than that stipulated

but also offered advice to the Admiralty upon the size and power of suitable vessels. The latter of tender, signed by Claxton, was as follows:

'Sirs,

I am instructed by the directors of the Great Western Steam Ship Company to express to their Lords of the Admiralty their willingness to enter into a contract for the conveyance of Her Majesty's mails to and from England and Halifax, Nova Scotia; but I am desired to state that the time specified in the form of tender is too short to allow them to make the necessary arrangements.

The experience of the last voyage of the *Great Western* has established, in the opinion of the directors, that no vessel of less than 1,000 tons register if built of iron, or 1,200 tons register, if of timber, and with engines of less than 350 horse power, will be adequate to the duty required, and three such vessels will be necessary.

The time required for the construction, equipment and trial of these vessels and engines will be not less than 18 to 24 months from the date of the contract.

From and after such a period, the directors will be willing to contract for monthly departures to and from England and Halifax, for the sum of £45,000 per annum; on condition that the contract remains in force for seven years from its commencement, and subject to all other conditions being agreed upon between the Board of Admiralty and the directors.'[30]

The Great Western Ship Company, with its experience of operating a steamship on the North Atlantic, was the only concern in a position to offer any advice on the matter then under consideration. Their Lords of the Admiralty, however, were not favourably disposed to a lecture upon maritime affairs, even though the lecturer had superior knowledge about the subject, and particularly when the lecturer was a half pay naval officer. On Janaury 10 1839 they declined the offer:

'Sir,

Having laid before my Lords Commissioners of the Admiralty your letter of 13th ultimo, stating the conditions under which the Great Western Steam Ship Company would be disposed to enter into a contract for the conveyance of Her Majesty's mails between England

and Halifax by steam vessels, I am commanded by their Lordships to aquaint you that they decline this offer.

I am, etc, John Barrow.'[31]

The tone of the rejection leaves little doubt about the feelings of the Lords Commissioners towards the party in Bristol. Sour would, probably, be too mild an expression.

The owners of *Great Western* heard nothing more until news leaked out that a Canadian, Samuel Cunard, had been awarded a contract for a twice monthly mail service between Liverpool and Halifax, with an extention to Boston. For the service Cunard was to be paid £55,000 per year; the rate actually being increased to £60,000 before the service commenced on July 4 1840. Not surprisingly the size and power of Cunard's vessels was almost identical to the figures suggested by the Bristol concern, as was the starting date and initial term of the contract. Though no public comment was made at the time the circumstances of the Cunard contract were viewed with suspicion. In 1841, following the first winter of operating the mail contract, Cunard realised that he could not keep up the winter sailing schedule and petitioned the Admiralty for a reduction to one sailing per month during January, February, March and April. For what now became 20 instead of 24 annual sailings Cunard was awarded an increase in payment to £80,000 per year, or £4,000 per voyage.[32] Obviously, the Lords of the Admiralty realised that if Cunard did not receive the increased payment and a reduction in the number of voyages he would, very likely, abandon the contract after the first year rather than suffer great financial loss. A premature termination of the mail contract would not have left 'my Lords Commissioners of the Admiralty' in a very favourable position. Rather than be compromised they gave Cunard all that he wanted — from public funds with neither the public nor Parliament having a say in the matter. It is only fair to state that the contract price included payment for a small steamer operating on the St Lawrence River carrying the mails between Pictou, Nova Scotia, and Quebec. Thus the actual rate per Atlantic voyage was a little below £4,000.

Three Cunard vessels, *Britannia, Acadia* and *Caledonia* commenced operating during 1840 with a fourth, *Columbia,* joining them the following year. From the beginning Cunard's vessels took passengers from *Great Western* although the effect in 1840 was not as noticeable as in subsequent years. Any passenger making use of the Cunard service tended to be going to, or coming from, Nova Scotia or Boston. Alternatively they were people on British government service who were instructed to use the mail steamers as the contract stipulated that passage rates for such persons had to be at a reduced level. From the passenger lists published by various newspapers it may be observed that the *Great Western* consistently attracted a greater number of passengers than any Cunarder sailing at about the same time as the Bristol ship. In fact, the Cunard management became so concerned at their poor passenger figures, due to the direct competition from *Great Western*, that they reduced their passage rates for sailings which took place within days of a departure of *Great Western*. The fares came down from 38 guineas to 30 guineas.[33] There was, however, little influence upon the respective shares of the available passengers. Receipts from the *Great Western* did fall due to the competition but the ship continued to attract a large proportion of the passengers and that fact may be taken as an indication of the vessel's popularity and as a compliment to its owners.

Although not in possession of a mail contract the Bristol steamer still carried mail, as she had done since commencing service. However, unless a letter was specifically marked to go by *Great Western*, or a special Post Office bag was arranged, all mail was sent by way of the contract steamers. Before the Cunard steamers came on the line the company's vessel would carry between 10,000 and 12,000 letters on each crossing; afterwards the figure fell to between 4,000 and 5,000. For each letter the company received two pence from the British government and a further two pence from the Americans following delivery at New York. Upon each eastbound letter the Americans paid a quarter of a dollar (one shilling) with a further two pence coming from the British Government.[34] Obviously, carriage of American mail was the more lucrative. Before the mail contract came into force the Great Western Steam Ship Company received letters through its own office. That practice later became illegal and all mail had to be forwarded through the Post Office. Such was not the case with parcels and the company had its own scale of charges depending upon size. Parcels with a maximum dimension of up to 6 inches were charged at 7 shillings;

for a maximum dimension of up to 9 inches the charge was 11 shillings, whilst parcels up to 12 inches long cost 16 shillings; for dimensions above 12 inches the rates were in proportion. Whenever necessary, both before and after the Cunard steamers appeared, *Great Western* carried British government despatches but her owners received not one penny for that service.

Despite the tribulations and setbacks the *Great Western* remained a profitable ship for, even though other routes were subsidised, the New York run was, by far, the most popular. Upon that line no other contemporary vessel could compete with her. The rewards were attractive and Cunard cast covetous eyes at the line. As far as the Great Western Steam Ship Company was concerned, however, other factors controlled its destiny.

Chapter 6

Structure of the *Great Western*

In 1836 the art of ship construction could be seen at its best in those vessels built for the Admiralty and so it is understandable that the Great Western Steam Ship Company should cast its net in that direction when seeking advice on the construction of its unique vessel. To resist the Atlantic weather a strong, rigid ship was a necessity. The Admiralty possessed such ships, designed to combat more than weather. The solution did not lie solely with the Admiralty, however, as the Navy possessed no steamships of the size envisaged. Ultimately, the design of the ship lay in the hands of the company.

During the early years of the 19th century the Admiralty became increasingly concerned about the growing shortage of good, long timber for the construction of its ships. Timber from overseas was increasingly employed by there was much wastage in the cutting of timber for frames. Traditionally, the frames or ribs of a ship had been formed from long section of timber, the joints in the frame being made by means of chocks or wedge pieces. This method not only consumed considerable quantities of timber but produced a relatively weak frame which was liable to decay where the grain had been cut. In 1820, Sir Robert Seppings, then Chief Surveyor to the Admiralty, advocated, in a paper to The Royal Society[1], a new method of constructing merchant ships based upon his recent naval practice, where he had produced stronger structures and saved timber. His method utilised shorter sections of timber joined by dowels to form complete frames; these frames were placed closer together and diagonal trusses fitted to produce greater strength and rigidity.

No one man had complete responsibility for the con-

structional design of *Great Western* but much credit is attributable to William Patterson who supervised the construction, probably did much of the design work and drew the lines for the hull; a signed copy of the lines is preserved at Bristol Museum. Brunel's skill and experience, particularly regarding the structural strength, must have played an important part in the final detail design and dimensioning, frames, etc. Less direct, but no less invaluable, assistance came from the works of Seppings as well as Sir William Symons and Oliver Lang, then at the Admiralty.[2]

Unfortunately no detailed drawings of the hull construction of the *Great Western* appear to have survived, that is if they ever existed in the first place. Understandably, the newspapers and periodicals of the day avoided technical descriptions whenever possible, confining their coverage to topics of interest to the general reader. Generally, the technical publications followed the same line. Regarding the construction, all that is available is a tantalising description, originally published by the directors of the Great Western Steam Ship Company in their report to the first Annual General Meeting held on March 1 1838.[3] That extract from the report was subsequently quoted in sections of the contemporary press, without explanation: '. . . Her floors are of great length and over-run each other, they are firmly dowelled and bolted, first in pairs, and then together by means of 1½ inch bolts, about 24 feet in length, driven in four parallel rows, scarfing about 4 feet. The Scantling is equal in size to that of our line-of-battle ships, it is filled in solid, and was caulked within and without up to the first Futtock Heads, previously to planking, and to all above this height of English Oak.

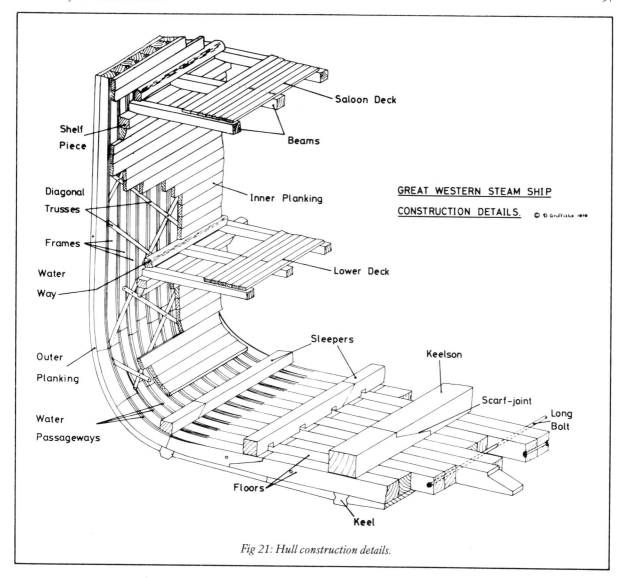

Shelf Piece

Beams

Saloon Deck

Diagonal Trusses

Frames

Water Way

Inner Planking

GREAT WESTERN STEAM SHIP
CONSTRUCTION DETAILS. © D Griffiths 1978

Lower Deck

Sleepers

Keelson

Scarf-joint

Long Bolt

Outer Planking

Water Passageways

Floors

Keel

Fig 21: Hull construction details.

She is most firmly and closely trussed with iron and wooden diagonals and shelf pieces, which, with the whole of her upper works, are fastened with screws and nuts, to a much greater extent than was hitherto been put in practice . . .'

Apart from indicating the care taken in ensuring that a sound vessel resulted from the labours of those employed in the yard of Patterson & Mercer, the above description does little to illustrate the hull construction except, possibly, to a trained naval architect. However, from that description, Seppings' paper and engine room drawings, which show some of the hull section,[4] the author has been able to reconstruct a section of the hull structure (fig No 21).

The 'floors' formed the lower portion of the frames and being of 'great length' they passed completely

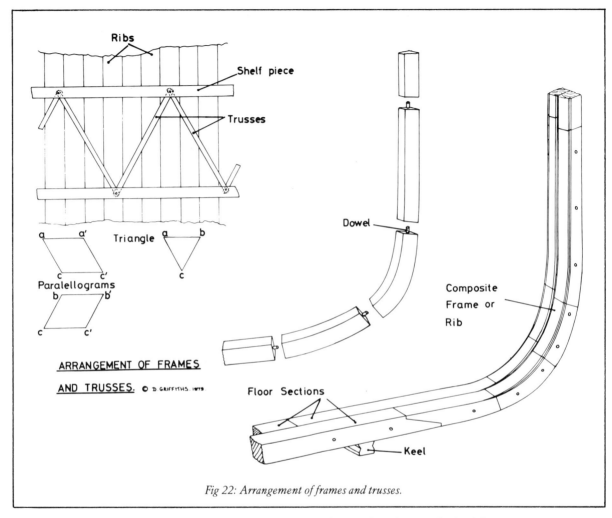

Ribs

Shelf piece

Trusses

Triangle

a   a'

c   c'

Paralellograms
b   b'

c   c'

a   b

c

Dowel

Composite
Frame or
Rib

ARRANGEMENT OF FRAMES

AND TRUSSES. © D. GRIFFITHS. 1979

Floor Sections

Keel

Fig 22: Arrangement of frames and trusses.

across the keel, thus avoiding a joint in a potentially weak region. By 'over-running' each other the joints in each adjacent pair of floors/frames were staggered thus avoiding another potentially fragile area. Although dowelled joints would have been employed for most sections of the frames, bolted scarf-joints were needed in the floors; the overlap of the joint being about four feet. Because of the necessity for great strength composite frames had to be used in order to provide for rigidity at the joints in the frames (fig No 22). This is indicated by the statement that the floors were 'firmly dowelled and bolted, first in pairs,'. Seppings' plan

advocated such a method of frame construction as it allows shorter lengths of timber to be used and provided considerable strength in the composite arrangement. By means of the 24 foot long bolts the composite frames were bolted together to form a continuous structure. The small gaps that existed between the frames were 'filled in solid' by hammering small pieces of timber into the gaps. All joints would be finally caulked with tarred hemp before internal and external planking was fitted. 'Shelf pieces' provided support for the deck beams but also added rigidity to the frame-work structure. In a heavy sea, however, movement of the frames could still take place and so diagonal trussing was applied. These iron and wood diagonals were connected to the frames along the sides of the hull. Together with the shelf pieces these trusses formed triangles and parallelograms firmly connected to the frames thus preventing each from moving relative to its neighbour.

The arrangement as shown provided an exceptionally strong hull which answered in every way the demands of the North Atlantic weather. As a protection for the timber against dry rot Brunel had all susceptible wood treated by Kyan's patent corrosive sublimate process.[5] This wood preservative Brunel had found to be effective from his work at the Monkwearmouth Dock, Sunderland. To protect the outer timber from the ravages of Toredo Navalis and other worms, the whole of the underwater section of the hull had copper sheeting firmly applied. Between each adjacent pair of frames a shallow channel would be left at the joint in order to allow any leaking water to fall to the bottom of the ship from where it would be regularly pumped overboard. Although shown, it is unlikely that inner planking was applied throughout the ship. In passenger areas such treatment would be essential but certainly not in the cargo and bunker spaces. As a protective measure the coal bunker spaces were encased in iron sheeting to prevent the coal from damaging the internal timber work. This 'tanking', however, appeared to have resulted in many erroneous statements in the newspapers of the day; probably all copied from the same source. The popular misconception was that the bunker 'tanks' would be filled with sea water ballast as quickly as the coal was used.[6] Certainly the available log books make no mention of such an important task as ballasting at sea. The log books do, however, indicate a draft change during the Atlantic crossing. This change corresponds to the amount of coal consumed, illustrating that no ballast can have been taken during the passage.[7]

The annual surveys conducted by the local surveyor to Lloyds' Register of Shipping, Mr George Bayley, confirms that the *Great Western* was truly a sound ship. In February 1841, after seventeen round trips to New York, he reported: '. . . In these places [the bottom outer planking] I found the caulking to be hard and sound, and the pitch in the butts and seams to be unbroken . . . The wood trussing being free from

movement or strain I directed my attention particularly to the state of the suspension truss bars, and selected a point where the strain is the greatest, and requested that two bolts might be driven out — they proved to be in perfect state . . . The holding down bolts do not show the slightest indication of movement, nor is there any appearance of straining in the scarphs of the keelsons or of the sleepers. She is, as far as can be seen, in a perfectly sound state, and free from the slightest indication of decay in all parts to which access was had.'[8]

The following year he wrote: 'We found no appearance of straining or working in any of the Butts or Seams of the bottom, the caulking was remarkably sound and hard, and had the appearance of having been done last year, instead of five years since . . . A yellow metal bolt driven out of the scarph of the keelson immediately abaft the Engine Room, it was quite perfect and free from corrosion . . . The scarphs of the Keelson, Engine Sleepers, Butts in the Bilge Planks, and the lower ends of the Trussing, are all quite close, firm and in a very sound state. The wood and iron trussing is all firm, shews no appearance of yielding or movement at its ends.'[9]

During the winter of 1842/3 no drydocking took place and so Bayley examined the ship whilst aground on the mud at Kingroad. His report was as glowing as in previous years; particular attention being directed in his survey to dry-rot: '. . . we could not discover the slightest trace of its existence, excepting a little fungus by the side of one timber on the starboard side forward. I recommend the fungus to be removed and the rooms (or spaces) between the timbers on each side filled with salt to some height above the point referred to. She has now been running five seasons, cross the Atlantic fifty-four times, and (as per log) traversed 166,687 nautical miles without requiring any material repair to the hull or to the machinery . . . she is still in a most efficient state.' In a postscript to the report Bayley wrote, 'To shew that no movement has taken place, I may just mention that in one of the store rooms, forward, a movement had taken place about three years since. The place was lime washed about two years since, and the last wash is still unbroken, shewing the ridge produced by the movement referred to.'

An interesting sentence in the report gives an insight to the actual materials used in the frame construction. The original statement from the company report of

1838 apparently indicated that only English oak was to be found in the framework below the first futtock heads. Bayley's report states, 'Her frame consists of one set of English oak timbers, fayed close with felt between them, and, I am informed, are coaked and bolted together, and one set of Danzig fir timbers, fitted and secured the same as the oak timbers.'[10] Evidently, the frame consisted of alternate oak and Danzig fir composite units bolted together.

Only good quality, sound timber could produce a sound vessel with the ability to resist the battering of the Atlantic waves. The Great Western Steam Ship Company chose only the best. For the hull alone some 36,702 cubic feet of oak, elm, hard pine (Danzig fir) and yellow pine were used. A complete materials list is given in Appendix No 4.[11] The actual volume of timber required for a hull 212 feet long, 35 feet wide and 23 feet deep illustrates clearly the loss of cargo/passenger/coal bunker space suffered by a wooden ship in comparison with an iron vessel of similar dimensions. This fact Brunel and Guppy were to seize on when planning the second vessel. Obviously, for strength the scantlings (dimensions) had to be large: 'The Scantling is equal in size to that of our line-of-battle ships.'[12] Some idea of the sections employed may be gathered from a statement in *Mechanics Magazine*, for September 23 1837: 'The paddle or main beams are formed from four pieces of timber each 12 or 13 inches square, confined together at the ends and separated to the distance of 6 or 7 inches at the middle length.'[13]

Nominally a wooden built vessel, the *Great Western* contained a considerable amount of metal in her structure. Apart from the engines and boilers, which weighed some 400 tons, and permanent iron ballast of 40 tons the iron work and copper in the hull amounted to 60 tons.[14] That iron work comprised of the trussing, coal bunker lining and fresh water tanks. Copper sheathing applied to the hull came in different thicknesses to suit the particular locality of application, the thickest being fitted where rubbing was most likely to take place. Grades were given in weight per square foot and those employed, 16oz, 18oz, and 22oz.[15] Bayley used the appearance of the copper as an indication of hull timber movement or damage and always reported that the surface was smooth. The considerable quantities of bolts, nuts and screws were either iron or brass, depending upon location, and water pipe-work was entirely manufactured from lead.

The initial Certificate of British Registry, issued at Bristol on September 2 1837, gives *Great Western* a burthen of 679 tons and indicated that she was carvel built with a rounded stern, mock galleries, a Neptune figure-head, standing bowsprit, schooner rigged with four masts and had two decks. The Registry Certificate gives the engine room length as 84 feet, but data issued by the company after the ship entered service show it to be 72 feet. The latter figure is likely to be the more accurate as the exact size of engine room necessary could only be determined after the engines and boilers had been constructed. The paddle wheel drive compelled the builders to position the engines amidships. Originally the idea had been to place the four boilers in pairs, one set before and one set astern of the engines; thus producing a two funnel appearance. Such an arrangement would account for the extra length of engine room on the Registry Certificate. Concerned that the aftermost boilers would lead to high accommodation temperatures in warm weather and that, perhaps more importantly, the would reduce the size of the revenue earning main saloon, a single set of four boilers placed before the engines was adopted.[16] *Great Western* became a single funneled ship.

The four masted configuration remained with the *Great Western* throughout her operating life. Only the fore mast was placed in front of the funnel and only this mast was equipped with square sails. As shown in the sail plan (fig No 7), spencer sails and trysails could be set on all of the masts with jib and stay sails available when needed. For operation in favourable light winds studding sails were provided, the gear being fitted, as required, to the fore mast.

Internal accommodation layout when the *Great Western* entered service has already been discussed in Chapter 3 and so further comment is unnecessary here. Apart from the cabins built on the saloon and lower decks, a poop or cuddy and a forecastle were provided on the main deck. Although no figures are given for the dimensions of these structures, contemporary paintings and prints show that the forecastle extended back over halfway to the fore mast, about 20 feet, whilst the poop reached almost to the after-most mast, again about 20 feet. The forecastle will have provided access to the crew and officer accommodation, situated at the forward end of the saloon deck and below the forward saloon. Certainly within the forecastle there would have been store rooms, chain lockers and, probably, workshops. The poop did not contain any passenger accommodation but is likely to have provided space for the galley, food stores (maybe an ice house) and a mail room. For the provision of milk and fresh meat and eggs, cows and other animals found themselves confined aboard the early steamships. Cow houses formed part of the deck buildings at a later date and it seems probable that provision was made for such animals from the outset. This being the case, the forecastle or, preferably, on the sponsons next to the paddle boxes would have been the most suitable site. Water closets, to save on pipe-work, will have been located in groups; those for the passengers within the accommodation and those for the officers and crew on deck, probably amidships.

As mentioned in Chapter 5, additional cabins were erected on the after deck just in front of the poop. This work occupied the time at Kingroad between the second and third voyages and produced six substantial, but temporary, two berth cabins. At the termination of her first season a completely new poop section became part of the *Great Western's* structure. This extended to the mizzen mast and contained cabins on either side with a central promenade area. In reporting these changes the *Bristol Mirror*, for January 26, 1839 stated that, 'The whole of the lower berths under the saloon have been thrown into cargo space, and passenger berths reduced to a number which must ensure every comfort and accommodation.' Later that 1839 season the *Great Western* carried 137 passengers, an impossible figure, even with the enlarged poop, if there were no under saloon cabins. It would appear, therefore that some of the under saloon cabins were retained whilst others gave way to cargo space. The berth plan for 1839 (fig No 8) has been redrawn from plans held by the Public Record Office and dates for voyages early in 1839.[17] These, however, must be the arrangement for late 1838 as they show only limited poop cabins and extensive under saloon berths. An interesting insert on the main saloon plan is the blocking in of the central recess areas for cabins. Although those elegant recesses featured extensively in the early publicity the Company soon became aware of their revenue earning potential and provided three two berth cabins in each alcove. Modifications made at this time also increased the cooking area and added to the deck houses,[18] the exact

purpose of which are unknown.

The winter of 1839/40 saw further extensive alterations in the accommodation arrangements, the last major changes to the structure whilst the *Great Western* remained in the hands of the Great Western Steam Ship Company. The directors informed the shareholders in their annual report: 'A Deck is now added to her forebody, and the Poop is extended 16 feet, by which means not only is the number of most desirable berths increased, but the sleeping or messing of the officers, cadets, clerk, firemen, stewards and boys, which were either beyond or under the fore saloon, are all placed in situations neither annoying to the passengers nor inconvenient to themselves, which they formerly were.'[19] The poop now extended from the stern to the paddle box whilst the new fore deck almost reached the funnel. With no crew occupancy, the section below the fore saloon became available for cargo. The addition of the new deck areas increased the tonnage from 1,340 when first in service to about 1,700 and the work carried out that winter cost the company in excess of £3,150.[20]

Press and company reports only outline the main changes which took place, they do not indicate the full details regarding the number and size of cabins or the layout. It is extremely unlikely that any major alterations took place in subsequent years as the company now had a vessel which, for its size, was ideal for the service intended. Perhaps, more importantly the company was preoccupied with the construction of the *Great Britain*, which soaked up all available money, and more. Throughout the next five years modifications must have been made to the fabric and layout of the *Great Western* but exactly what they were and when they took place does not appear to have been recorded. During early 1844 new boilers, which were more compact, replaced the originals, possible resulting in a slight repositioning of the funnel. Fortunately, when the *Great Western* came up for sale in 1847 the Royal Mail Steam Packet Company inspected her prior to purchase. The report of the RMSPC secretary gives details of how the ship looked in her last year of service with the Great Western Steam Ship Company and, conceivably, her general arrangement from 1840.

The forecastle and quarter deck were of such proportions as to provide a complete spar deck apart from a 40 foot section amidships. As a means of obtaining additional space the sponson areas had been utilised to

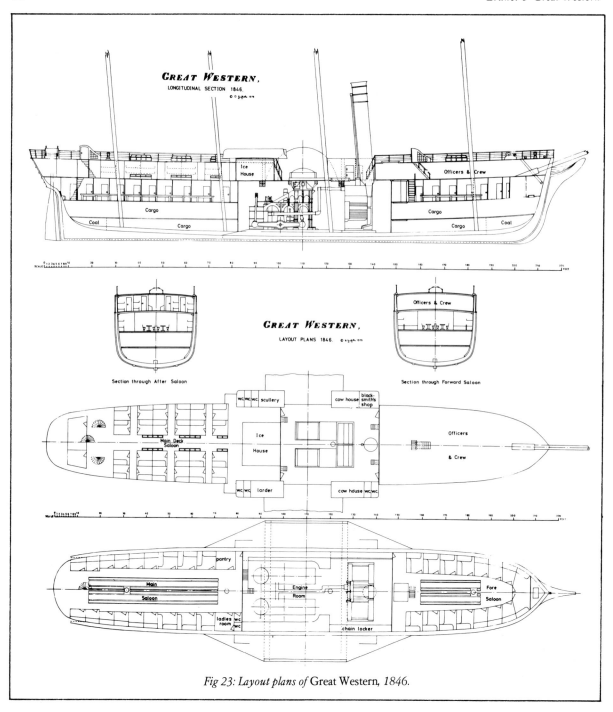

GREAT WESTERN,
LONGITUDINAL SECTION 1846.

Ice
House

Officers & Crew

Cargo

Coal   Cargo   Cargo   Coal

SCALE

Officers & Crew

GREAT WESTERN,
LAYOUT PLANS 1846.

Section through After Saloon

Section through Forward Saloon

wc wc wc   scullery   cow house   black-smith's shop

Ice

House   Officers

& Crew

wc wc   larder   cow hduse wc wc

pantry

Main
Saloon   Engine
Room   Fore
Saloon

ladies wc
room wc   chain locker

Fig 23: Layout plans of Great Western, *1846.*

erect a number of houses. Resting comfortably outside the main hull structure on the port sponson were two passenger water closets, a cow house, an iron lined blacksmith's shop, a scullery and the captain's water closet. Opposite these, on the starboard side, could be observed a similar array save that water closets for the officers and engineers replaced the blacksmith's shop and captain's water closet, whilst a larder replaced the scullery. Situated amidships, but not actually part of the structure of the ship was an immense ice house. The ice house contained about seven or eight tons of ice and was held onto the deck by means of cleats and stanchions.[21] It must have been close to the quarter deck otherwise it would have obstructed the engine room skylights and ventilators. This region also contained the galleys for passenger and crew food preparation. Passenger galley positioning had to be such that the food did not become cold when being moved to table. Situated at the forward end of the main deck saloon the passenger galley would be within easy reach of scullery, larder, ice house and pantry for the main saloon dining tables. Separate crew galley and mess facilities had to be provided as the crew certainly did not enjoy the fare supplied to the passengers. Being coal fired, the galley ranges needed a constant supply of fuel which could be easily brought to a midship position, from the boiler room, without having to pass through the passenger areas. During hot weather, being close to the engine rooms, the galleys must have been uncomfortably hot, but in winter months quite cosy.

Without an accompanying plan, the RMSPC report gives the following account of the accommodation: 'The principal Saloon is 60 feet long, with a double rank of tables the whole length and four stern windows. The sleeping cabins are all fitted with two or more bed places, they are on each side of the Saloon, on each side of the main deck above and on the Saloon deck forward, the main deck forward being appropriated exclusively to the Officers, Crew and servants.

The passenger accommodation, therefore, at present consists of:—

19 Cabins in Saloon,	42 Bed places.
24 Cabins Main Deck aft,	48 Bed places.
16 Cabins Fore Saloon,	40 Bed places.
Total 59 Cabins.	130 Bed places.

There is a very large Steward's Pantry before the Saloon on one side, and a Drawing room with a water closet for the Ladies on the other side.'[22]

Utilising the information given in the report and the known shape and dimensions of the *Great Western* it is possible to reconstruct a plan of the ship as she stood in 1846 (fig No 23), presuming two and three berth cabins only.

Features such as the steward's pantry, ladies' drawing room and central dining tables survived from the 1838 layout. From the given number of cabins and berths, the main saloon must have contained 12 two berth cabins and six three berth units. All cabins on the main deck contained two berths, whilst the fore saloon was fitted with eight two berth cabins and the same number containing three berths. For a full complement of 130 passengers the double row of tables in the main saloon could not have provided sufficient places at a single meal sitting. Further seating arrangements must have been made, possible in the fore saloon. Cabins were small; for two berths about 6 feet 6 inches by 7 feet, whilst for three berth about 8 feet by 7 feet. In the two berth cabins the beds would have been built one above the other to save space. A similar construction must have existed in the three berth rooms with a third bed along another bulkhead. As may be realised, not all rooms were rectangular due to the curvature of the ship's sides.

On the main deck cabins could not have been built along the sides of the vessel. 24 rooms set out in blocks, as shown, allow a more satisfactory usage of available space. Skylights in the spar deck and in the main deck provided illumination for the main saloon, although even with these the place must have been pitifully dark by modern standards. At night only candle or oil lamps allowed some semblance of social life to exist. In keeping with his rank the Captain of such a vessel always had a cabin in the best passenger area. Such a room with an office is likely to have been placed at the forward end of the main deck saloon — a chart room, as an extra or built into the office, would be essential. From here the Captain could readily reach, or be called from, the navigation/lookout position on the paddle boxes. In fog or ice Hosken, when Captain of *Great Western*, habitually spent long hours on one, or other, of the paddle boxes.[23] As both a surgeon and a purser were carried, rooms must have been set aside for their work—possibly near the Captain's quarters or possibly at the after end of the same deck, where the curvature of the ship and the rudder tiller prevented the use of the space for passenger cabins. Internal staircases of the semi-spiral type — as extensively fitted aboard *Great Britain* — provided a satisfactory means of connection between the decks without occupying too much space. Although not clear in the RMSPC report, the various houses on the sponsons had to be arranged conveniently. Passengers' and Captain's water closets, scullery and larder connected directly with the main deck saloon. At the forward, working, end of the ship the cow houses and blacksmith's shop would cause little inconvenience to the passengers.

No details are available of the fore deck officer and crew accommodation. Except for the senior officers, individual cabins are unlikely with various sections of the crew being allocated particular mess and sleeping areas, probably with bare bunks; each man supplying his own mattress or hammock. As passenger's servants were charged a lower fare, their accommodation would be more spartan. Highly likely were male and female dormitories in the forecastle area. The engineers and stokers probably slept and messed in the fo'c'sle. However, during the first voyage the stokers complain about the heat in their accommodation.[24] From this it appears that they occupied, initially anyway, the empty spaces below the main deck around the boilers. The engineers were probably positioned likewise but in the cooler regions at the after end of the engine room. Such quarters would be conveniently located for work. Although not mentioned anywhere an enclosed passage through the engine room must have connected the main and forward saloons. Without such, movement between the two chambers on a stormy might might try the patience of the staunchest passenger or skilful steward with a tray of hot food. Subsequently, the spaces alongside the engine room became chain lockers,[25] although an enclosed passageway must have been retained.

Consequent upon the building of the new decks and the erections of the sponsons, the *Great Western* developed a disconcerting tendency to roll heavily. The solution to the evil came from the fitting of bilge keels.[26] None of the survey reports makes any mention of these devices and the conclusion must be drawn that they were fitted during, or after, 1844 as the last available survey report for the ship is dated February of that year.

Well aware of the safety requirements in the event of their ship foundering, the Great Western Steam Ship Company provided large life boats from the outset. All early prints and paintings show two large quarter boats in davits. A painting, by Walters, of the first arrival at New York indicates a smaller boat behind the port paddle box — possibly duplicated on the starboard side. By 1846 the situation had changed; one iron and three wooden quarter boats graced the ship's sides. The RMSPC report provides a further interesting piece of information; 'There is also over the immense Ice House Amidships a huge Iron Life Boat, stored bottom up, about 28 feet long by 10 feet broad. This Boat floated full of water, with 90 men in her.' The *Great Britain* had been equipped with similar iron boats, built at the company's yard in accordance with a patent taken out by Guppy. The patent, No 9779, of 1843 covers the construction of iron boats and the iron buoyancy which make up part of their construction. The iron boats on the *Great Britain* were 30 feet long, 8 feet broad and 5 feet deep.[27] Allowing for the estimated figures of the Royal Mail report, it seems that the iron boats aboard both ships were identical. As the Great Western Steam Ship Company wound down its operations at its Bristol yard towards the end of 1844 when the *Great Britain* left, the iron life boats must have been completed before then. *Great Western* did not return to service until June 1844 and could have carried with her the iron life boat. Certainly, with a passenger capacity of about 150 and a maximum crew of about 70 the four quarter boats and the iron life boat should have been sufficient, if all could be launched. If each quarter boat carried 50 people, the total boat capacity approached 300. Rarely did the total number on board exceed 200 people indicating that the *Great Western* was much better prepared for saving life than many of her larger successors on the North Atlantic. Fortunately, the boats were never needed.

Upon entering service the *Great Western* had cargo spaces provided below the crew accommodation forward and underneath the lower saloon aft. Subsequent changes during the next few years opened up the decks above for cargo. The exact arrangements of these spaces are not known, nor do they matter. Cargo varied considerably and was always loose stowed, allowing full utilisation of the space available. Packages had to be fairly small in order to pass through the confined hatches provided in the decks. Whilst lying alongside a berth small, light, packages could be brought on manually but when at Kingroad, or for heavy and bulky items, derricks had to be employed. A drawing of the *Great Western* at Kingroad shows loading/discharging taking place. A derrick may be clearly seen operating on the fore-deck, between the funnel and fore-mast. The painting of the arrival at New York shows what appears to be a derrick attached to the mizzen mast. Hatches, positioned close to the engine room would give ready access to the cargo space without too much disruption of the passenger spaces.

Two particular items of cargo required individual attention; namely mail and specie (gold and silver coin). Often, the specie value exceeded that of the remaining cargo. During the second outward passage, over 10,000 oz of gold coin were in the charge of Captain Hosken.[28] Such coin, and other valuables, must have been secured in a safe which was, more than likely, fixed in the Captain's quarters. In order to protect the leather mail bags from the attention of rats, the mail room had to be lined with zinc — a task assigned to the joiner on at least one occasion.[29] Mail, consisting of letters, newspapers and parcels could be heavy and valuable, necessitating a large and secure room. No sources of information indicate the location but the tweendecks aft would have been ideal.

Coal bunkers occupied those regions of the ship which were irregularly shaped and so unsuitable for other purposes. Extreme forward and after lower hold sections are known to have provided bunker space, as is the midship area surrounding the boilers. There seems little reason why such conditions should change during the service life of *Great Western*. In order to avoid spreading coal dust whilst bunkering, each bunker space was probably fitted with one, or more, bunkering hatches. Coal could be simply tipped through the hatch and down a chute into the relevant bunker.

After purchase by the RMSPC alterations were made to the *Great Western*, the major ones being carried out at the end of 1847. Apart from the main deck, which had to be replaced, the hull was found to be structually sound. A completely new spar deck was also laid, this one extending the whole length of the ship and thereby, changing the external appearance somewhat.[30] It is difficult to imagine what modification, if any, took place in this, now enclosed, midship section. Certainly, engine room skylights and ventilators must have been extended upwards to the new upper deck level. The complete spar deck gave the passengers a promenade over 200 feet long. In the tropics the after end of the spar deck is likely to have been covered with a canopy supported by a removable wooden framework. Internally, the accommodation layout will have changed slightly to suit a different service but the main and forward saloons were retained for passengers[31] as must have been the main deck cabins.

When new boilers were fitted in 1847 the engine room length was reduced from the 65 feet it had been in the later years on the North Atlantic, to 58 feet. New boilers, closer to the engines, may have allowed the funnel to be moved slightly towards the stern.

Chapter 7

Propulsion machinery

All early commercial steamships were propelled by means of paddle wheels set at, approximately, mid-length. This form of propulsion requires a slow running engine capable of providing a high torque. Although many engines fell into this category the side lever engine was, by far, the most commonly adopted. Adapted from the Watt beam engine, which had a large beam above the steam cylinder and a crank driven flywheel, the side lever engine combined low height with the ruggedness of its progenitor. A form of the beam engine, called the walking beam engine, survived as a power unit for American paddle steamers until the end of the 19th century.

The side lever engine, as its name implies, replaced the large overhead beam with two smaller beams, or levers, positioned as low as possible alongside the cylinder (fig No 24). A bearing pin placed at about mid-length provided a fulcrum about which the relevant lever could pivot. The piston rod connected with the side levers by means of a crosshead and two side rods. At the other ends of the levers a similar crossbar, called a cross-tail, attached the side levers to the paddle crank via a long rod called the connecting rod. In most cases, a number of pump drives were taken from the side levers.

A steam cylinder of a side lever engine was double acting; that is, steam pressure alternately forced the piston downwards when given access to the top of the cylinder and upwards when allowed into the lower part. So as to maximise the effect of the steam on the piston, and hence gain more useful work, the side of the piston not subjected to steam pressure was maintained at a very low pressure. The use of a condenser made very low pressures possible. A slide valve, placed alongside the cylinder, controlled with the correct timing, admission of steam to one side of the piston and connection of the opposite side to the condenser. An eccentric on the paddle shaft operated the slide valve drive. The condenser chamber converted the steam back into water, thereby reducing its volume by about 1,700 times. Thus the pressure within the condenser fell considerably.

As the piston reciprocated it rocked the side levers and these in turn rotated the paddle shaft through the action of the connecting rod and crank. Many bearings had to be provided where moving parts connected with stationary or other moving parts. All required careful lubrication and, for most engines, were a major source of trouble.

The sea water supply for the condenser spray came directly from the sea through a valve in the ship's side; correct regulation of the sea water quantity being of supreme importance. If too little sea water was used all of the steam in the condenser did not turn back to water and so the back pressure on the piston rose. With boiler steam pressures being, generally, below 5 lb/in² even a slight increase in condenser pressure would produce a considerable loss in power. Too much sea water spray would flood the condenser and cylinder causing the engine to stall, possibly resulting in damage. All engines were equipped with a pipe connecting the bilge with the water spray box on the condenser. The idea was that in the event of the bilge pumps failing to remove sufficient water from the bilge, due to mechanical breakdown or hull damage, the low pressure in the condenser would draw in bilge water. This pipe and its connection to the condenser were known as the 'bilge

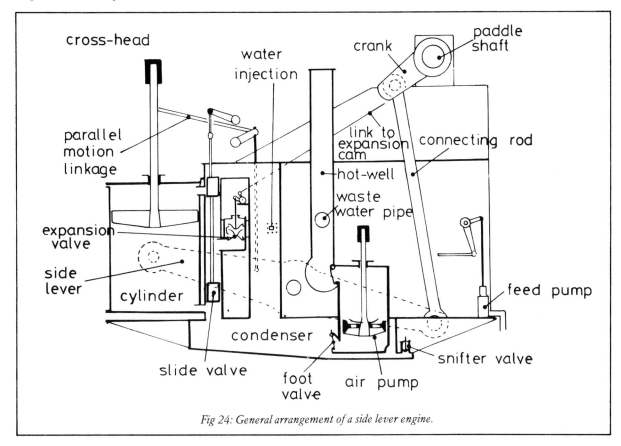

Fig 24: General arrangement of a side lever engine.

injection', a term still used on ships today to refer to the largest direct bilge pipe connection to the bilge pump; the association with the condenser having long since ceased.

Any air trapped in the steam flow would soon destroy the vacuum in the condenser thus seriously affecting the engine's efficiency. Removal of the air preserved the vacuum. Fitting an air pump achieved this as well as the removal of water from the condenser. Operation of the reciprocating air pump came from the side levers through a set of side rods and a crosshead; guide rods ensured that the crosshead, and hence pump piston, maintained a true vertical motion. Water and air from the pump discharged into the hotwell, a tall elliptical cylinder above the pump, through a non-return valve at the top of the pump cylinder. Feed pumps, also operated by the side levers, took water from the hotwell

and forced it into the boiler; as the pumps generally supplied more water than the boiler(s) needed at any one time, relief valves, on the feed pipe-lines, allowed the surplus to return to the hotwell. Taking boiler feed water from the hotwell allowed for greater operating efficiency as it was hotter than water taken directly from the sea. A waste pipe, passing through the ship's side, discharged the hotwell water overboard. As only the water above this waste pipe was discharged, a constant water level was maintained in the hotwell. On many engines of this type, the top of the hotwell cylinder opened into the engine room thus allowing air to escape. However, the cylinder had to be tall enough to prevent water from flowing into the engine room when the ship was fully loaded. Also connected to the side levers were the bilge pumps, but the actual arrangement differed with the engine builder. Most fitted

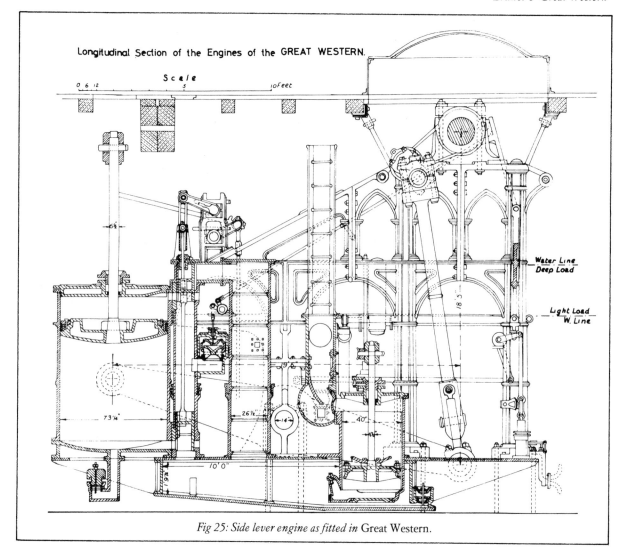

Longitudinal Section of the Engines of the GREAT WESTERN.

Scale

0 6 12   5   10 Feet

Water Line
Deep Load

Light Load
W. Line

Fig 25: Side lever engine as fitted in Great Western.

these pumps on the opposite side lever to which the feed pump was connected as this preserved some form of balance.

The above is an account of a typical side lever engine arrangement and operation. It was this type of engine that Maudslay, Sons and Field contracted to supply for the *Great Western* steamship, based upon the specification (Appendix 1).

In effect the 'engine' consisted of a pair of side lever

engines coupled to the same paddle shaft. (At that time each cylinder was considered to constitute a separate engine.) Actual engine details are given in Appendix 7. The combined indicated horse-power of 750 does not show the actual effective output of the engines as that figure, used for commercial purposes, is the result of calculations involving engine dimensions and maximum steam pressure. A more realistic and useful figure for the power output to the paddle shafts is given by the nominal horse-power of 450; this takes account of losses in the system. Although of conventional side lever form, the engines did incorporate some novel features for that time.

The design of side lever engine frames, which supported the crank shaft and other running gear, caused much controversy in early years, as engineers appeared to be more concerned with the relative aesthetic charms of Gothic arches and Doric columns than with the functional performance of the frames themselves. Certainly, the cast iron Gothic arched frames of the *Great Western's* engines possessed beauty, but they must have been rather costly. The inherent weakness of cast iron for engine frame-work quickly revealed itself. After two years exposure to the rigorous Atlantic weather, the brittle cast iron developed cracks.[1] Replacements, using the same materials, would have been expensive and would have similarly cracked within a few years. The Great Western Steam Ship Company decided to repair the frames with wrought iron brackets and braces around the fractured sections. These repairs, to top and bottom framing, lasted for the remainder of the ship's service with the original owners. The efficiency of the repairs may be gauged from a survey report of early 1847. This stated that the fractured parts did not appear to have moved for some time and that the frames would, probably, last as long as the hull itself without being taken out.[2] They did.

With side lever engines there was very little headroom available for the provision of piston rod guides above the cylinder; such being necessary to maintain the piston/piston rod motion vertical. True vertical motion was essential in order to minimise the wear on piston, piston rod, cylinder and gland thus reducing the frequency of overhaul. A system of linkages, known as a parallel motion mechanism, performed the same function as guides but with less height. The arrangement favoured by Maudslay, Sons and Field is shown in fig No 26. Each linkage had to be of specific length, for that size of engine, in order to ensure that an exact parallel motion existed between the piston and its crosshead. Provided that the designer correctly determined the linkage dimensions, the ship's engineer had few problems with the mechanism. This appears to have been the case with the *Great Western*.

Joshua Field had invented, and patented, a device for conserving heat when boiler water was blown out of the boiler. This blowing down of the boiler had to be carried out at frequent intervals in order to prevent the heating surfaces of the boiler from becoming encrusted with salt due to the increasing salinity of the boiler water. At that time most ships still employed sea water feed to the boilers. The blowing down procedure consisted of opening the blow down valve fitted on the boiler shell and a cock on the ship's side, thereby allowing the steam pressure within the boiler to force some of the boiler water overboard. If carried out regularly, particularly in conjunction with the use of a hydrometer, which measured the degree of saltiness of the boiler water, encrustation of the boiler inner surfaces could be minimised. Although satisfactory, the above system operated inefficiently as cold sea water was used to replace hot boiler water. In order to improve the efficiency, Field adopted a heat exchanger to transfer heat from the escaping boiler water to the incoming feed water. Instead of passing directly to the boiler the feed water passed through a number of small

Fig 26: Parallel motion mechanism.

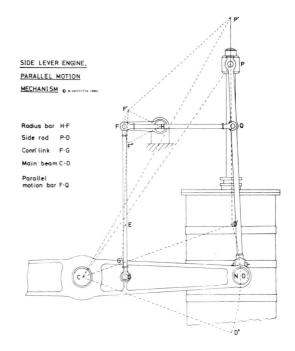

SIDE LEVER ENGINE.
PARALLEL MOTION
MECHANISM © D GRIFFITHS 1980

Radius bar H-F
Side rod P-D
Conn' link F-G
Main beam C-D
Parallel
motion bar F-Q

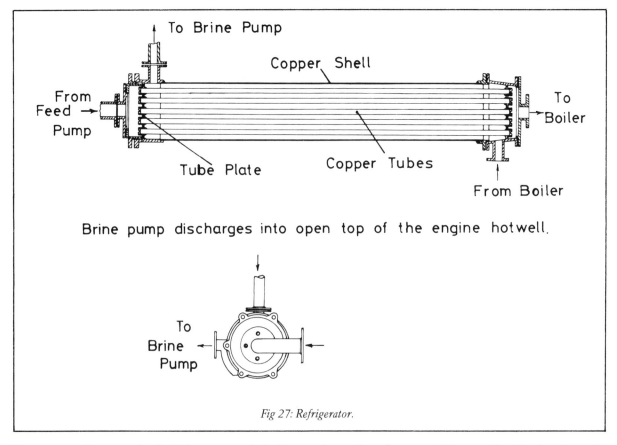

To Brine Pump

Copper Shell

From Feed Pump →

To Boiler

Tube Plate

Copper Tubes

From Boiler

Brine pump discharges into open top of the engine hotwell.

To Brine Pump ←

Fig 27: Refrigerator.

bore copper pipes contained within a copper shell. Hot blow down water from the boiler circulated around these tubes, imparting some of its heat, before being discharged overboard by one of the brine pumps.[3] The heat exchanger was referred to as a refrigerator (fig No 27). Careful regulation of the equipment enabled the boiler water levels to be maintained as well as the degree of saltiness. Tests carried out showed that a temperature increase of about 70°F could be expected in the feed water when the device operated.[4]

At the crankshaft end on each engine three pumps, driven from the outboard side lever, acted as brine pumps (two) and deck water supply pump. Each brine pump served one of the four boilers via its relevant refrigerator. The idea was that the brine pump would assist the blowdown operation by extracting the warm blowdown boiler water from the refrigerator and pump

it overboard — possibly not directly, but into the hotwell from where it would eventually pass overboard. Brine pumps were essential to the efficient operation of the system as the low boiler pressure was not sufficient to force blowdown water through the refrigerator at a high enough rate to heat the incoming feed. Available drawings show the suction pipes for the deck water pumps to have connections from the hotwell and direct from the sea. Brine and sea water pumps could be disconnected from the drive whenever they were not required.

Safe and efficient ship's side connections for water admission and blowdown had been a problem with all steamships until 1837 when John Kingston, of Portsmouth Dockyard, developed the valves which subsequently bore his name. These consisted of a gunmetal tube fitting through the hull and a screw operated

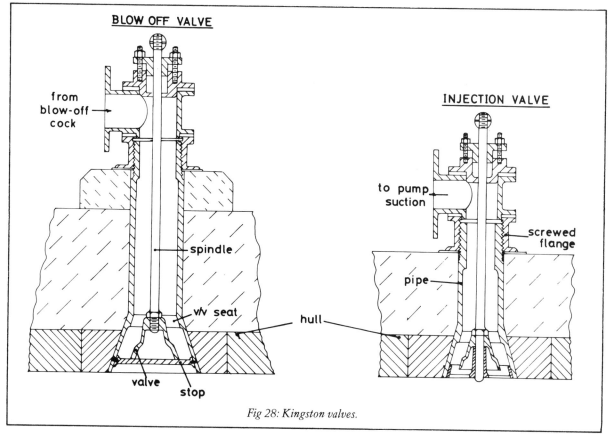

BLOW OFF VALVE

from
blow-off
cock

spindle

v/v seat

hull

valve

stop

INJECTION VALVE

to pump
suction

screwed
flange

pipe

hull

Fig 28: Kingston valves.

gunmetal valve, which seated within the tube and opened outwards. The valve (fig No 28) could be closed at will and, in the event of the spindle breaking, would act as a non-return valve preventing water from flowing back into the pipes. This valve found immediate favour with the Admiralty and it is likely that the Great Western Steam Ship Company had them installed in the *Great Western* before she was launched. Certainly they were in place in 1846.[5] Throughout the ship all pipes were of copper or lead and all fittings of brass.

Perhaps the most significant feature of the *Great Western's* engines was the expansive working of steam in the cylinders. Up to the time of *Great Western* most marine engines, and many of their land based counterparts, supplied steam to the cylinder for almost the entire piston stroke. As exhaust to the condenser commences soon after the steam supply valve closed, an

unnecessarily wasteful consumption of steam ensues. Through the use of an instrument called an 'indicator' (fig No 31), diagrams, showing the variation in cylinder steam pressure as the piston moved, could be obtained. Such diagrams were of immense benefit, as the area enclosed by the pencil line on the paper related, directly, to the amount of work being produced by the cylinder. The indicator, a simple device to operate, enabled quick and regular checks to be made on the engine's performance. Fig No 30 shows a typical indicator diagram for the space on one side of the piston; it may be seen that comparatively little of the area is above the atmospheric line, illustrating that little of the work was obtained from the steam above atmospheric pressure. In fact the majority of the engine power came as a result of the condenser vacuum. The lower the pressure on the side of the piston connected to the con-

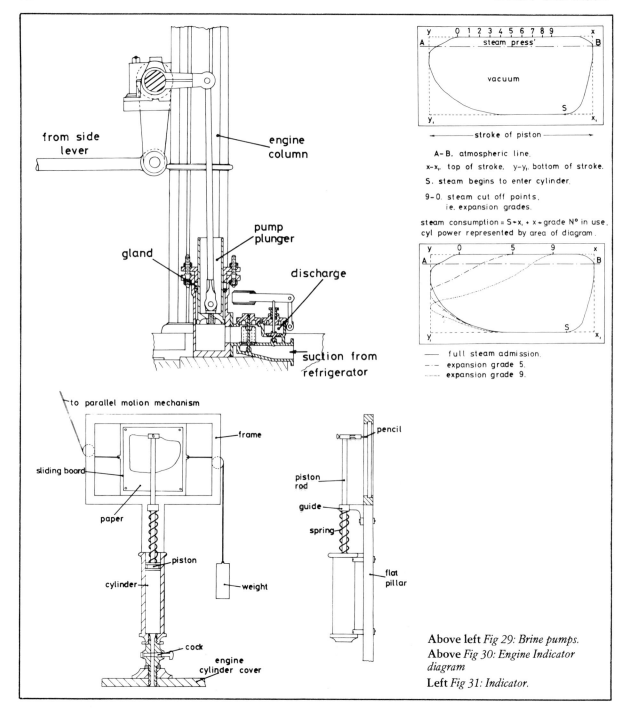

from side lever

engine column

gland

pump plunger

discharge

suction from refrigerator

y 0 1 2 3 4 5 6 7 8 9 x
A B
steam press'
vacuum
S
y₁ x₁

stroke of piston

A-B. atmospheric line.

x-x₁. top of stroke. y-y₁. bottom of stroke.

S. steam begins to enter cylinder.

9-0. steam cut off points,
ie. expansion grades.

steam consumption = S→x, + x→grade N° in use.
cyl power represented by area of diagram.

y 0 5 9 x
A B
S
y₁ x₁

—— full steam admission.
—·— expansion grade 5.
······· expansion grade 9.

to parallel motion mechanism

frame

sliding board

paper

piston

cylinder

weight

cock

engine cylinder cover

pencil

piston rod

guide

spring

flat pillar

Above left *Fig 29: Brine pumps.*
Above *Fig 30: Engine Indicator diagram*
Left *Fig 31: Indicator.*

denser, the less the back pressure acting against that side of the piston under steam. Lowering the condenser pressure produced the same effect as raising the boiler pressure. This demonstrates the necessity for preserving a good vacuum, as allowing the back pressure to increase due to inadequate condensation or air build-up, reduced the amount of energy released by the steam when in the cylinder.

With reference to fig No 30, it may be perceived that steam began to enter the cylinder just before the piston reached the end of its stroke, (at x-x) and the supply was maintained until just before the end of the next stroke (at y-y), when the exhaust would be opened. With the piston forced down, work would be done, however, the steam retained much of its energy until, as exhaust, it entered the condenser. Here the energy released from the steam simply heated the sea water. By cutting off the steam supply to the cylinder earlier in the stroke, a reduction in steam, and hence coal, consumption could be obtained. Power developed by the cylinder also fell although not to the same extent. Fig No 30 illustrates the merits of cutting off steam supply earlier in the stroke. Cutting off the steam at say grade 0, produced a diagram with a smaller area, giving less work, but steam consumption was reduced considerably. Expansive working, as this was termed, had particular benefit when wind conditions allowed advantageous use of sails. During the first crossing to New York, Pearne conducted tests to determine the relative coal consumption and power developed at different expansion valve settings. These tests required the weighing of coal consumed over a particular period together with the taking of indicator diagrams to determine the power developed. The following values were obtained:[6]

Steam consumption	Grade No	Engine Speed rpm	mph	Coal cwt/hr
Full steam at 3½ lb/in²	0	15½	12¾	28
8/10 full steam	2	15	12½	27
7/10 full steam	3	14	12¼	26
5/10 full steam	5	13	11	23

With greater degrees of expansion further fuel savings could be made. The Engineer's log for the first voyage shows that the expansion grades were continually being changed to suit prevailing wind conditions.[7]

An expansion valve (fig No 32) positioned between

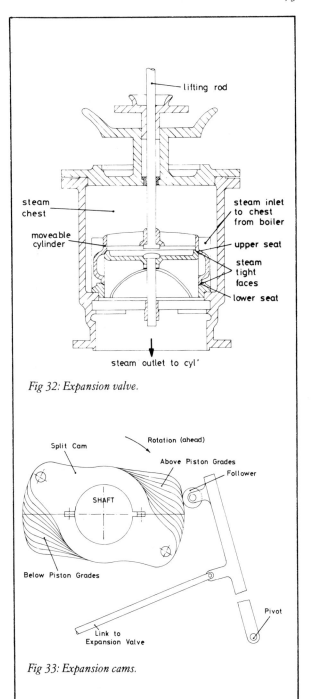

Fig 32: Expansion valve.

Fig 33: Expansion cams.

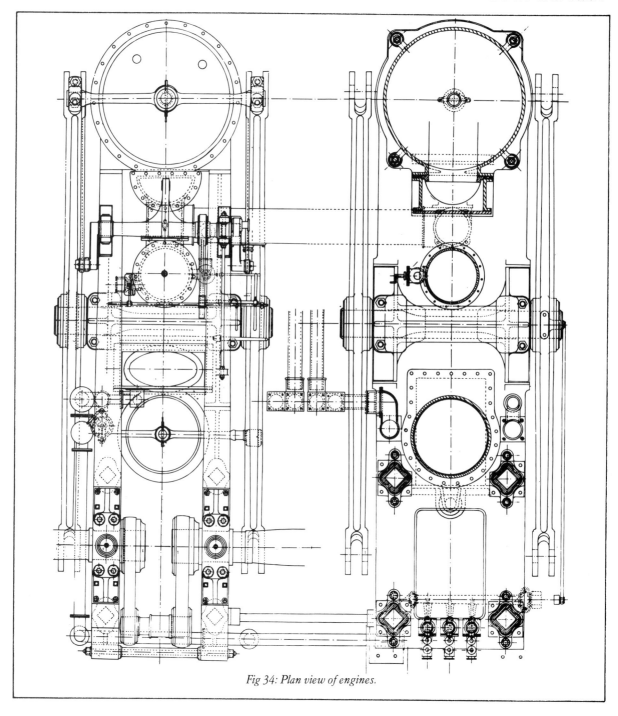

Fig 34: Plan view of engines.

the main steam supply pipe and the slide valve, allowed the steam flow to the cylinder to be interrupted even though the slide valve was in the open position. Such a valve took little power in its operation as it was balanced; the working mechanism was a cylinder upon which steam acted with equal force upwards and downwards. A system of cams (fig No 33) operated the expansion valve via a linkage, the cams being keyed onto the crankshaft.[8] Moving the cam follower from one cam to another altered the period during which the follower was in contact with the raised portion of the cams and hence the period for which the expansion valve remained open. The raised portions on the cam profiles all began at the same position but all ended at different grades, 9 to 0, thus giving the ten grades of expansive working. On any piston stroke, therefore, steam entry to the cylinder always commenced at the same point but could be made to cease at any of ten positions in the next stroke. Because the engine cylinders were double acting above and below piston grades had to be fitted to each cam.

Expansive working of steam, with a consequent reduction in fuel consumption, was fundamental to the economic operation of oceanic steam ships. Had Lardner considered the implications of its employment he would probably have avoided committing himself to such a specific position in the debates upon the feasibility of Atlantic steam navigation.

Apart from the air pump, deck water pump and brine pumps each engine also operated a bilge pump and a boiler feed pump, both of the reciprocating type. Two methods of driving these pumps found extensive use on this type of engine, namely from the air pump crosshead or direct from the outside of the side levers. In the case of the *Great Western* the former appears to have been the preferred system. A plan view of the engine (fig No 34) makes it clear that the pump barrels were situated between the two side levers. Sectional and side views of the engines show pump barrels positioned near the top of the air pump cylinder. Placed here, actuation could only be by means of the air pump crosshead. As bilge and feed pump barrels were slightly offset from the transverse centre line of the air pump cylinder, a small twisting moment must have been exerted on the air pump crosshead when the pumps operated. Guide rods, shown in a sectional view of the engines, would have exercised a restraining effect on

the twisting. With pumps placed at that height attention to valves and glands could be readily given. It seems likely that these pumps operated continuously with the engine. Relief valves diverted any water not needed by the boilers, back to the hotwell thus allowing the feed pumps to run constantly without suffering damage or overfilling the boilers. Similar operation of the bilge pumps only served to maintain the bilge spaces in a dry condition.

During the early years of steam navigation, engine bearings created many problems. In this respect those of the *Great Western* were no exception. Understandable, perhaps, as the engines of that ship exceeded in size any then built. Tallow or oil lubricated the brass bearings, extreme care being essential to ensure that sufficient reached the correct regions. Particularly problematic were the crankshaft bearings and those on the connecting rod — crank end and crosstail end. Plummer blocks not only supported the crankshaft and paddle shafts but also acted as thrust blocks in that they transmitted, to the hull, the thrust due to the reaction of the paddles on the water. Because of tightness or inadequte lubrication, bearings would overheat; a problem encountered by the *Great Western* on her first return from New York. The usual practice was to play a jet of cold sea water over the heated bearing in order to cool it. Unfortunately, the not infrequent result was broken brasses or housing. Should a plummer block fail, both engines had to be immobilised in order to facilitate a repair. If, however, a crank bearing, or any other bearing not associated with the support of the crankshaft, failed that engine could be disconnected and the ship powered by one engine until a repair could be carried out. In order to minimise the drag effect of the paddle wheels with the engines stopped and the ship under sail, many engine builders fitted disengaging gear to the paddle shafts. This enabled the paddle wheels to be disconnected from the engines and allowed to free-wheel. It is uncertain whether, or not, the *Great Western* had such devices. Certainly, no mention is made of them nor do any of the surviving drawings show them.

The main shafting of *Great Western's* engines consisted of two paddle shafts and an intermediate shaft. Acramans, of Bristol, had forged both paddle shafts and they travelled with the ship as cargo when she made the voyage to London for her engines. Each paddle shaft

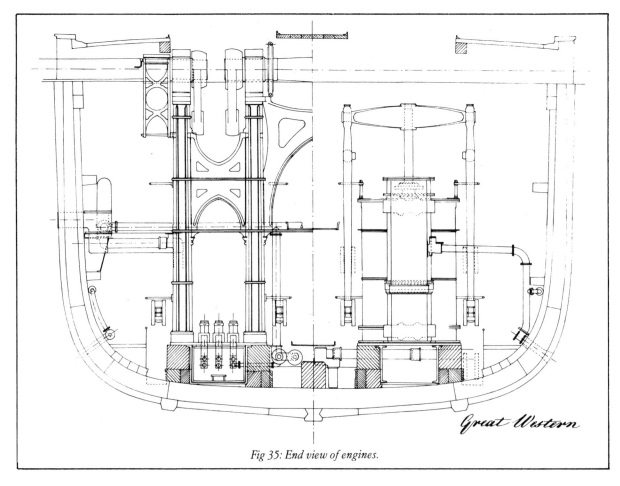

Fig 35: End view of engines.

weighed 6½ tons and the intermediate shaft 4½ tons.[9] Shrink fits connected crank webs to the relevant ends of the paddle and intermediate shafts; each pair of webs being united by a machined crank pin. The intermediate shaft joined the shafting of the two engines together. Cranks on the engines were set at 90° to each other thus allowing the engine group to be started from any position. Each engine had its own eccentric drive for operating its slide valve. Eccentrics clamped onto the intermediate shaft inboard of the main bearing. A strap around the eccentric moved a linkage when the engine turned and this, through a system of levers, moved the slide valve up and down with the correct timing. Expansion cams had a keyed connection with the

intermediate shaft adjacent to the eccentric. Common practice of the day allowed shrink and force fits to be strengthened by the use of wedge keys, locking pins and 'rusting in'.

Firm fixing of each engine to the hull required a rigid mounting platform and that came from the provision of two longitudinal wooden sleepers at bottom of the ship. Upon these sat the engine bedplate. Naval steam ships employed a number of brass holding down bolts which passed through hull, sleepers and bed plate before being secured by a nut above the bed plate. In keeping with their policy of adopting the best systems, the owners of the *Great Western* utilised the idea for their steamer. Rigidity for the upper section of the framework, essential for correctly supported shafting, resulted from a number of stay bolts, secured to brackets on main deck beams. Two long bolts also connected the engine framework together at the bearing supports.

Engine speed adjustments were achieved by throttling the steam supply to the cylinders; the less steam supplied, the lower the engine speed. Each engine had its own throttling valve and could be regulated independently. Alterations in steam supply to the engine had to be matched by changes in condenser sea water provision rate; if this were not so, condenser flooding took place. At slower speeds the air pump removed less water from the condenser than it did at the higher speeds, hence the flooding. If such an occurrence took place when entering, or leaving harbour, the resultant stalling of the engines could endanger the ship with a strong tide running and no assistance from tugs. Starting of both engines and subsequent speed adjustments could be achieved by one engineer. All main engine controls were conveniently positioned together just above the inner side lever pivot. The three main controls were: the steam throttling valve; the cylinder slide valve manual operating handwheel; and the condenser water valve control lever. Obviously, the assistance of other engineers was essential for checking the operation of the engines and ensuring that the boilers supplied the necessary steam and functioned normally.

When starting from cold, the engine was initially flooded with steam; both sides of the piston and throughout the condenser. This could be accomplished by overriding the eccentric operation of the slide valve and moving it manually by means of a cam segment turned by a hand wheel. With that step completed, the slide valve had to be placed in the correct position for the engine to turn in the desired direction. Opening the sea water spray valve allowed cold water into the condenser, thereby producing a vacuum. As the slide valve had been set in a particular position, the cylinder on one side of the piston was connected to the condenser and so the piston would move in that direction. Once the engine started, the eccentric would have taken over control of the slide valve and the manual arrangement disengaged. As both engines were physically connected by the crankshaft, only one engine had to be started by this means as the other would rotate when the crankshaft turned. On this second engine only the steam and water supply required adjustment.

Correctly positioned platforms around the engines allowed the engineers to attend to the machinery without hinderance. Lubrication of bearings and attention to glands occupying much of the time. A clockwork index or revolution counter, fixed to the engine frame, enabled the engineers to determine the exact number of engine revolutions turned during any period.[10] Such information was of considerable importance as it allowed an estimation of the ship's speed to be made during adverse conditions and also enabled a value for the slip of the paddle wheels to be obtained.

The engines of Maudslay, Sons and Field remained in the *Great Western* until she went to the shipbreakers in 1856, performing excellently and, after the initial running in period, giving very little trouble. Log books for voyages Nos 23 and 43 indicate no engine malfunctions. During voyage No 28, from Bristol to New York via Madeira, the engines ran continuously for over 20 days, (Funchal to New York) no trouble being experienced.[11] This was the longest period of continuous service that any marine engine had then made. The engines attracted comment and praise from various quarters and appear to have been looked upon as the ultimate of their type. In 1844 *The Artisan* commented: '. . . indeed, machinery of this quality is very well able to speak for itself. . . we do not know of any production in steam machinery that is in every respect more creditable'.[12] Researching the voyages of the *Great Western*, apart from the first voyage, the author has been able to uncover only one recorded incident of engine failure of a major nature. That occurred near the end of voyage No 49, between the West Indies and Southampton. Nearing Southampton, on passage from Bermuda, the starboard engine crank pin fractured disabling the engine. That engine had to be shut down but the port engine could still power the paddle wheel on that side of the ship.[13] Considering that the engines were of unprecedented size and power, when built, their performance record was examplary.

Maudslay, Sons and Field always considered their engines to be superior to any then available and, with justification, were of the opinion that they played an important role in the success of the venture. Additionally they felt that due credit had not been given to the engineers and the engines. That fact was made clear to

Brunel in a letter from a Mr Young, of Maudslay, Sons and Field, who, in November 1838, wrote, '. . . there has, throughout, seemed a studied omission of all mention of the fair share of merit due to the engineers'. Certainly, Maudslay, Sons and Field had cause to feel aggrieved that little of the published praise, so freely given during the first year of operation, happened to be directed at them. It is, however, unlikely that this came about by design. The building committee were conscious of the importance of good, efficient engines to the ultimate prosperity of the ship and its owners.

Before concluding the discussion about the engines, it is worth mentioning that relations between the Great Western Steam Ship Company and Maudslay, Sons and Field were, during 1838, rather strained. There had, since the end of 1837, been considerable debate between the parties regarding the matter of 'extras'. Which items actually constituted the extras and could be charged for as such resulted in much correspondence. Engine builders did charge for extras but, apparently, the contract did not make the situation clear. In the first letters between the company and Maudslays' it had been mentioned that the usual practice of charging for extras would be set aside,[14] this, however, was not included in the contract. The items classed as extras also caused some sharp words between the two concerns. Brunel, disagreeing with the engine builders, did not consider that the paddle wheels or the change water apparatus constituted extras as they were basic to the propulsion plant as contracted for.[15] Agreement on a price for the machinery was, eventually, reached but it must have been a compromise and below the valuation of the builders. Brunel later stated that they, Maudslays', could not have afforded to make a second order as low as the first.[16] The Great Western Steam Ship Company appear to have obtained a bargain, not only in terms of cost but also with regard to quality.

At the time the *Great Western* was built, except for a few installations, all marine boilers operated on sea water feed. Not for any advantage possessed by the sea water but because of the impracticality of carrying large quantities of fresh water on board. Avoidance of salt scale build-up within the boilers became a major preoccupation of the marine engineer. Thick deposits of such scale resulted in overheating and eventual failure of the metal. Salinity of the boiler water could be kept within reasonable limits by regular blowing down or the use of brine pumps and refrigerators. Until about 1840, almost all marine boilers were of the flue type, although tubular boilers had shown themselves to be highly efficient in locomotive practice. Flue boilers contained rectangular passages, flues, through which the hot combustion gases flowed, there being a number of changes of direction as the hot gases wound their way from the furnace to the funnel uptake. The longer the gas path, the greater the heat transfer and the more efficient the boiler; at least in theory. Flues were tapered towards the top so as to allow steam bubbles, as they generated, to break away from the outer surface readily. Regular cleaning of the gas side of the flue promoted good heat transfer and was as important as maintaining the water side reasonably scale free. To facilitate this cleaning, flues were just wide enough to accommodate a man; a small man.

Riveted construction applied to all joints in the boiler shell and flues. Even if made with care, joints were never very good and many of them 'weeped' for a while when the boiler came under pressure for the first time. Caulking of the major leaks at the joints was the only practical way to stop them as to remake the joint necessitated partial dismantling of the boiler. Weeping at joints soon ceased as the salt scale and rust acted as a sealant.

A major problem with all early boilers was corrosion, the chemical reactions of which were not understood. No corrective action could, therefore, be taken. The severest corrosion always occurred within the steam chest and not, as expected, below the water level. This puzzled the engineers for many years until, towards the end of the 19th century, the effect of oxygen upon the corrosion of iron became understood. Below the water level corrosion within the boiler caused very little trouble, the iron in this region being protected by the thin layer of salt scale. In fact, this sea water scale was considered to be such a good protective layer that, as late as the middle of the 20th century, shell boilers of the Scotch type were frequently filled with sea water prior to being put into service so as to form such a layer. External corrosion of the upper part of the boiler came as a result of water dripping from the deck above. Suitable lead sheathing on top of the insulating felt minimised the problem. Boiler bottom plating frequently lay below the bilge water level and as that water was highly acidic on wooden hulled ships corrosion became rapid. Mastic cement, in which the boilers were set upon their sleepers, helped to protect the lower plating. Steam space corrosion limited the life of marine boilers, at that time, to between five and six years.[17]

Maudslay, Sons and Field supplied four flue type boilers for the *Great Western*. Operating pressure was a modest 5 lb/in² but the boilers, like the engines, were huge for the day. Each boiler could be fired separately so that one, or more, could be shut down and the plant operated more efficiently on those remaining in service. Three large furnaces were fitted to each of the boilers, all furnaces connecting with the base of the flue

passage-way at the back of the boiler. The flue passage wound around the boiler shell above the furnaces before connecting with a common funnel uptake set at the inside rear of each boiler. Although boiler water level would vary in operation depending upon the steam demand and the feed water supply rate, the nominal level was set 12 inches above the highest flue.[18] This afforded protection for the flues since if the tops became exposed the cooling effect of the water would be lost, overheating and possible collapse would quickly result. A large volume steam receiver, mounted on the top of each boiler shell, provided sufficient steam capacity to meet fluctuations in demand without allowing adverse changes in boiler pressure. The flue

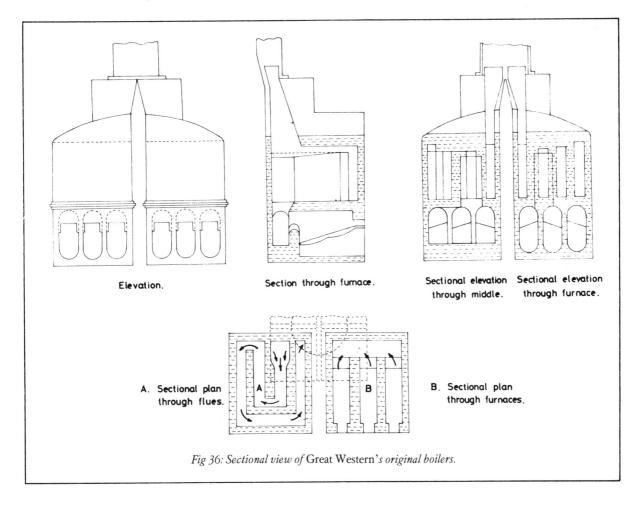

Elevation.   Section through furnace.   Sectional elevation   Sectional elevation
                                                          through middle.   through furnace.

A. Sectional plan   B. Sectional plan
   through flues.   through furnaces.

Fig 36: Sectional view of Great Western's *original boilers.*

uptake passed through each receiver providing a drying effect upon the steam. Separate valves controlled the steam supply from the individual receivers to the single main steam pipe. The steam side of each boiler could, therefore, be isolated allowing a boiler to be shut down for repair whilst the others remained under steam.

Supplying large quantities of steam to the powerful engines necessitated a heat transfer area within the boilers of, hitherto, unimagined proportions. A fire grate area of 202 square feet consumed coal at the average rate of about 30 tons each day. The furnace area of 890 square feet and flue area of 2,850 square feet allowed steam to be generated with ease, provided that coal could be fed to the furnaces at a high enough rate.[19] From the difficulties encountered during the first crossing it was evident that the factor governing steam generation rate was not how fast the stokers could fire

the boiler furnaces but how quickly coal could be fetched from the bunkers at the extreme ends of the ship. Even a very large heating area had no effect if the fires burned low. A large flue area did not emanate from length, rather from width. In fact, the short flues were a major factor in the lack of soot deposits on the heating surfaces.[20] Even though pressures were low — maximum 5 lb/in^2 — the flat flue surfaces required support otherwise the steam pressure would result in collapse. A great many stays — bars with screw threads at each end — supported the flues and boiler shell by connecting these flat plates and so making the structure more rigid. A drawing of the boilers in *Practical Mechanic's & Engineer's Magazine* for November 1842 shows the positioning of some of these stays.

Fig Nos 37 and 38 show the layout of the boilers in the ship. Placing them in the manner shown required the

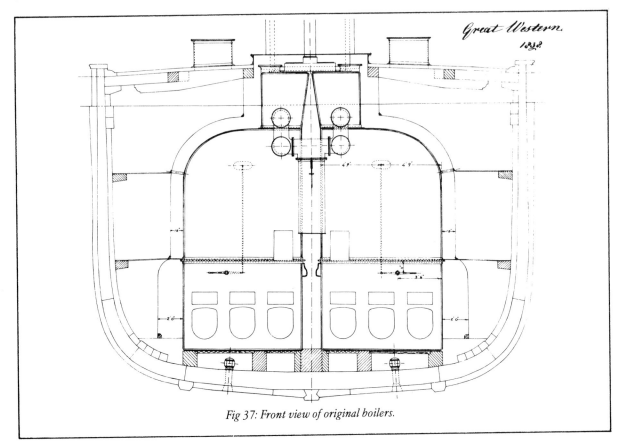

Fig 37: Front view of original boilers.

provision of two stokeholds. Little space existed between the boilers but a two foot wide passage-way can be seen between the boilers and engine room bunker spaces. Barely enough room for a man to walk let alone push a wheelbarrow full of coal or haul sacks of ashes. All ashes had to be hauled to the deck for disposal overboard. From the known length of the boilers and of the engine room, allowing for the length of the engine leaves but a short space available for each stokehold. Obviously, shovelling coal required skill and patience.

Mounted upon the top of the steam receivers were safety valves, one for each receiver. A single steam waste pipe, abaft the funnel, carried the steam away from the two after valves, whilst a waste pipe in front of the funnel served the two forward valves. The design of the safety valves is unknown but it was, probably, of the dead weight type. Dead weight safety valves were fitted to boilers installed later in the ship's life. Water level within the boiler had to be kept within strict limits; one drawing of the boilers shows a gauge glass arrangement. The boiler drawings in the Science Museum indicate floats within the boiler water spaces. An internal system of levers terminates, outside the boiler with, what appears to be, a handle. Land boilers, at that time, utilised such arrangements for indicating water level but the practice does not seem to have extended to the marine field. A possible use was for the automatic operation of the feed water supply valve to the boiler; also found on shore plants. The latter could be the case as the boiler drawings in *Practical Mechanic's & Engineer's Magazine* show the feed water pipes to have some connection, possibly a valve, where the float lever system ends. In either case operation would have been seriously affected by variations in water level as the

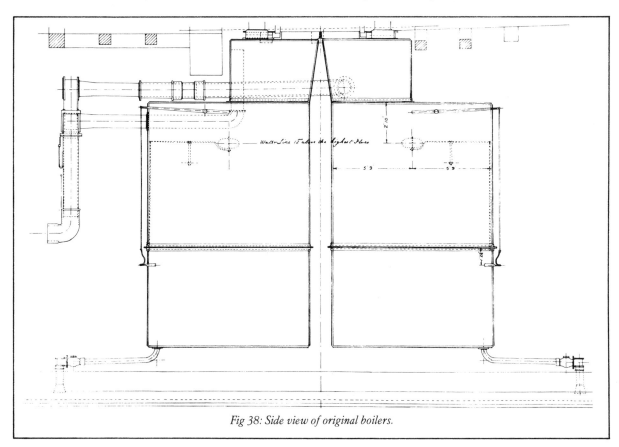

Fig 38: Side view of original boilers.

vessel moved in a seaway. Another lever on the outside of each boiler appears to terminate nowhere. This may have been a lever system for manually lifting the safety valves in an emergency as these valves were, on occasions, known to stick in the closed position. Unfortunately, no written explanations for these fitments is available.

At the bottom, towards the front, the boilers were fitted with connections for blow-down. This was simply a pipe outlet from the boiler with a blow down cock fitted somewhere between the boiler and Kingston valve. Other outlets from the bottoms of the boilers connected with the refrigerators on Field's apparatus for changing the boiler water. To control the feed water input a valve or cock would be necessary. Whether manually or automatically operated this need not have been directly connected to the boiler; the feed pipes must have been. Steam pressure was measured by means of a U-tube full of mercury. One end of the type opened into the steam pipe to the engine, whilst the other end held a float with a pointer. As the pressure rose the mercury in the free end of the U-tube was forced upwards displacing the float. The pointer, against a suitable scale, indicated the steam pressure. A mounting, not shown on any of the drawings but essential, had to be provided in order to prevent the formation of a vacuum as the boiler cooled down. A reverse or atmospheric valve allowed air into the boiler thereby avoiding the problem.

The flue boilers served well and, apart from the blocked cocks of the first crossing, gave few problems. They did, however, over the years deteriorate, mainly due to corrosion, and their performance fell off as a result of salt scale. In September of 1843 the company's engineer, Thomas Guppy, reported to the directors on the state of the boilers in the *Great Western*. He informed them that for the outlay of about £1,000 they could be made to operate efficiently for another year or two. (They had already reached the end of their expected life of six years.) Guppy did, however, recommend that they be replaced. After much thought the directors, anxious to avoid expense, adopted his advice and decided to fit new boilers of the tubular type. Guppy, in his recommendation, informed the directors that the new design of boiler would require little more than half the space of the originals, thereby increasing cargo capacity, and gave an estimate for their

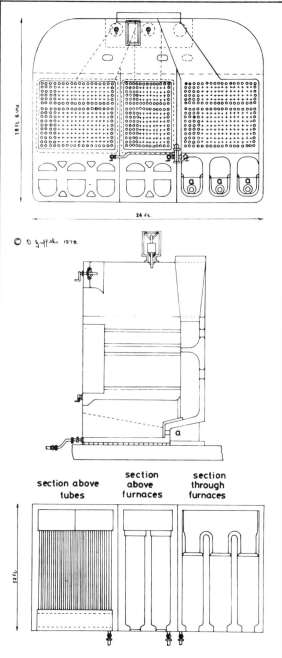

Fig 39: Sectional view of tubular boilers as fitted in 1844.

construction of £3,000, a very optimistic figure.[21] These boilers the company would construct itself, in the yard set up to repair the machinery of the *Great Western* but now occupied in building her sister.

The new boilers comprised essentially of one single unit, 24 feet wide, 12 feet deep and 18 feet 6 inches tall, with three seperate sections. The outer section contained three furnaces whilst the inner section had two (fig No 39). Furnaces remained separate until the back of the boilers where those for each boiler combined into a smoke box. Iron tubes, three inches internal diameter and eight feet long, carried the gases to the front smoke box which acted as a bend and returned the gases to the back of the boiler through an upper set of identical tubes. From the only available drawing of the boiler[22] there appears to have been a total of 750 tubes, 258 on each of the outer boilers and 234 on the centre. It would also seem that more tubes existed in the lower bank than the upper, the upper bank containing six rows to the lower's ten. The tube heating area of 5,900 square feet would have been provided by the 750 tubes if the thickness of the tube walls measured 3/8 inch; a not unreasonable figure. Full data on the boilers is given in Appendix No 7.

No indication has been made available as to the arrangement of the boilers within the ship. Certainly space saving could only have been accomplished with the 24 feet width athwartships. Whether the furnaces faced forward or aft is unknown. Positioning the furnaces facing the engine would not only allow the engineers to watch both engines and boilers more conveniently, but also enable shorter steam and feed water pipe runs to be used. For these reasons the drawings of the 1846 ship layout (fig Nos 23a & 23b) indicate the boilers to be arranged that way. The usual boiler mountings had to be connected as for the earlier steam generating plant.

Not only were the tubular units smaller and lighter than the flue boilers but they consumed less fuel per horse-power output, the important factor as far as the owners were concerned. Efficiency of operation was not matched by steaming capability. A fact that Guppy readily admitted.[23] This scarcity of steam gave an excuse for the government surveyor to reject the ship when a sale to the P & O Company had been arranged soon after the new boilers were placed on board. How great an influence the steam shortage had on the service speed cannot really be known, but it did affect it. Passage times between Liverpool and New York, and vice versa, were one or two days longer for the years after the boiler replacement than for the years prior to it. This slight increase in passage time concerned the directors but the reduction in fuel costs of about £275 per voyage and the potential increase in revenue, because of the additional cargo space from the reduced size of the new steam plant, mollified them.[24]

Steaming performance worried Claxton and towards the end of 1845 he solicited the assistance of Brunel. After discussing the problem with Joshua Field, Brunel suggested to Claxton that a small auxiliary boiler be placed on board to generate steam which was to be blown up the flue to increase the furnace draught. Brunel also suggested that a more lively coal might be burned thereby encouraging a draught but, at the same time, increasing coal consumption.[25] That the advice was not taken is indicated in the report made by the Secretary of the RMSPC just over a year later. The report commented, 'The boilers are Tubular and defective in form.' John Bourne, in his book *A Treatise on the Steam Engine* (see ref No 19), considered that the deficiency of steam had its roots in the fact that the boilers possessed a very large heating area compared with the grate area. The actual heating area to fire grate area ratio for the tubular boilers standing at a phenomenal 49.5 to 1 whilst that for the original boilers was only 19.2 to 1. Essentially the new plant extracted too much heat from the gases — it was too efficient. Cold funnel gases, he presumed, could not maintain sufficient furnace draught. He, like Brunel, advocated a steam blast up the funnel in the manner of a locomotive. A simpler suggestion proposed the cutting of a hole through the water box, which separated the rear smoke boxes for the upper and lower tube banks, thus allowing some of the gases to bye-pass the upper tubes and so enter the funnel hotter. Such a plan would, probably, have worked as the smaller number of tubes in the upper bank must have restricted the gas flow in comparison with the lower bank, thereby adding to the effect of the cold gases. Allowing some of the gas to take an easier route to the funnel would have provided an increased flow area. Any reason for such vastly different numbers of tubes in each bank is difficult to imagine. Provision for forced air draught to the furnaces was made on the boilers, possibly the first instance on a

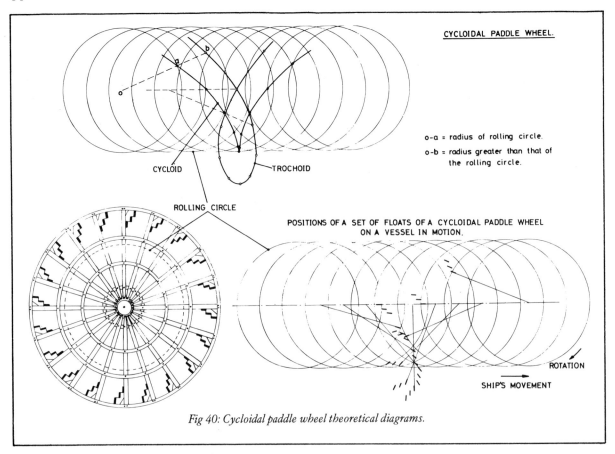

CYCLOIDAL PADDLE WHEEL.

o-a = radius of rolling circle.

o-b = radius greater than that of the rolling circle.

CYCLOID   TROCHOID

ROLLING CIRCLE

POSITIONS OF A SET OF FLOATS OF A CYCLOIDAL PADDLE WHEEL ON A VESSEL IN MOTION.

ROTATION

SHIP'S MOVEMENT

Fig 40: Cycloidal paddle wheel theoretical diagrams.

marine installation. The plan called for air to be forced into the space below the grate through holes at the back of each ashpit. Probably never implemented, the idea was workable but inconvenient. With furnace doors open for firing, the blast would force smoke into the engine room.

Purchase for the Mail Service gave the Admiralty a say in the equipping of the ship. They did not like the boilers and so they were replaced. Unfortunately, little information exists on the steam generating plant installed by the RMSPC in late 1847. Designed by the engineer of that concern, Mr Mills, they followed the acceptable flue principle and were constructed at Southampton by the firm Smith & Ashby, Engineers and Boilermakers.[26, 27] There were four boilers with a single stokehold, the operating pressure being 5 lb/in².

No mention is made of replacements and it appears likely that these boilers remained in the *Great Western* until she was broken up in 1856.

Paddle wheels provided the final and essential part of the propulsion equipment. The wheels fitted in London were of the cycloidal pattern; an arrangement devised by Joshua Field in 1833 but patented by Elijah Galloway in August 1835. Conventional wheels employed single boards, or floats, mounted at the circumference. With this type considerable shock resulted when the float hit the water causing vibration within the ship and wasting energy due to the splash produced. The idea of Field, and Galloway, was to employ a float which entered the water smoothly. Instead of a single float a number of smaller boards were fitted at each station. These boards were mounted on the wheels in a step fashion towards the circumference.

Any point on the circumference of a rolling wheel scribes out a cycloid (point 'a' in fig No 40). In the case of a rolling wheel no slip occurs and the circumference is also the rolling circle. Another point, 'b', outside of the rolling circle scribes out a trochoid. Plain paddle boards have points mainly outside of the rolling circle, which lies some distance in from the wheel circumference. Slitting the floats into a large number of shallower boards and mounting them in a curve rather than a straight line allows them to produce a section of a trochoid where entry to the water takes place. Thus all of the shallow floats enter the water at the same place. Employing this principle the cycloidal, or perhaps more accurately trochoidal, paddle wheels were produced. Rather than a number of shallow boards a single board of a particular curvature would give the same result but cause energy loss at exit from the water; split boards allow the floats to leave the water cleanly. Production and mounting of such floats would present difficulties. Fig No 40 shows a section of trochoid scribed out by a rotating wheel with only three float boards.[28]

Maudslay, Sons and Field fitted cycloidal wheels 28 feet 9 inches diameter to the *Great Western* in 1838 (fig No 41). Full details of the wheels are given in Appendix No 7, but it is interesting to note that four floats of different depths were used, the outer one, 4½ inches deep, being of iron to counteract the heavy shock effect on the first float to enter the water. Wooden construction sufficed for the remaining float boards. A riveted and bolted form of construction provided the wheel skeleton, there being three circular sections to the completed wheel; the third wheel section was placed equidistant from the two outer sections. Paddle boards connected onto the wheel spokes, or paddle arms, at the stools. Long hooked bolts held each float board in place. This method of connection did not prove efficient as nuts frequently became loose resulting in the ship having to be stopped to retighten them. Prior to entering Bristol dock system for a winter overhaul, the lower section of the paddle wheels needed to be removed so that the *Great Western* might negotiate the locks at the Cumberland Basin. This, obviously, had some effect upon the constructional efficiency of the

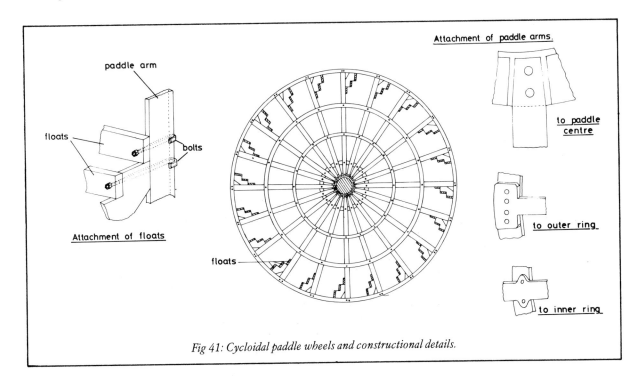

Fig 41: *Cycloidal paddle wheels and constructional details.*

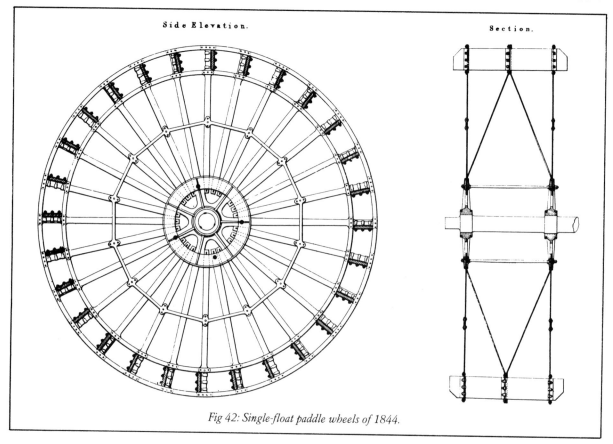

Side Elevation.

Section.

Fig 42: Single-float paddle wheels of 1844.

wheels. From the first voyage the wheels were a continual source of expense and, at the end of 1843, Guppy reported that they had gone too far to be worth repairing.[29] He planned new wheels which, he hoped, would stand up better to the wear and tear experienced by an Atlantic voyager. Actually Brunel had at one time proposed changes in the cycloidal wheels in order to improve speed and, possibly, to try out designs for the paddle wheels of the new ship; at that time, December 1839, still to be paddle propelled. One idea was to reposition the outer float on each arm between the main arms.[30] It is unlikely that this was even tried out as no mention is made of the step, not even in Brunel's report

on the screw propeller, which contains references to tests carried out aboard the *Great Western*.

Of the more conventional single float type, the new wheels had 28 floats riveted to the support arms at the outside and centre. As with the new boilers, these wheels were constructed at the company's works in Bristol. *The Artisan* for October 1844 published an illustration of the wheels and made the comment, '. . . we think it is the best wheel that has come under our observation'. These wheels appear to have given no trouble and the absence of adverse comment in the RMSPC documents gives reason to believe that they remained with the ship until the end of her career.

Chapter 8

A move to Liverpool

The foresight shown by the guiding fathers of Liverpool docks contrasts sharply with the reluctance of their brothers from Bristol. Steam powered harbour and coastal craft had graced the murky waters of the Mersey for many years prior to any scheme aimed at extending their operations west of Ireland. When such propositions began to take shape Liverpool, unlike other ports, seized its opportunity. A new steam dock would take time to construct and so a stop-gap measure had to be found. The berths set aside for steam ships engaged in the coastal trade could not accommodate the larger Atlantic ships then envisaged. During the early part of 1838 the Liverpool Dock Committee requested its surveyor to prepare plans for a large steam dock which might be available within a short period of time. On July 12 he submitted his design for new piers and gates to be placed at the entrance to the outer basin at the south end of Queen's Dock. With an entrance 70 feet wide all paddle steamers then envisaged could gain access and lie afloat at all states of the tide. A week later the committee approved the plan at its estimated cost of £35,400 for gates and piers and £1,915 for excavating the bottom of the basin.[1] This new dock would have an area of 23,623 square yards and a quay length in excess of 1200 feet. Additionally there was quay space for the storage of considerable quantities of bunker coal, an essential as far as steam trade was concerned. Following the marriage of Queen Victoria to Prince Albert of Saxe Coburg and Gotha, the Dock Committee decided to name their new dock in honour of the prince, hence Coburg Dock was born. When the Cunard mail steamers commenced service in 1840 they made use of its facilities and continued to do so for many years after.

Falling passenger numbers — due mainly to the competition provided by the Cunard vessels — and the absence of any relief from crippling port dues at Bristol led to the managers considering an alternative terminal port for the *Great Western*. As an experiment they decided that Liverpool and Bristol should alternate as the arrival and departure port during the year 1842. Unlike Bristol, Liverpool provided safe enclosed berths for its steamers and also held out better prospects for cargo and passengers. With lower inland transportation cost between the factories of the North and Midlands and the docks at Liverpool, improved cargo figures could be expected. The difference in dock dues and other expenses — barges, small steamers, etc, — meant that *Great Western* could be clear out of Liverpool £200 per voyage cheaper than from Bristol.[2] However, much of the agency business at Bristol in the hands of the company itself, was lost to Gibbs, Bright & Co of Liverpool. During 1841 this had been worth £452 in commission.[3] The move to Liverpool did not find favour with all of the shareholders as many felt that the company had been formed to benefit Bristol as well as themselves. Notwithstanding, profitable commercial interests prevailed and Bristol lost its grip on the Atlantic trade.

Fortunately the log book which records that first voyage to the new terminal has survived and is preserved at Bristol Museum. Thus some interesting events may be recounted. With 69 passengers, a mixed cargo and a heavy mail the *Great Western* steamed out of the Avon at 1.30 pm on April 2 1842. Just after 9 o'clock that evening, off Lundy Island, the pilot was safely decanted into a pilot skiff conveniently anchored nearby.

Obviously the company had now dispensed with the expensive, and needless, practice of carrying a Bristol Channel pilot on board. Later that same evening an unscheduled ten minute stop took place in order to cool a connecting rod bearing on the port engine. It is recorded that Joseph Williams, the second engineer, suffered injury whilst working on that engine, probably whilst endeavouring to cool the bearing.

The early part of the voyage progressed steadily with reasonable weather and a speed varying between eight and nine knots. By the seventh day, however, strong gales had blown up; high head seas and little sail set resulted in the speed falling below six knots. Within two days conditions improved and normal speeds were achieved. On April 12 a number of icebergs were in sight, except when the fog came down and avoiding action necessitated many course changes. Thick fog and icebergs provide probably the most dangerous combination of elements that any ship has to face, certainly in peace time. Surprisingly, the log book indicated that no speed reductions took place during this period; the speed actually rising above nine knots. At 10.20 am on Sunday April 17 the New York pilot embarked and guided the *Great Western* to her berth at the foot of Clinton Street. This was a few hundred yards further up the East River than her original berth at the foot of Pike Street. Berthing could not take place immediately due

to the fast current and so she lay off until slack water in the early afternoon.

Normal ship board duties of coaling, cargo work, painting, etc, occupied the crew during the stay, except for one seaman, J. Jones, who sought to pass his time in the company of a liquor bottle. His persistant intoxication is well highlighted in the log book, warranting no less than five separate entries for the eleven full days in port. On each of those occasions he was found to be drunk and incapable of performing his duties. Jones probably enjoyed his stay in New York but it is unlikely that he remembered much of it. During the night of Sunday 24 and Monday 25 Frederick Bowden, the cook's mate, absconded taking with him all of his clothes. This was a not infrequent occurrence as there were many who found it an inexpensive way of emigrating. Fortunately, willing hands were always available for a passage in the other direction; possibly some were those whose earlier 'emigration' had not worked out. On April 23 to mark St Georges Day and the fourth anniversary of the ship's first arrival at New York the *Great Western* was draped overall with flags and bunting. A number of those on board had actually made that first passage and were justifiably proud.

Departure from New York, on April 28 had to be delayed for half an hour beyond the normal sailing time of 2 o'clock whilst a replacement pilot was sent for. The

Fig 43: Track of Voyage No 23 across the Atlantic.

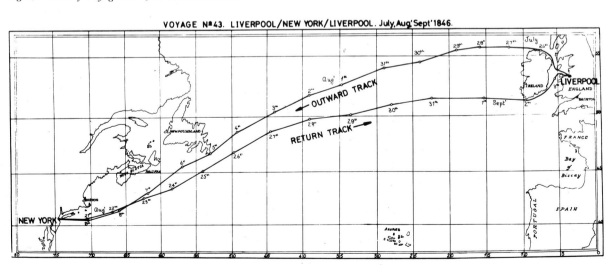

VOYAGE N°43. LIVERPOOL/NEW YORK/LIVERPOOL. July, Aug'Sept'1846.

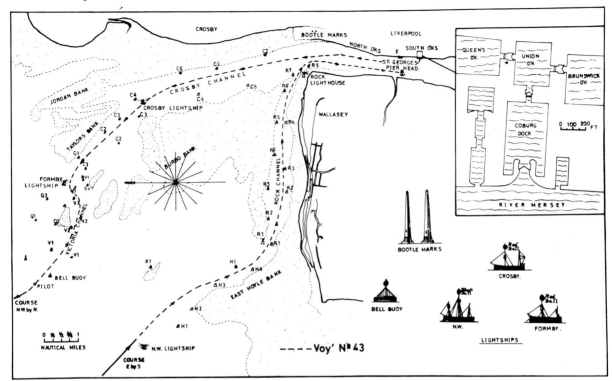

Fig 44: Mersey Estuary and Coburg Dock.

first, when he arrived at 1.00 pm, being so inebriated that Hosken would not entertain him on board. Seemingly a man after the fashion of seaman J. Jones. Because of the ice encountered during the outward passage Hosken took his ship further south on the return crossing and added about 200 miles to the journey. In favourable weather *Great Western* made a fast, if uneventful, run towards Liverpool, the speed frequently exceeding 11 knots and sometimes 12 knots. One discomforting incident occurred on May 6 when, with a high following sea and gale force winds, a wave broke over the poop smashing the cuddy windows and allowing a considerable quantity of water to enter the after accommodation. No doubt dinner that evening was a very damp affair.

Tuesday May 10, the day before arrival at Liverpool, produced a rather unusual and enlightening incident. At 6.30 am whilst off Kinsale in Ireland, Hosken ordered that the engines be stopped. The reason was to put a Mr Towers of Ireland, at his own request, into a fishing boat that had been signalled to come alongside. Obviously, that passenger wished to avoid a further steamer journey from Liverpool to his home country and hence save upwards of three days, not to mention the extra cost. Unfortunately, in attempting to come alongside the fishing boat hit the larger steamer causing herself damage. Hosken, after ascertaining that the damage to the hull and mast was not serious, employed another fishing boat to tow the damaged vessel into port, leaving Mr Towers to sort out any problems. An hour after stopping, the *Great Western* proceeded on her way to the Mersey. The incident illustrates either the lengths to which steamship masters would go in order to please their passengers, or the persuasive power of Mr Towers' wallet; or both.

Having picked up a pilot off Anglesey the Bristol steamer had to anchor off the North West Light Vessel until high water approached. Prior to entering the docks a tug came alongside and took off some of the passengers. Many remained on board until the ship berthed, unassisted, on the north side of Coburg Dock.

The Albion for May 16 reported the arrival: 'This far famed Steam Ship, under the command of Lieutenant Hosken RN, arrived for the first time in the waters of the Mersey on Wednesday morning last. She passed the town a few minutes after 8 o'clock, firing her signal gun as she steamed up to the sloyne, where she remained at the moorings until high water when she entered the Coburg Dock.

The *Great Western* left New York on the afternoon of 28th ult' and arrived off the Northwest Lightship early on the morning of 11th instant. The passage occupied, therefore, 12 days 7½ hours, but the distance from New York to Liverpool, as compared with that of Bristol, is at least equal to 6 hours steaming.

This is the shortest passage ever made notwithstanding she went well to the southward to avoid ice, thereby increasing the distance 200 miles beyond the direct line. The average speed has been a fraction less than 11 knots or nautical miles per hour.'

The performance figure given does not take account of the fact that over an hour was lost in the Irish Sea when Mr Towers took his leave of the vessel. The same edition of the paper records that the Cunard ship *Britannia* arrived at Liverpool on the night of May 15 with 33 passengers from Halifax and Boston.

Widespread interest in the *Great Western* prompted the company to throw her open to public gaze on May 17-18. Throughout the first day admission cost one shilling and on the second six pence; all proceeds being distributed between the Northern and Southern Hospitals.[4] The directors were extending the charity they had shown at Bristol and at the same time gaining publicity for their vessel. At Liverpool the process was somewhat easier as the ship lay at a berth close to the town centre. Later that year, on August 29-30, the citizens of Liverpool had a further opportunity to inspect the ship when, during her second visit, she was once again thrown open for the same worthy cause.[5] This benevolent action probably took place at other times in the future as the *Great Western* developed into a popular 'Liverpool' ship. The visits enjoyed by the public, no doubt, inconvenienced the running of the ship. No other contemporary vessel appears to have served local hospitals so well.

Alternate sailings from Liverpool illustrated the advantages of that port compared with Bristol. Although bunker coal had to be shipped a greater distance bunkering costs must have been comparable as no loading barges were required at Liverpool. For similar reasons costs of cargo operations were lower and such operations more convenient. Passenger figures for 1842 show no general increase, or decrease, from the use of Liverpool as a terminal. Cargo figures at that time were distorted by a new import tariff imposed by the USA authorities and so no conclusions could be drawn from them even if they were available.[6] The directors, however, concluded that Liverpool's potential exceeded that of Bristol and planned for the UK terminal to lie on the Mersey. In the mean time they attempted to sell their only source of income, the *Great Western*.

A not insignificant group of shareholders became increasingly alarmed at the escalating construction costs of the new iron ship and the plummeting value of their shares; with a paid up value of £95 they could, in November 1842, be obtained for between £22½ and £25. Rather than tie the company in debt through excessive borrowings they proposed the disposal of their paddle steamer.[7] This the directors assented to and during the latter part of 1842 and early 1843 they attempted to find a buyer. Nothing concrete transpired from these efforts. The seriousness of the directors in their endeavours is open to dispute; certainly the events which took place at a public auction on October 17 1842 cast doubts on their willingness to part with the *Great Western*. Conditions of the proposed sale indicated that any purchaser must complete the voyage already arranged and imdemnify the company against any loss that might result from its completion. Following a description of the vessel, bidding commenced at £16,000 and rose quickly to £40,000, at which price the ship was 'knocked down'. Upon repeated requests to name the buyer, the auctioneer informed the assembly that the ship had been purchased for the proprietors but that he would be pleased to arrange a sale by private contract.[8] This was a clear attempt by the directors to obtain a market value for their ship, but that value is unknown as the final bona-fide bid was not disclosed.

Whilst attempting to effect a sale and scrutinise applications for a charter, the managers could not plan for the 1843 season, if there was to be one. Eventually they decided to arrange a February passage to New York by way of Madeira and, more importantly, planned that Liverpool would become the sole British terminal for their ship. It was not until late January that the sailing date of February 11 could be set, thus restricting the likely passenger numbers. A creditable 58 booked for New York at 41 gns with a few more to Madeira at £24 10s; both including the stewards fee.[9]

Without substantiating evidence any theories regarding the reasons for an early season voyage to New York via a southerly route must be speculative. Considerable cargo might be offered, as at that time of year the sailing packet times tended to be variable and prolonged. The directors may also have considered that such a cruise-like voyage would have attracted a larger than expected number of passengers. In fact, the total booked earnings for the outward crossing amounted to £3,275, which exceeded by £456 the earnings from the first voyage of 1842 and was only £600 below the average for that year.[10] Fuel, crew and victualling costs must have been greater than average due to the longer passage envisaged. Certainly, a succesful winter voyage would only enhance the standing of the ship when it came to any negotiations for a sale.

Departing from Kingroad between 4.00 pm and 5.00 pm on Saturday February 11, the *Great Western* headed south, encountering gales almost immediately. After a rough passage she reached Funchal at 4.00 pm on the eighth day out from Bristol. During the stay of 30 hours some 70 tons of coal were taken in very difficult conditions. A number of other vessels had to slip their cables to contend with the stormy weather. It took nearly a week more of bad weather and head winds before conditions improved and the temperature rose, producing a holiday atmosphere on board. A long passage and the hot conditions resulted in the melting of the ice packed within the ice house. Towards the end of the passage the thermometer in that compartment registered 70°F. Fortunately, more than adequate provisions had been put on board.[11] *Great Western* passed Sandy Hook at noon on March 12 after a run of 20 days from Funchal, during which the engines had operated continuously. In all she had steamed 4,700 miles on the passage from Bristol and consumed 660 tons of coal[12] — some seven miles per ton.

After a fast turn around of four days the foremost Atlantic liner headed homewards and immediately misfortune struck. Through the incompetence of the New York pilot she touched a shoal whilst leaving the harbour and, although no damage could be detected then, or on the homeward passage, the insurance underwriters insisted upon a drydock inspection before the next voyage. Unfortunately, two Cunard steamers occupied the large drydock at Liverpool so the *Great Western* had to travel to South Wales where the Admiralty had made available their facilities at the Royal Dockyard, Pembroke. Investigation showed the damage to be trivial but the delays encountered did not allow the vesel to resume her arranged sailing schedule. New sailing dates were set and the company offered a refund to those passengers who could not wait the two weeks until April 29 when the next sailing was to take place. At the same time they announced a fare reduction to 30 gns.[13]

As a result of the enforced drydocking and the retimed sailings, that first voyage of the season made a loss rather than the profit envisaged. Repair and docking expenses, including passages to and from Pembroke, amounted to £606, whilst the directors estimated the loss of earnings at £1,500. That year only five round trips were completed instead of the possible six and this would also have reduced the profits made. Because of the 'wilful or ignorant conduct' of the pilot at New York the company felt called upon to 'make such representations at New York as would lead to his suspension.'[14] Some New York pilots did not endear themselves to those who had charge of the steamship *Great Western*.

The remaining voyages of the 1843 season progressed without any real incident. Passenger figures improved on the previous year and crossing times held up very well. Significantly, from April 1 1843 advertisements for Cunard sailings included a statement to the effect that fares on certain sailings to Halifax and Boston would be reduced to 30 gns. Those sailings just happened to be about the same time as the *Great Western* took her departure from Liverpool. Freight rates also fell to £3 10s per ton; less than that charged by the Bristol company. Only once that year did any Cunard vessel, out or home, carry more passengers than *Great Western* and that was the new ship *Hibernia* on its second voyage, when it took out 87 passengers compared with 67 to New York three days earlier. The following trip saw the situation reversed as 124 persons took berths on *Great Western* whilst the *Hibernia,* sailing two days later attracted forty fewer. Eastbound crossings produced even greater differences between the ships; arriving at Liverpool on June 13, the *Acadia* brought 63 passengers whereas five days earlier the Bristol steamer landed double that number from New York. At the end of the season 99 passengers travelled on the steamer from New York whilst the *Acadia*, arriving a day later from Boston and Halifax, only managed to attract 26 passengers.

Admittedly the first four Cunard steamers were smaller than their Bristol built counterpart and could not carry as many passengers. That, however, was not the case with the larger *Hibernia* and later *Cambria*. It must also be accepted that passengers to and from inner Canada and America could find better connections at New York, making that terminal more attractive.

Over the next three years passenger numbers varied but *Great Western* consistently drew more passengers than any other Atlantic steamship arriving or sailing at about the same time. During 1845 and 1846 the newspapers did not often mention passenger numbers for ships sailing in competition with *Great Western* although, generally, those for the latter were given. It may be concluded that the Cunard company did not issue figures for fear of damaging comparisons being made. However, to be fair, the newspapers probably felt that with five regular Halifax and Boston steamers a single one was not as newsworthy as the sole survivor on the New York run.

The fare cutting actions of the Cunard company well illustrate the benefits of competition. They also indicate a certain ruthlessness as reduced rates only applied to particular sailings. Such actions may have been good business practice if the intention was to drive the Bristol concern from the North Atlantic. Cunard received a subsidy, from the taxpayer, of over £4,000 per voyage and, therefore, did not rely solely upon passenger and cargo revenue for survival. When questioned at the parliamentary select committee on the Halifax and Boston mails, in July 1846, Samuel Cunard was not completely forthright in his answers. To the question, 'At the period last year when the *Great Western* sailed nearly at the same time as your vessels, had you altered your fares?', Cunard replied 'Yes; and I have been sorry for that since. I was in Halifax at the time, and it was done here without my concurrence. I

regretted it, and it will not be done again. I thought it looked like an opposition, which I was sorry to see.'[15]

Cunard, however failed to mention that the same fare alterations took place during 1843 and 1844. Certainly as a busy shipowner he cannot have spent all of his time, during those three years, hidden away in Halifax and oblivious to what transpired at the Liverpool base. His memory again appears to have conveniently deserted him when the committee chairman raised the matter of freight rates: 'Has your rate been uniform', — 'Yes £7. We always go at £7.' 'You have not altered it in any way?' — 'No, not that I recollect.' 'You have not made bargains varying from your professed rate, to compete with other vessels that happened to be sailing at the same time?' — 'No, I have not any recollection of making any alteration whatever.'[16] The half price offers on freight made during 1843 and 1844 were expediently forgotton, but one member of the select committee must have been aware of the reduction to phrase the questions in those terms.

Understandably, *Great Western* and the Cunard ships drew supporters who championed their favourite in numerous verbal battles. Both they and the gambling fraternity rejoiced at the prospect of transatlantic race. Such 'races' could never be definitive in deciding the better class of ship. Firstly, the finishing (or starting) posts, at New York and Boston, were separated by some 200 miles and so the route followed differed to an extent. Secondly, weather conditions varied considerably with location — hence the importance of the course followed — and with the time. One ship might enjoy a fine crossing whilst another, separated by only a couple of days and a few hundred miles might experience exremely rough seas and head winds. *Great Western* suffered the additional disadvantage of having a deeper draft through the carriage of more coal than her 'competitors'. This presented problems as the dip of the paddle wheels changed considerably during the passage, altering the propulsive efficiency.

On September 3 1842, *Great Western* left Liverpool and the Cunard ship *Acadia* sailed within 18 hours of her. Many bets were laid that the latter would take less time to reach Boston than the former would in making New York. Quay to quay, the passage to New York occupied 14 days 10 hours, whilst that to Boston took 14 days 2 ½ hours, thus winning the bet for the supporters of the *Acadia*. Such examples do not illustrate the superiority of one ship over the other as New York was a further 20 to 24 hours steaming from Boston. Newspapers, in comparing the two performances failed to mention that fact. They also omitted any reference to the return passages when *Great Western*, arriving at Liverpool on September 29, took 13 days 4 hours from New York, whilst *Acadia*, arriving three days later, took 13 days 23½ hours from Boston.

Similar widely publicised betting took place in August of the following year. The wager centred on the contention that news by the *Hibernia*, a new ship, would reach New York, via Boston, before the arrival of the *Great Western*. This was, perhaps, a more significant contest as far as the American mail and passenger connections were concerned. *Hibernia*, with just over 80 passengers left Liverpool on August 4 and arrived at Boston on the 17th at 10.00 pm — a passage of 14 days 10½ hours.[17] Sailing the next day, *Great Western* carried 124 passengers to New York and arrived early on August 21 after a crossing of 15 days 16 hours. The newspapers do not record which ship won. Certainly the *Hibernia* had the advantage with her day's start and allowing for the stop at Halifax her time was very good.

From the passage times available for the ships, there is little to choose between them on performance up to 1844. After that date, with her new, more economical boilers, the timings of the *Great Western* fell off somewhat. There is, however, no doubt that the Bristol steamer was the more popular ship in that she had a greater passenger appeal.

Claxton frequently complained that press reports concerning the possible sale of the *Great Western* or the impending dissolution of the company cost the ship passengers.[18] This cannot be denied, but the main architect of the confusion was the company itself. Through its frequently announced decisions to offer its paddle steamer for sale the Great Western Steam Ship Company sowed, in the minds of potential passengers, the seeds of doubt as to the advisability of booking a passage. Public infighting at shareholders' meetings gave rise to the impression of an unstable concern. Growing debts, as a result of the escalating cost of the iron ship, indicated, to many, approaching bankruptcy. At a meeting in August 1842 there were calls for the winding up of the company before shareholders lost all of their investment.[19] Not surprisingly, the press

were excluded from most meetings after that year. Fortunately, well meaning shareholders provided the newspapers with details.[20] The company, therefore, had only itself to blame if published reports reduced the number of passengers attracted to the *Great Western*. Generally, newspaper coverage of the Atlantic steamships was completely unbiased.

In view of its expanding service east of Suez the Peninsular and Oriental Steam Navigation Company were interested in purchasing good steamers for their services to the Mediterranean and between Suez and India. During April 1844 they agreed to purchase *Great Western* for £32,000 and decided to place her on the Southampton to Alexandria service.[21] Due to her proposed employment under a government mail contract a very stringent survey had to be arranged prior to completion of the purchase. This carried out on May 18, she passed in all respects but one; her new tubular boilers were reported to be short of steam.[22] Following adjustments and modifications, the Great Western Steam Ship Company awaited a second survey by the government surveyor. However, despite fervent correspondence between the parties, no surveyor arrived. Rather than wait any longer, losing revenue, the company decided that P&O was no longer interested in the ship and advertised her for an Atlantic voyage from Liverpool on June 22. The Peninsular company took offence, rather than steps to arrange a re-survey, and applied to the vice chancellor's court for an injunction to prevent *Great Western* from sailing. On June 10 Sir L. Shadwell granted P&O its injunction.[23] Needless to say the company immediately took steps to have the injunction dissolved and in the mean time *Great Western* sailed for Liverpool. After hearing further evidence on the matter, Sir L. Shadwell cancelled his injunction; the grounds being that a defect in the contract did not bind the P&O Company to purchasing the vessel and so the Great Western Steam Ship Company should similarly not be bound. Sale negotiations ceased.[24]

Though the new tubular boilers were not able to provide steam at the same rate as the original flue boilers they still allowed good service speeds to be maintained. These speeds were as good, if not better than, those produced by P&O ships already in service. One report has it that an average speed of over 13 knots was obtained during a 12 hour trial under the direction of the government surveyor.[25] If that was true, then the proposed purchasers must have had some other reason for attempting to delay the sale. Possible a price reduction?

The intended purchase price of £32,000 was to have been paid one half in cash upon completion of the negotiations and the remainder by a bill six months later. Although they accepted, the company did think their vessel to be worth more. They even approached one of Cunard's partners for a grant of £3,000 or £4,000 for removing the *Great Western* from the Atlantic. Neither Cunard nor his partners were interested.[26]

Hosken had, in the mean time, been appointed to command the *Great Britain* and so Barnard R. Matthews became master of *Great Western*.[27] Hosken, accompanied by 33 passengers, sailed with the ship on June 22 in order to arrange berthing facilities for the *Great Britain* at New York. On her return *Great Western* brought 66 passengers whilst the final two outward crossings of that year each attracted in excess of 130 passengers, despite fare reductions on the corresponding Cunard steamers. Though her steaming capability may have been diminished, her popularity certainly was not.

A berth on the north side of Coburg Dock provided ideal accommodation for *Great Western*. More than adequate quayside storage area existed for coal yards and cargo handling, with coal, mainly from the Cunard steamers, taking up the greater share of the space. Brunswick Dock, Dock Master's record books for the 1842 to 1846 period[28] contain references to the regular arrival of colliers from South Wales. These were, obviously, replenishing the coal depots of both Atlantic steamship companies which made use of the facilities in Coburg Dock. Passengers generally boarded *Great Western* whilst she lay within the dock although on a number of occasions departure for a river anchorage took place a few days before departure from the port.[29] This was necessary if the berth had been booked by another vessel. Four and later five, Cunard steamships berthed alongside the same quay, which could only take two such large ships at any one time, and at regular intervals sailing colliers had to find space between them. Infrequently, the dock had to be run dry in order to allow necessary maintenance to take place but the books do not record that sort of incident affecting *Great Western*. With the ship at anchor, mails and passengers were brought aboard by means of one of the many small steamers which plied the Mersey.

No record of the use of tugs for docking or undocking appears to exist and it is almost certain that such assistance was never necessary. The high degree of manoeuvrability of the ship allowed her to negotiate the ample width of the dock entrance and turn in the river, provided that too fast a current was not running. A Liverpool turn-round generally exceeded seven days, as did that at New York, but between voyages No 38 and 39 it occupied the short period of four and a half days. Discharging and loading of the cargo as well as the bunkering and revictualling of the ship must have been carried on at a hectic pace.

Shortly after *Great Western* sailed on her 38th voyage, on July 5 1845, her consort, *Great Britain*, arrived in Liverpool for the first time. The sailings from Liverpool of both vessels were staggered and so they did not berth together in Liverpool until the end of that season. *Great Western* only remained on the Mersey for two days before returning to Bristol for her winter overhaul. As *Great Britain* underwent repair and modification at the end of her first, rather short, Atlantic season she is unlikely to have been in Coburg Dock when her older sister returned from New York. Returning to Liverpool on March 10 1846, *Great Western* brought with her the replacement screw for *Great Britain*; this had been manufactured at the company's Bristol workshop.[30] For the fitting of this screw the iron ship must have occupied a dry dock and so it is improbable that the Bristol sisters graced Coburg Dock together.

The screw propulsion of *Great Britain* attracted considerable interest. Those on board *Great Western* had, however, encountered that mode of drive in October 1843. An American warship, *Princeton*, fitted with a 14 feet diameter Ericsson screw, had 'raced' with the wooden paddle steamer whilst she was leaving New York on October 19 1843. Hosken reported that the American ship achieved a speed close to 11 knots whilst his own could only manage just over 9 knots.[31] Although an interesting comparison of the two methods of propulsion no conclusions could be drawn regarding the superiority of the American ship. She was a sprinter on a short course whilst the British steamer was a long distance performer, with bunker space for an Atlantic crossing. The event attracted the attention of the American public and received wide coverage in the New York newspapers.

On October 20 the *New York Commercial Advertiser* described the event thus; 'The *Princeton* had been plying about the river and bay during the morning. About a quarter before three o'clock the *Great Western* came down the East River, with apparently a good head of steam on, and all sails set, to make the most of the breeze which was blowing fresh and favourable, in wafting her out to sea.

'After the *Great Western* had passed the Battery, the *Princeton* some distance astern, and without a single sail set, gave chase, and both ships headed for the quarantine. The *Princeton* rapidly gained on, and finally passed the *Great Western*, thus giving evidence that those who had spoken most highly of the speed of the former had not in the least overrated her powers.'

The newspapers then went on to add a paragraph in defence of the Bristol ship.'

'It is but justice to state, that so far as the *Great Western* is concernd, there could be no concerted race between the two vessels. It is contrary to the express orders of the company by whom the vessel is owned, and the agents here positively deny that any preparation was made by Captain Hosken to test the sailing qualities of the vessel which he commanded with those of the *Princeton*.'[32]

That final paragraph illustrates the caution which the

Great Western Steam Ship Company demanded of its servants in the handling of its ships. The significance of the episode did not escape Hosken who, before dropping the pilot, penned a note to the New York agent with a copy for Claxton. In it he stated his opinions: '. . . It is true that the *Great Western* is deep in the water, rather more so than usual; still it convinces me, and will, I think, the public also, that our iron ship, the *Great Britain* will, to a moral certainty, surpass every steam ship that has gone before her.'[33]

A terminal at Liverpool could be reached from New York by passing north or south about Ireland; the reverse route from Liverpool provided the same alternatives. Going north about was the shorter of the two passages but there was also a greater risk of bad weather and ice, at particular times of the year. There appears to have been no company policy regarding the course to be taken. Hosken, and later Matthews, would have had the digression to take either route depending upon prevailing circumstances. During voyage No 43, for which a log book still exists,[34] the outward crossing to New York passed north of Ireland whilst the return took the southerly route. Whenever the northerly route was taken the Liverpool pilot would be dropped, or picked up, near the Bell Buoy, close to the present Bar Lightship, whilst going south about the pilot station, positioned off Angelsey.[35]

Voyage No 43, during July and August 1846, pro-

Fig 45: Track of Voyage No 43 across the Atlantic.

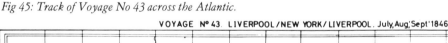

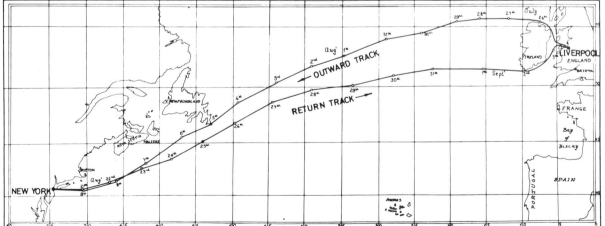

gressed without much incident. With a well filled passenger list of 138 outwards and 75 on the return the company would have been pleased, particularly as bookings for *Great Britain* showed an increase.[36] Though the weather varied from severe gales to foggy calms the *Great Western* turned in commendable times of 15 days 12 hours to New York and 14 days 2 hours for the return. However, the situation changed drastically next voyage.

Great Western departed from Liverpool at 4.00 pm on Saturday September 12 and for the first week encountered very favourable weather conditions. The following Saturday commenced with fine clear conditions but by late evening a full gale was blowing. The next forty-eight hours saw the most terrifying storm that the ship had ever encountered. It brought fear to those on board, caused considerable damage and delayed *Great Western* for a number of days. Extracts from the ship's log book and the personal observations of some passengers were published in the American newspapers shortly after the Bristol steamer arrived at New York; the British press repeated them when *Great Western* arrived home. The peril faced by the 211 souls on board — Captain, five officers, five engineers, 74 crew and 126 passengers — is well illustrated by an article in the *New York Tribune* for Thursday October 1 1846.

The Captain's log describes the commencement of the storm; 'Sunday 20 (September), the sea rising frightfully and breaking over and against the ship. At 4.00 am the wind increased to a heavy storm and the sea running most furiously at the ship. A great quantity of water got into the engine room from the sea breaking over the ship . . . Sunday morning most of the passengers assembled in the cabin and saloon. Their haggard faces told too surely of the sleepless and anxious night that had passed. Even those most ignorant of nautical affairs could not fail to discover that we were in the midst of great peril. Few could dress with their accustomed care, owing to the violent pitching rolling of the vessel. The stewards abandoned any attempt to lay the breakfast table.'

As the day progressed the situation became more serious and the passengers more alarmed. The log continues: '11.00 am. A heavy sea broke over the fore part of the paddle box, this started the ice house and large iron lifeboat from their fastenings and with much diffi-

culty they were temporarily secured . . . 11.30 am. The lee quarter boats were torn from their davits. Word was passed among the passengers that two of our boats were gone and that the others were likely to follow, the davits and bolts beginning to give. But not a remark was made; each spoke to the other only through the eye. And the ominous silence which pervaded the whole company told how sensibly all felt themselves in the very presence of the King of Terrors, uncertain of their doom.'

Those on board must have resigned themselves to the loss of the ship and their own lives. Matthews' log goes on to relate his own observations and a telling conversation with a passenger: 'Every heart was occupied with its individual griefs and memories as if not another shared the peril. Home, with its loved ones and a thousand cherished hopes and joys, rose fresh to the view and, with a power like the storm, swept over the mind and left it, like the ocean tempest, lost and troubled . . . "See", said a Gentleman to me, "no one converses, no one reads, all are engaged each with his own thoughts; and I confess, if my wife and children were here, my feelings would be of the most distressing character." "But", said I, "they suffer in your loss." "Very true; and yet it is only a question of time, and, whether sooner or later, God's will be done." '
Clearly, at least privately, Matthews was not at all optimistic about the situation.

The gales continued throughout the day. A breaking sea demolished the port paddle box, a piece of timber from it striking Matthews. The force and the effect of the sea carried him overboard. Fortunately the netting around the ship's sides saved him.

An unknown diarist described the scene in the saloon when a particularly bad wave struck: 'Most of us were seated in agonising suspense in the lower cabin, holding fast to the tables and settees; a sea struck the vessel and a tremendous crash was heard on deck. Instantly the cabin was darkened and torrents of water came pouring down upon us through the skylights . . . Scarceley had the waters reached the floor when all in the cabins and state-rooms sprang to their feet and simultaneously, as if by concert, the ladies uttered a scream of agony, so fearful and so despairing, the sound of it will never be forgotten; and Heaven grant that such a wail of anguish may never again be heard by me. Several fainted — others clasped their hands in mute despair, while many called aloud upon their Creator.'

In the saloon and throughout the accommodation, husbands comforted wives, fathers consoled their daughters and mothers wept for the families they might never see again. Night brought no respite. The diarist continued; 'As darkness came, clustering together in the cabin, we all thought and reflected on our fate. Most, if not all of us, had given ourselves up for lost. For what with the heavy labouring of the ship, the terrible noise and howling of the wind, the continued thumping of the sea, the quivering and shaking, the groaning of the timbers, the carrying away of so many portions of the vessel's upper works, and the knowledge that we were, perhaps, for another night to be exposed to the full power of a raging hurricane, left us little to hope for.'

The four members of the clergy on board found themselves well occupied with their ministerings. On Sunday evening the Reverend Balch conducted Holy Communion in the cabin. Upwards of 60 persons attended, many of whom received communion for the first time. After communion, the diarist returned to his state-room: 'The gentleman who shared it with me had gone below (into the main saloon) to die, as he expected, in company with his daughter and son-in-law. Left, therefore, alone, taking a last look at the pictures of my little family and commending them, and all dear to me, to the grace and protection of God, I laid down and slept peacefully.'

Throughout the night the storm raged in all its fury. At 5.00 am the ship was in the greatest danger when a tornado struck. Mr Stevens, one of the passengers, described the incident; 'A peculiar lifting of the haze in the East, with an appearance of an amber coloured belt of light, low down on the horizon, warned us of an approaching blow. Presently it came, a perfect tornado, driving before it the clouds of spray, and as it neared us, fairly lifting up the white foam from the waves, like a shower of rain. As the squall struck us, the ship careened over and buried her gunwales in the ocean, and lay for a few moments stricken powerless and apparently at the mercy of the savage waves that threatened to engulf us. This was the trial, the last round fought between the elements and our gallant vessel. At this critical moment the engine was true to her duty. Still went on her revolutions, and round and round thundered her iron water-wings. Gradually

recovering her upright position, the good ship with head quartering the sea, came up to her course, and all was well. It was the climax of the storm.'

By mid-day on Monday the seas had calmed enough to allow passengers and crew to move about the ship in relative safety. Brunel's ship and her crew were up to the task and, although a little battered and bruised, came through the trial commendably. Nine days later, on September 30, *Great Western* proudly entered the port of New York. Her leaking hull and wrecked upper works bore witness to the recent turmoil. The damage could be sooon repaired but those on board would long remember their ordeal.

As a mark of gratitude the passengers collected £200 10s for distribution between captain, officers and crew, all of whom had played their part in the battle against the elements. Having been so close to a watery grave, the fortunate passengers also felt concern for the families of those who had perished at sea. Before the end of the voyage they had collected nearly six hundred dollars to be placed in a fund for the relief of those families whose heads and supporters had been lost at sea. The fund was to be called the *Great Western* Fund. In accepting the monies from the passengers, Matthews thanked them for their kindness and indicated his own throughts upon their deliverance from the jaws of death; 'It is to Divine Providence alone that we are all indebted for our safety. For during my long experience at sea I never witnessed so severe a storm, and were it not for the good qualities of my noble ship, under the direction of God, she could not have weathered it'[37] Whilst the brave *Great Western* steamed away from her ordeal with the deep, an incident over a thousand miles away was sealing her fate as an Atlantic liner.

With 180 passengers on board the steamship *Great Britain* departed from Liverpool shortly before noon on September 22. Taking the northerly route Hosken steered his ship to take her south of the Isle of Man. After passing the Calf of Man a northerly course would bring the ship around the Ulster coast. A navigational error resulted in *Great Britain* going ashore in Dundrum Bay at 9.30 pm that night. Early hopes of a quick salvage and return to service were unfounded. The iron vessel was grossly under insured and the company had no money with which to fund a salvage operation. *Great Western* had to be sold to repay debts and provide much needed capital for the removal of her younger sister from the Irish beach. This step doomed the company for they no longer had a revenue earning asset. Actually the continuation of both vessels on the New York station was very doubtful following the outcome of the parliamentary select committee enquiry into the Halifax and Boston mails. The company had received no hopes of any share in the mail contract to New York thus leaving them at mercy of the subsidised Cunard ships when they entered service. Under such conditions the Great Western Steam Ship Company decided upon the prudent step of abandoning New York before their vessels were forced off the line. 1847 was to have been the final year of operation on that route. Events at Dundrum hastened the end by one year.[38]

After the accident to *Great Britain*, *Great Western* completed one more round trip, returning to Liverpool for the last time on December 12 1846. A week later, after discharging cargo and some stores, Brunel's first steamship bade farewell to the Mersey and headed for Bristol and a lay-up berth in the Floating Harbour.

Chapter 9

Rivals

The *Great Western* steamship came into being in order to provide an Atlantic passenger, cargo and mail service in competition with the sailing packets, then in sole possession of the route. Sailing ships operating the liner services were well equipped for fast running and passenger comfort; at least to a degree better than that offered by other ships. Although the service life of the ships was limited due to the rigours of the Atlantic weather and the way in which they were pressed, the operating companies could afford regular replacements. Ships changed but the companies did not. Set sailing dates and fairly fast crossings appealed to passengers and cargo shippers alike; the ships made money and the trade expanded.

Sailing packets varied in size from about 600 tons to over 1,200 tons. After the steamers appeared even larger packets were built — but they all had two fundamentals in common; scheduled sailings and speed. Speed was relative to the direction of travel and the vaguaries of the wind. Under favourable conditions eastward crossing times exceeded only marginally those of some early steamers. That fact together with more frequent sailings and, generally, lower charges allowed the packets to maintain healthy passengers lists even when the steam services came about. The fear of boiler explosion haunted many people who, for that reason alone, preferred the sailing packets. Others, after an unpleasant experience aboard a steamer, restored their loyalties to canvas power. A notable member of the latter brigade was Charles Dickens. Crossing the Atlantic for a lecture tour in America, Dickens booked his outward passage aboard the Cunard ship *Britannia*. Following a particularly cramped and harrowing crossing he decided upon a more leisurely return on a sailing packet.[1]

Operating services between a variety of American and British ports, the sailing packet companies had the lucrative end of the North Atlantic trade to themselves for over twenty years until the steam ships appeared on the scene. American dominance through the sailing packets gave way to British control via the steamers. However, sailing packets plied the Atlantic prior to *Great Western* entering service and they remained long after she departed. Over the years competition from steamships caused the sailing packet owners to amend their fare rates downwards and to concentrate more on the lower priced steerage end of the market. As a way of reducing costs many of the packet companies merged, completely in some cases, but in others the amalgamations were for promotional and advertising purposes only. They did however compete with the steam ships and for the whole of *Great Western's* North Atlantic service they competed well. In fact, as far as the Bristol ship is concerned, for the major part of her Western Ocean operations the packet ships provided the main opposition. It has been necessary to consider the sailing packets as a collective body for no individual vessel acted alone against the ventures of *Great Western*. Sailing ships came and went during the eight years of North Atlantic operations but, as a force, the sailing packets were ever present taking passengers and cargo that the company might have expected for its vessel.

When dealing with the competition provided by rival steam ships the matter is less vague. Primarily because there were fewer of them and individual details are more readily available. Although a number of steam

Fig 46: Sirius (Courtesy Merseyside County Museums).

powered vessels crossed, and recrossed, the Atlantic during the period 1838 to 1846 not one came into direct competition with *Great Western* whilst she occupied the Bristol/New York or Liverpool/New York routes. Any comparisons have to be, therefore, general rather than specific when performances are considered. It is opportune to treat the other steamships individually on an operating company basis rather than chronologically as they entered service. The *Field Papers,* at the Science Museum Library, London, contain a detailed contemporary description of the early Atlantic steam vessels in a volume entitled *Glances at Atlantic Steam Navigation.* Unless otherwise credited all details in the following section have been drawn from that source.

Although *Sirius* beat *Great Western* to New York her challenge as an Atlantic steamer was not real; she completed only two round trips to the new world before resuming her short sea duties. However, as a part of the history of the Western Ocean merit is due to *Sirius* and her crew. Delays during the construction of their first vessel prompted Junius Smith's partners in the British and American Steam Navigation Company to seek a steamer with which to steal, from the Bristol company, the honour of being first on the Atlantic. Three of the directors, Messrs Pim, Beale and Twigg, were also directors of the St George Steam Packet Company.[2]

That concern possessed some large ships, the biggest and newest of which was the *Sirius.* Built by Menzies, of Leith, the 700 ton *Sirius* had a length of 178 feet and a width of 26 feet. Her side lever engines provided 320 horse-power, giving the ship a speed of 10 knots in good conditions.[3]

Advertisements in the London and New York papers indicated that *Sirius* would sail from the Thames on March 28 and call at Cork on April 2. Departure from New York for the return crossing was set for May 1. Three classes of accommodation were offered; after cabin at 35 guineas, fore cabin at 20 guineas, and steerage at 8 guineas. From New York the fore cabin berths were to cost 140 dollars with the after cabin berths being charged at 8 dollars; no steerage passengers were expected homeward. Sailing from Cork two days later than scheduled *Sirius* carried 11 passengers in the after cabin, eight in the fore cabin and 21 in steerage. *Sirius* was shockingly overloaded with 453 tons of coal occupying all available bunker and cargo space as well as a considerable amount of deck area. The crossing, in mainly rough weather, took 18 days 10 hours from Cork to Sandy Hook. During this period the boilers consumed all but 22 tons of the coal and 43 barrels of resin. Resin was used to mix with the ashes thereby enabling even the fine particles of coal which passed through the grate to be burned.

With a total of 47 passengers on board *Sirius* returned to England in 18 days, encountering contrary winds and rough weather. Before proceeding to London the coastal steamer landed her mails and some passengers at Falmouth. During the passage an interesting encounter took place. On May 16 1838 *Sirius* came across the government mail brig *Tyrian* en route from Halifax, Nova Scotia, to Falmouth. The brig, twenty days out from Halifax, lay becalmed. Amongst her passengers were two notable members of the Canadian judiciary, namely Judge Joseph Howe and Judge Thomas C. Haliburton. The latter had an international reputation as a humorist and satirical author.[4] His most famous work to that date being *The Sayings and Doings of Samuel Slick, Slickville*. Later, as a result of crossing aboard the steamer *Great Western*, he was to write *The Letter Bag of the Great Western, or Life in a Steamer*, a humorous collection of imaginary letters from equally imaginary travellers aboard the Bristol ship. Captain Jennings, of the *Tyrian* asked Captain Roberts, of the *Sirius*, if he would take charge of the Halifax mails. Roberts readily agreed and the mails were transferred. The two judges hitched a ride to the steamer with the mails. After a very quick inspection of *Sirius* they returned, without much enthusiasm, to their, by now, seemingly outdated mode of transportation. With their influence it is almost certain that the judges played a part in the decision of the British government to invite tenders for a steam propelled mail service across the Atlantic. Two days after the chance meeting *Sirius* encountered fog off the coast of England and only a fortuitous clearing saved a disastrous termination of the voyage on the rocky outcrops of the Scilly Islands.[5]

The second, and final, Atlantic voyage of *Sirius* began at London on May 26. Captain Stephen Mowle, her master during her coastal voyages, took charge as Roberts had been relieved in order to take command of the *British Queen*, recently launched.[6] Leaving Cork on the last day of May, *Sirius* reched New York in 17 days. The return crossing to Plymouth took one day less. With relatively few passengers and no cargo both voyages made a loss for the charterers, the British and American Steam Navigation Company. A loss of some £3,500 in all.[7] Following her historic Atlantic crossings *Sirius* returned to coastal work between England, Scotland and Ireland but not before she had been tried on a new line between London and St Petersburg. On June 16 1847, en-route from Glasgow to Cork in thick fog, she ran onto the rocks in Ballycotton Bay, Ireland, and became a total loss.

Junius Smith's first steamer, for which *Sirius* was an expensive and temporary stop-gap, had been ordered from Curling and Young, of Limehouse, shortly after the building of *Great Western* had commenced. Smith wanted elegance and got it. The lines of his ship were superb and for costliness the fittings of the accommodation vied with those of Brunel's wooden vessel. Fortune, however, did not favour the ship, intended to be called *Royal Victoria,* as, with her machinery over half completed, the engine builders, Claude Girdwood and Co, went into liquidation. Smith's company searched around for another marine engine builder and eventually settled upon the Clydeside firm of Robert Napier. The delay brought about by the bankruptcy of Girdwood removed the vestige of any possibility that the ship would be ready to compete with *Great Western*. Hence the charter of the little *Sirius*.

With the accession to the throne of Queen Victoria the British and American Steam Navigation Company decided upon a different name for its vessel. Amid scenes of great celebration and in the presence of the Prime Minister, Lord Melbourne, *British Queen* was floated off her building dock on June 23 1838. Considered to be the largest ship then afloat she had two decks, together with a poop and forecastle, and a length of 275 feet. At 40 feet 6 inches her breadth exceeded that of *Great Western* by more than five feet. The main dining saloon was 60 feet long and 30 feet wide, allowing the cabins to be placed along the ship's sides with an opening into the saloon. Saloon berths numbered 104 whilst a further 103 were provided foreward of the engine room. Like the Bristol ship *British Queen* received lavish praise for her decor. The saloon was decorated in Elizabethan style with imitation tapestries draping the walls and the ceilings and woodwork painted to imitate oak. Sofas and chairs were covered in velvet and handsome carpets extended throughout the accommodation. For cold weather a Sylvester coal-fired stove provided heating. A ladies cabin, 16 feet square and placed at one end of the saloon, contained a library and piano. All decoration lay under the command of a Mr Simpson, of London, and was carried out in Scotland by a team of craftsmen sent from London.

Decoration proceeded with the installation of the machinery. For this purpose *British Queen* had been despatched to the Clyde shortly after her launch. As with most steamers of the period side lever engines drove the paddle wheels. *British Queen's* engines not only exceeded, in size and power, any then in service but differed from most in one fundamental respect. Instead of the conventional sea water spray condensers, Hall's surface condensers were fitted — similar units were to be found in the engines of *Sirius*. A nest of small bore copper tubes, through which sea water circulated, occupied space in the greatly enlarged condenser. Exhaust steam, from the engine cylinder, coming into contact with the cold outer surface of the tubes condensed resulting in the desired pressure drop. The absence of a sea water spray meant that the boiler feed water remained uncontaminated thus preventing salt scale formation within the boiler. Such an arrangement required that a reserve supply of fresh water be carried in order to make up any loss from the system due to leakage or evaporation. Ships later that century were able to make fresh water from sea water by means of an evaporating plant, there is, however, no evidence that any equipment of that nature was fitted in *British Queen*.

At the time in question arguments abounded in the technical journals regarding the merits, or otherwise, of Hall's condensers. Certainly they kept the boilers free from salt scale but before engineers appreciated the causes of corrosion, and its remedies, this was actually a disadvantage. Boiler corrosion resulted, primarily, from oxygen dissolved in the water and the open top to the hot well allowed the oxygen concentration to be maintained. Conventional systems utilising sea water spray for condensation allowed a salt scale to build up on the boiler plating thereby affording a measure of protection to those surfaces below water level. A further disadvantage of the surface condenser arose from the use of tallow and oil to lubricate piston rods and valve rods. Some lubricant found its way into the cylinder and then into the condenser where it coated the copper tubes and reduced their effectiveness.

Each of the two engines produced 250 horse power from a 77½ inch diameter cylinder with a 7 foot stroke. Four simple long flue boilers provided steam at 5 psi. The two outer boilers contained four furnaces each whilst the two centre boilers each had one furnace less.[9] Floats 9 feet 6 inches long were fitted to the 31 feet diameter paddle wheels. Originally there were three floats at each arm on Galloway's cycloidal principle.

Fig 47: British Queen *in a storm, from a painting by Samuel Walters* (Courtesy Walker Art Gallery, Liverpool).

Following later patent infringement problems the floats were modified with a loss of efficiency.

British Queen left the Clyde on June 30 1839, calling at Liverpool before arriving in the Thames on July 5. She looked every bit a strong and powerful ship with three masts, two abaft the single funnel, carrying a wide expanse of sail. Her attractive lines were completed by the figurehead, a full length image of Queen Victoria. After taking on stores and bunkers *British Queen* set out on her maiden voyage from London six days later. With a call at Portsmouth for passengers and mail she arrived in New York on July 27, 15½ days from her last British port. The return passage attracted much interest as *Great Western* had been scheduled to depart from the American terminus on the same day, August 1. Both ships had good crossings but the Bristol ship arrived at the Avon on the evening of August 14 whilst *British Queen* reached Portsmouth early next morning. Both sides claimed victory but, taking into account the slightly different distances, the contest should be declared a draw. A second voyage in September and October of that year returned similar crossing times. The third and final round trip that year was disastrous. An outward passage of 20 days 7 hours was made to look good by the return of 23 days. Clearly the ship could not cope with very rough weather. *British Queen* had cost £90,000 and for speed or the ability to attract passengers she could not match her Bristol rival. Coal consumption was prodigious. During the fourth voyage in March and April 1840 some 635 tons were consumed outwards (16 days) whilst over 613 tons were burned on the return (14 days 7 hours).[10] The remaining voyages that year returned varying times which were generally in excess of those achieved by *Great Western*, whilst in November that same crossing took 20 days — *Great Western* arrived two days later in 16¾ days. No homeward crossing that year was less than 14 days whilst the longest, in December, occupied no less than 21 days — the Bristol ship arriving home two days later, on December 24, took 14 days 10 hours.[11]

British Queen had a tonnage of 2,016 tons but the engine room, in volume terms, occupied 963 tons of this. A cargo space for 500 tons was originally provided but the excessive coal consumption and abnormally long passages necessitated that some of this be made over to coal; not that a full cargo could ever be expected. When the ship was built a bunker space for 750 tons coal

had been constructed.[12] Notwithstanding the efforts and exertions of her crew Smith's ship could not compete with the original Atlantic steam liner. Described as 'Fast when light and light stern breeze'[13] *British Queen* was unsuitable for work on the, almost permanently, rough Atlantic. The reasons, whether poor sea keeping, inefficient machinery or paddles, not enough sail or incorrect hull form, cannot be determined from this distance as little information has survived.

December 1840 saw an injunction granted against the British and American Steam Navigation Company preventing them from making use of Galloway's cycloidal paddle design unless royalties were paid. Unwilling to pay such fees to a Mr Routledge, proprietor of Galloway's patent, Smith ordered that the wheels on the company's two ships be modified. A few days after leaving Portsmouth, on March 10 1841, *British Queen* encountered serious trouble. Badly fitted paddle floats on the port wheel began to work loose and fall off. By the 16th of that month not one float remained on that wheel. Half of the floats from the starboard wheel were transferred but barely had this task been completed when a tremendous hurricane struck. The storm continued unabated for nearly ten days. To facilitate repairs and preserve his ship from a worse hammering the Captain headed for the nearest port, Halifax, which they reached on March 30. Eventually the *Queen* made New York on April 4 after a total passage of 24 days 12 hours. The return crossing in 16 days 18 hours proved to be the last that *British Queen* made under the flag of her original owners.

That tremendous storm encountered on the outward passage, it appears, claimed the sister ship, *President*. The British and American Steam Navigation Company could not stand the loss and *British Queen* had to be sold. She had returned some profit for her owners but certainly not enough to offset her high original cost. For her nine voyages the average receipts had been £9,111 4s 8d whilst the average expenditure, neglecting repairs, amounted to £7,854 11s 2d.[14] For the same period the receipts are similar to those for *Great Western* but the expenditure is much greater allowing the Bristol ship a higher profit level each voyage.

Until August 1841 *British Queen* remained in dock at Liverpool. Like the Great Western Steam Ship Company at a later date, her owners had decided that the Mersey offered the better prospects as a British terminal. Purchased by the Belgian government Junius Smith's surviving steamer made for Antwerp. The government of the infant Belgian state retained British officers and engineers for their maritime status symbol and, perhaps surprisingly, also retained the name, *British Queen*. Following some conversion work, in April 1842 the ship was advertised for a service between Antwerp, Cowes and New York. The fare to America was to be 20 guineas with a half guinea stewards fee. A departure from the traditional shipboard arrangement was that these fares did not include provisions. As in an hotel meals could be purchased separately. 1s 6d for breakfast or tea and 3s for dinner. Parties were able to contract for favourable group rates for travel and meals.[15] Although novel the idea did not prove a success. *British Queen* only made three round trips for her new owners, never carrying more than 50 passengers. Passage times did not improve, the fastest being 17 days from New York to Cowes whilst the slowest, her last crossing, took 26 days to Cowes including a stop at the Azores for fuel. Laid up at Antwerp at the end of 1842, *British Queen* was scrapped two years later.[16]

The career of Junius Smith's second steam vessel was even shorter and even more inauspicious. *President*, as the new ship was to be called had been ordered from Curling and Young, the builders of *British Queen*, and laid down shortly after that vessel was floated out of her building dock. *President* differed from all of her Atlantic contemporaries in that she had three decks. This gave her the appearance of a very large vessel though, in fact, her length happened to be somewhat less than her elder sister. An extreme length of 268 feet, breadth of 41 feet and midship depth of 23 feet 6 inches — the depth from the spar deck being 32 feet 9 inches — gave her a tonnage of 2,336 tons, somewhat greater than *British Queen*. Floated out of her building dock at Limehouse on Monday December 9 1839, after an attempt the previous Saturday had failed through insufficient height of the tide,[17] *President* had to make a trip to the Mersey for her machinery, constructed by Fawcett and Preston of Liverpool, to be fitted.

The passage to Liverpool, in December 1839, met with misfortune soon after it commenced. Considered by many to be ill-adapted for fast sailing, *President* was certainly top heavy, especially without her machinery, and rolled excessively even in moderate seas. Severe damage in the English Channel resulted in a call at the Naval Dockyard, Plymouth, for repairs, before she could safely continue the voyage to Liverpool. A pair of conventional side lever engines, bore 80 inches and stroke 7 feet 6 inches, produced 540 horse power, totally inadequate for that size of vessel. Schooner rigged with three masts, two abaft the single funnel, *President* looked much like a frigate, particularly as she was painted in the fashion of a man-of-war with imitation gun ports. A main saloon aft measured 87 feet in length and 41 feet at its widest. Leading from this were two and four berth cabins for a total of 110 people. Forward of the engine room were second class or servant's cabins with accommodation for 44 persons.[18]

The maiden voyage, departing from Liverpool on August 1 1840, attracted only a few passengers as *Great Western* and the Cunard *Acadia* sailed at about the same time. Both outward and return crossings took a disappointing 16½ days each. Sailing on October 1 the second crossing to New York lasted 16 days 10 hours but the return proved very unfortunate. After a six day battle against heavy seas and gale force winds *President* was forced to put back to New York where she arrived on November 6. The progress made in that time amounted to a meagre 300 miles. Eventually she arrived at Liverpool on November 27 after another 16½ day passage. If nothing else *President* was consistent.

The delay resulted in a planned December voyage being cancelled. Dissatisfied, the owners wanted a scapegoat and found one in the commander. Originally a Captain Fayrer had been appointed to the command but the disappointing maiden voyage resulted in his replacement by Captain Keane. The disastrous second voyage guaranteed that his tenure would last no longer than a single voyage. In desperation the British and American Steam Navigation Company transferred an unwilling Captain Roberts from *British Queen*. Aware that efficient machinery was a prime factor in the operation of any Atlantic steamer Roberts requested that Mr Peterson, Chief Engineer on *British Queen*, should accompany him to the *President*. This the owners acceded to.

With modified paddle wheels *President* set out on her third voyage from Liverpool towards the middle of February 1841. She reached New York on March 3 following a dreadful 21 day crossing. Eight days later, with an almost full cargo and a total of 136 persons on

Fig 48: President (Courtesy Merseyside County Museums).

board *President* sailed out of New York into oblivion. During March severe gales were to be encountered throughout the entire North Atlantic; *British Queen* experiencing the effects of them at that time. Apart from one sighting *President* was never seen again. As she became overdue at Liverpool rumours abounded causing both confusion and anguish. Undoubtedly the terrible storms, which almost finished off her sister, claimed the unfortunate *President* and all on board. No wreckage was ever found and her actual fate must be speculation. Captain Cole, of the packet ship *Orpheus*, is reported to have seen *President* on March 12 between Nantucket Shoals and George's Bank. When observed the steamer was labouring heavily and shipping large quantities of water on her deck.[19] Undoubtedly *President* could not manage the storm conditions and succumbed to the elements. Though constructed in a substantial manner using the finest materials, the stability of the *President* was frequently questioned. This and her undoubted lack of power were the probable reasons for her inability to weather the storm.

Neither *British Queen* nor *President* offered much of a challenge to *Great Western* as far as their ability to attract passengers was concerned. Cargo presented a different picture as manufacturers were predisposed to make use of the most convenient ship to get their goods to market in America as early as possible. This being so, *Great Western* could more than hold her own against Smith's ships, or any other contemporary vessel for that matter. The sad loss of *President* and subsequent removal of *British Queen* from the line possibly helped the Bristol concern in the long term although initially there was a detrimental effect. With Atlantic steam navigation still in its infancy the loss of a vessel such as the *President* deterred many who, instead, remained with or returned to the tried and trusted, though equally susceptible, sailing packets.

The third of the pioneering Atlantic steam ship companies had its base at Liverpool. A number of directors of the coastal ship owners City of Dublin Steam Packet Company had aspirations westward. From their efforts the Transatlantic Steam Ship Company came into being. Late on the scene and anxious to make an impression this Liverpool company decided to charter a vessel to test the waters of the Atlantic. Needless to say the City of Dublin Steam Packet Company provided that vessel, *Royal William*. Built by Messrs Wilson of Liverpool the 617 ton *Royal William* had a length of 175 feet, a breadth of 27 feet and a depth of hold of 17 feet 6 inches. Her 270 horse power side lever engines, built by Fawcett and Preston of Liverpool, drove paddle wheels 24 feet in diameter. As with *Sirius* cargo did not figure seriously in her revenue earning capability. On her first voyage *Royal William* arrived in New York on July 24 1838 after a stormy 18 days 23 hour crossing. During the passage she consumed just over 351 tons of fuel and still had almost 60 tons on board, enough for a further 600 miles. Some of that fuel, however, was not coal but compressed peat. Experiments carried out on board suggested to the master that 1 cwt of peat saved 3 cwt of coal. A rather optimistic figure. With its lower density peat, for an Atlantic crossing, would have presented stowage problems even for a large vessel. For the small *Royal William* the experiment must have proved that the only suitable fuel available was coal. The return took nearly 15 days.

Royal William made two further Atlantic voyages before returning to her coastal duties between Liverpool and Dublin. Passage times for both were in excess of the respective times for the maiden voyage on the Western Ocean. Following service as a coal hulk *Royal William* eventually reached the hands of the shipbreaker in 1888.[20] Not a success on the Atlantic, *Royal William* did allow the Transatlantic Steam Ship Company to gain a foothold before their own ship was ready. Such experience should have been valuable.

Aware of its lateness on the scene the Transatlantic Steam Ship Company decided to save some time and purchase a vessel already in an advanced stage of construction. Suitable ships were, at that time, not in abundance but, fortuitously, a vessel of the desired size lay on the stocks in the yard of Humble and Milcrest at Liverpool. Originally laid down to the order of Sir Jon

Tobin, acting for the City of Dublin Steam Packet Company, the vessel was launched on October 14 1837 and named *Liverpool*. This 1,050 ton vessel had a length of 223 feet, breadth of nearly 31 feet and hold depth of 21 feet, making her the smallest of the ships actually purchased for the formative transatlantic services. Her tastefully furnished cabins and saloon provided accommodation for 98 first class passengers. Forester and Company, of the Vauxhall foundry at Liverpool, supplied the 468 horse power side lever engines. These had cylinders of 75 inches diameter and 7 feet stroke. Unlike *Great Western* the two distinct sets of boilers had separate flues thus making *Liverpool* the first twin funnelled Atlantic steamer. The two funnels, one each side of the paddle wheels, and three masts, two abaft the funnels, gave an impression of power and speed; a completely false impression as it turned out.

Liverpool, with between 50 and 60 passengers on board, departed from the port after which she was named on October 20 1838 and headed into the Atlantic for the first time. At the commencement of that voyage she had 563 tons of coal on board, there being space for 600 tons, but after six days battling against a tremendous gale *Liverpool* was forced to put back to Cork due to increasing anxiety about the fuel consumption. Upon reaching the Irish port only 350 tons remained, not enough for a crossing to New York. Departing from Cork on November 6 she eventually reached New York in 16 days 17 hours with a coal consumption of almost 465 tons, a not unreasonable figure. The return to Liverpool occupied 14 ½ days with a fuel consumption of just over 445 tons.

Six outward voyages in 1839 all took in excess of 16 ½ days, three of them taking 18 ½ days. The fastest return crossing occupied 13 days 17 hours. *Liverpool* fully justified the description 'Slow and crank' given to her by a contemporary analyst.[21] On December 16 1839 *Liverpool* began her final return crossing of the season, her final Atlantic crossing as it turned out. Severe gales and head winds depleted the bunkers at an alarming rate and on December 30 she put into Fayal in the Azores. A three day wait for bunkers preceeded a dismal passage to Liverpool where she arrived on January 11 1840. A total crossing time of 27 days.

Slow crossings failed to attract sufficient passengers and the accommodation offered could not compete with the other steamers then on the line or about to appear. At the end of the 1839 season the Transatlantic Steam Ship Company decided to make their vessel more attractive. *Liverpool* underwent extensive alterations during which she was widened by some seven feet and had a spar deck fitted. With alterations almost complete the directors of the Transatlantic Company decided that they would not be able to compete successfully on the Western Ocean and, in July 1840, sold their interests to the Peninsular and Oriental Steam Navigation Company. P&O had just been awarded the government mail contract to carry mails from Britain to India by way of Alexandria. The enlarged *Liverpool,* now some 1,300 tons, became *Great Liverpool* and continued on the Southampton to Alexandria service until wrecked off Cape Finisterre on February 24 1846.[22] At the time of its dissolution the Transatlantic Steam Ship Company was in the process of having a second vessel built. This larger vessel, to be named *United States,* also fell into the hands of the P&O Company and became their 1,787 ton, 420 horse power *Oriental.*

Whilst the original Atlantic steamship companies were suffering their many trials and tribulations at the dawn of a new transport era, the opportunist Canadian, Samuel Cunard, was not idle. It is unnecessary to detail the berth of the Cunard Company as any volume concerned with the history of the Western Ocean generally contains a full account. The present work will involve itself only with a comparison between *Great Western* and the early Cunard steamers. These comprised the *Britannia* class of 1840, namely *Britannia, Acadia, Caledonia* and *Columbia* (1841) together with the identical *Hibernia* (1843) and *Cambria* (1845).

The *Britannia* class vessels were identical wooden paddle steamers of 1,150 tons. All were built on the Clyde but by different ship builders; *Britannia* at the yard of Duncan and Company, *Acadia* by J. Wood and Co, *Caledonia* by R. Wood and *Columbia* at Steel's yard. This rather unusual arrangement expedited delivery of the vessels in order to meet the terms of the mail contract which required, initially, a bi-monthly service to commence before the end of 1840. Each vessel was powered by a pair of side lever engines developing some 440 horse power; Robert Napier being the builder of all sets of machinery. With a length, between perpendiculars, of 206 feet, an extreme breadth of

Fig 49: Liverpool (Courtesy Merseyside County Museums).

Fig 50: Britannia *at Boston* (Courtesy Merseyside County Museums).

34 feet 6 inches and a hold depth of 22 feet 6 inches the Cunard quartet were but smaller versions of the *Great Western*. They did not advance the level of nautical science as neither their construction nor machinery differed, in principle, from those employed in building similar ships years earlier. In fact these mail steamers were, in many respects, inferior to the Bristol vessel.

As has already been discussed, there was little difference between the performances of *Great Western* and the four original Cunarders. In view of the shorter track, and hence smaller change in paddle wheel dip during a voyage, *Britannia* and her sisters should have been capable of consistently faster crossings than Brunel's paddle steamer. This was not so. Available information would indicate that *Great Western* had the edge over the early Cunard vessels particularly as her machinery had to operate for longer periods. It should be borne in mind, however, that the Cunarders operated throughout the year though, like their Bristol rival, they still only performed five or six round trips each year.[23]

From the outset Cunard showed no interest in decorative frills for his ships which, in comparison with the opulence of the accommodation aboard the original Atlantic steamers, could be described as basic. Charles Dickens, following a crossing aboard *Britannia*, gave

the following pen picture of the accommodation: 'Before descending into the bowels of the ship, we had passed from the deck into a long narrow apartment, not unlike a gigantic hearse with windows at the sides; having at the upper end a melancholy stove, at which three or four chilly stewards were warming their hands; while on either side, extending down its whole dreary length, was a long, long table, over each of which a rack, fixed to the low roof, and stuck full of drinking glasses and cruet-stands, hinted dismally of rolling seas and heavy weather.' His cabin was even worse; 'That this state room had been specially engaged for "Charles Dickens, Esquire, and Lady" was rendered sufficiently clear even to my scared intellect by a very small manuscript announcing the fact which was pinned on a very flat quilt, covering a very thin mattress, spread like a surgical plaster on a most inaccessible shelf.'[24]

Dickens was not at all impressed with the accommodation provided, particularly as it differed so drastically from the artistic impression on view at the London agency. By modern standards the accommodation offered on board *Great Western* would be considered austere but by the standards of the day it was excellent and much superior to that on the Cunard vessels. This is probably one of the main reasons why *Great Western* could attract passengers from the mail steamers whenever sailings occurred close together. Standards of catering and service are unknown, but from Cunard's attitude to the accommodation on board his ships it is likely to have been good but not excessive and somewhat below that offered by the Bristol company.

With a growing awareness that four steamers could not maintain the mail service for which they had contracted, the Cunard company arranged to build further tonnage. Entry into service of the fifth vessel, *Hibernia,* proved to be fortuitously timely. No sooner had she returned from her maiden voyage, on May 28 1843, than *Columbia* prepared to depart on what was to be her last. Setting out for Liverpool on July 2 1843 *Columbia* hit the rocks at the entrance to Halifax harbour and again reduced the Cunard Atlantic fleet to four ships. *Cambria,* an identical vessel to *Hibernia*, was quickly ordered to make up for the loss, entry into service being in January 1845.

Both later ships were but larger versions of the original quartet, their side lever engines giving a designed service speed of 9½ knots. At 1,400 tons they were only slightly larger than *Great Western* and, certainly, represented no advance in the design or construction of ocean going ships. Considering the marine advances embodied in Brunel's iron masterpiece, the construction of which was almost complete when *Cambria* was ordered, the Cunard company obviously had no intention of becoming a maritime innovator. It could afford to play safe with basic less costly vessels, possession of the mail contract guaranteed survival without the need to attract more than a minimum of passengers or cargo. Little is known of the internal arrangements of the new ships but it would seem likely that cabins and decor closely followed the pattern of *Britannia* and her sisters.

Comparison between the performance of *Great Western* and the Cunard vessels has already been made in a previous chapter, the conclusions being drawn that there was little to choose between the individual protagonists. Popularity with passengers and merchants certainly favoured the Bristol ship indicating a superior service to that offered aboard the mail steamers and on that account alone *Great Western* must be considered a better ship than its government sponsored rivals. Voyage for voyage her earnings from passengers and freight greatly exceeded anything achieved by the contemporary Cunard ships. In fact, had it not been for the large mail subsidy the Cunard company could not have

survived, its non-mail revenues from the early ships being exceedingly poor.

When, in 1845, the Great Western Steam Ship Company placed its iron wonder on the Liverpool to New York service it was confidently predicted that she would soon cream off the bulk of the lucrative first class Atlantic passenger trade. All rivals would suffer, including her now aging sister. Rich Atlantic voyagers were, however, not so fickle. They knew *Great Western*, liked her and trusted her. More importantly they maintained their patronage. Despite having a much greater passenger capacity, only once did *Great Britain* manage to attract more passengers, during similar periods of the year, than *Great Western*. That was for the fateful passage to New York in September 1846 during which disaster struck at Dundrum Bay.

There is no doubt that the iron ship was the better of the two vessels which the Bristol company owned both with regard to potential performance and passenger comfort. Unfortunately, *Great Britain* never had chance to prove herself before all hopes and dreams were dashed on the beach at Dundrum. It is pointless to describe the features of Brunel's iron ship as this would be repeating that which has already appeared in print many times. For a thorough description of the ship and her varied career the reader is referred to the definitive work on the subject; *The Iron Ship* by Dr Ewan Corlett, published by Moonraker Press in 1975. Fortunately, following an operational life which stretches fictional plausibility *Great Britain* rests in her building dock at Bristol being lovingly restored as a monument to her designer, original owners and the skill of the craftsmen a century and a half ago.

Following the cessation of her North Atlantic service *Great Western* found employment upon routes further south. Whilst her new owners operated other ships on the same services they were consorts and not rivals. In effect *Great Western* only experienced serious competition whilst she operated the line to New York. This she met, matched and, in most respects left far astern. Considering that she was the prototype for the Western Ocean steamship service, only one other vessel, her iron sister, could be said to be an improvement, at least during her nine years occupation of the line. A remarkable record considering the importance of the waterway and the changes in the subsequent nine years.

Chapter 10
Life on board

On board any passenger ship there are essentially two distinct worlds, the leisurely one of the fare paying traveller and the confined, perhaps harsh, existence of the crew. Aboard *Great Western*, and other early steamships, the gulf was enormous, as it not only separated customer from servant but also the classes. Few were able to straddle the divide and those that did, Master and some senior officers, tended to have more in common with the passengers than their fellow seafarers. Company rules and regulations were drawn up to ensure that neither group had much contact with the other. For the crew member, infringement of the regulations resulted in loss of pay and dismissal. By modern standards passenger conditions would appear to have been rather primitive and those for the crew harsh and intolerable. However, circumstances are relative to the situation prevailing at the time. For his fare a passenger enjoyed service and a menu equal to that provided by the best hotels whilst even the lowest crew member tended to be better off than his contemporary ashore.

Unfortunately few accounts of life on board the *Great Western* have survived, at least publicly, but from available records as well as books and newspapers of the period it is possible to obtain a fair indication of life aboard *Great Western*. Before beginning the description reference must be made to one such book briefly mentioned in an earlier chapter. A notable and proud citizen of Nova Scotia, Judge Thomas C. Haliburton had published a light-hearted, but informative, imaginary account of life on board the Bristol ship as seen through the eyes of a number of equally imaginary passengers. *The Letter Bag of the Great Western* was well received for its satirical view of the steamer patrons.

Many letters make no reference to the ship and are merely a commentary on events at that time. Other letters do contain remarks about the ship, its crew and its owners. Though not definitive in content they provide certain pieces of general information which may be taken as factual because of repetition in different letters and because of agreement with information relating to other early steamships. For its own sake as a piece of very amusing literature the book is well worth reading.

In passenger terms *Great Western* catered for the rich and the very rich. She had accommodation for first class voyagers only; a limited number of berths being available for their servants, in less attractive conditions of course. The lower North Atlantic fare of 30 guineas was way beyond the capabilities of all but the most affluent; at that time this represented almost a year's earnings for an unskilled worker. Seaman aboard *Great Western* were then receiving £3 per month. Anyone desiring to emigrate to America had to suffer the insalubrious conditions in steerage aboard one of the sailing vessels plying between the old and new worlds. It is interesting to relate that the Great Western Steam Ship Company at one stage considered tapping that sector of the passenger market. Following the stranding of *Great Britain* and an unsuccessful sale in 1848 the company considered the retention of the ship and conversion to sail alone. William Patterson was requested to prepare an estimate for conversion with a view to the operation of a triangular service Liverpool/New York/New Orleans/Liverpool. Some 800 emigrants were to be carried to New York at £5 each and a cargo of cotton brought from New Orleans.[1] The idea of 850 souls (50 crew) aboard a ship the size of *Great Britain* would give some impression of conditions on a slaver and is best left to the imagination of the reader.

Though *Great Western* offered only first class accommodation, cabins were small. Less than eight feet square, they offered the two, three or four occupants little space to move, dress or attend to their ablutions. The cabins were basically places in which to sleep. Charles Dickens described his cabin aboard the Cunard vessel *Britannia* in the following fashion: '. . . utterly impracticable, thoroughly hopeless, and profoundly preposterous box.'[2] Cabins aboard *Great Western* were undoubtedly larger, but not very much so. With an assortment of cabin trunks in place, movement about the confined compartment must have presented something of an obstacle course. Sole occupancy of a double cabin could be had for a little less than double fare. Only the very well-to-do and those concerned about the habits of their fellow occupants were at all likely to adopt such a course of action. At favourable rates the company did allow family occupancy of suites of cabins. Certainly the risk of sharing a room with a total stranger for two weeks could have uncomfortable consequences particularly if his/her personal hygiene was not all that it might have been. One of Haliburton's correspon-

dents, Captain Haltfront, describes a particularly obnoxious companion who not only made use of his (Haltfront's) towels and brushes but snored 'like a Newfoundland dog' and refused to make use of the available appliances during bouts of seasickness. Passengers not satisfied with a 'cabin mate' did request, and whenever possible were granted, alternative accommodation. Captain Hosken, in his autobiography, relates one incident concerning a coloured passenger, a rarity because of the fares charged. The passenger assigned the same cabin as the coloured gentleman complained about it and was found an alternative room, the coloured gentleman then having sole occupancy of his cabin, no doubt, much to his delight.[3]

The saloons provided more space in which passengers could move about and entertain themselves. Permanent dining tables did take up a considerable amount of room in the main, and possibly the forward, saloon thus inhibiting freedom. Smoking was only allowed on the upper deck in order to minimise the risk of fire and ensure a reasonably breathable atmosphere in the saloons. Such a situation would not have found favour with some of the ship's patrons. The provision of fresh air was always a problem on board passenger ships before forced air circulation came into common usage.

Fig 51: Great Western *at sea, contemporary print* (Courtesy City of Bristol Museum and Art Gallery).

Ventilators in the skylight allowed for a reasonable air change but when the upper deck cabins were added this must have reduced the amount of fresh air reaching the main saloon. Use of the skylights particularly those on the spar deck, had to be restricted during stormy weather in order to prevent quantities of water flooding into the accommodation. It is almost certain that the cabin ports could not be opened and so cabin ventilation would be totally reliant upon the saloon air circulation. With a full passenger complement, eating in the main salooon during bad weather conditions must have been stifling. Good ventilation is, in any case, a personal matter and many a heated discussion will have resulted from the opening, or otherwise, of the skylights.

During cold weather a passenger would be faced with the alternatives of suffering a stuffy atmosphere or putting on more clothing to combat the icy blast of fresh air. Accommodation heating presented a problem on all wooden steamers due to the considerable risk of fire, the seafarers dread. The coal fired stoves that Dickens found aboard *Britannia* produced some warmth during a cold Atlantic passage. Similar units in the saloon of *Great Western* are assumed for no other source of heat could be safely provided at that time. Adequate illumination of the below decks accommodation was a convenience demanded by the passengers, particularly those who had paid a first class fare. During good weather the port covers could be raised allowing light into some of *Great Western's* cabins. Skylights afforded the same facility for the saloons. During the hours of darkness only artificial illumination could be available. The only available contemporary picture of the main saloon shows oil lanterns fitted to the deckhead at regular intervals. These together with similar lanterns fitted to the bulkheads will have lightened the gloom but, by modern standards, *Great Western* and all early steamers were poorly lit. Cabin illumination for those retiring was essential and such was, probably, provided by the employment of candles. Naked flames were, and still are, extremely dangerous aboard any ship and close watch on the use of candles or lamps was necessary for safety. One of the ship's junior officers will have been assigned the duty of ensuring that all lights were extinguished at a set time.

The Royal Mail Steam Packet Company adopted stringent conditions for cabin illumination aboard its early wooden steamers. Lamps were placed in the bulkheads between alternate cabins in such a manner that they could only be reached from outside. By this means the cabins could be illuminated and the person designated to extinguish the lights was able to do so easily at the appointed hour.[4] Such duty fell to the fourth officer, the time, for light-out being 11.00 pm.[5] When *Great Western* entered the service of the RMSPC accommodation modifications took place. One of which will almost certainly have brought her lighting arrangements in line with that prevalent throughout the rest of the fleet.

It can with certainty be stated that passengers enjoyed, in abundance, the best food that could be provided. Fresh meat was available through the carriage of live animals which were housed on deck. During the early North Atlantic voyages a wide variety of beasts were put on board but with the provision, at a later date, of an ice house the necessity of carrying so much meat 'on the hoof' disappeared. At least two cows provided fresh milk throughout the crossing, this milk being intended primarily, for the women and children. Whilst on the New York run cows were taken aboard at that port.[6] Whether or not these animals were landed following the outward passage is unknown. Poultry provided fresh eggs as well as fresh meat. Ships of the RMSPC carried live sheep and pigs in addition to being furnished with a large ice house.[7] No meat at all was allowed to be taken on board if it was already packed in ice, only fresh meat could be placed in the ice house.[8] Someone in authority was well aware of the possibility of dubious quality meat being obtained. Fresh fish occupied a considerable amount of space in the ice house but it became common practice, whenever convenient, to exchange some commodity with a local fishing boat for part of its catch.

Generally three main meals were offered to passengers with a cold supper being provided for those who wished further nourishment before retiring. The bill of fare matched that available in the very best hotels ashore. An indication of the food on offer may be gathered from the following list which was to serve 87 passengers.[9]
'Breakfast: 6 dishes boiled ham, 6 dishes fish, 6 dishes mutton chops, 100 eggs in omelettes, 6 dishes devilled legs of poultry, 6 dishes Indian meal.
Dinner: 6 tureens of mock turtle soup, 2 dishes venison,

4 roast turkeys, 4 couple of ducks, 4 dishes roast beef, 4 dishes cod fish, 4 couple of chickens, 6 dishes of fried oysters, 4 dishes stewed oysters, 4 dishes boiled mutton, 4 dishes maccaroni.
Vegetables: 6 dishes baked mashed potatoes, 6 dishes mashed turnips, 6 dishes mashed potatoes, 6 dishes parsnips, 6 dishes plain potatoes.
Pastry: 6 plum puddings, 6 custard puddings, 6 raspberry pies, 6 apple pies, 6 cranberry pies, 2 cherry pies.
Wines in abundance'.

From the variety of dishes served there must have been something to satisfy even the most fastidious palate. The main problem was not, however, the choice but the placing of the dishes on the tables. Should a favourite delicacy be laid some distance from an individual the chance of obtaining more than the less appetising cuts appears remote. An individuals' fortune in the dinner table stakes could, no doubt, be increased by a gratuity to an obliging waiter. With such an extensive menu it is likely that some of the dishes were relatively cold upon reaching the table. This does not appear to have caused too much concern as, from newspaper accounts, the passengers were eager to offer testimonials to the master at the culmination of each voyage. At the end of voyage No 5 the passengers commented, '. . . unvaried civility and attention has been paid to us, and that the table has been most liberally and profusely supplied during the passage.'[10]

From the available crew lists it seems that one waiter to about ten passengers maintained an adequate saloon service. For the 138 passengers on the return leg of voyage No 43 there were 13 waiters, three cooks, a baker, a pastry cook and a butcher.[11] Separate galley staff provided food for the crew. Ships in the service of the RMSPC also carried a French cook thereby allowing for greater variation in the menu offered.[12] After table meals had ceased for the day passengers could always obtain light refreshments from the saloon steward, though it is difficult to imagine a need for further sustenance following a normal day's eating. Alcoholic drinks could be obtained from the saloon bar steward until the bar closed, at about 10 o'clock each evening. During periods of inclement weather many passengers had cause to be grateful for the soporific effect of alcohol.

Rough weather brings heavy pitching and rolling. Coupled with a wet deck this makes for difficult movement about the ship. Many passengers will have enjoyed a regular constitutional about the upper decks but only the more spartan could avail themselves of the extensive deck area during adverse conditions. Confined below deck passengers had to entertain themselves as best they could. Many kept diaries or some form of journal, this being a common pastime during the Victorian period. Unfortunately few of these records seem to have been preserved. Reading, even in the poor light of an oil lamp, passed many an hour for most of the passengers. *Great Western*, like the sailing packets, carried a rather limited library from which the weary traveller could choose a book, generally one unlikely to be given shelf room when ashore. Some, of course, brought their own literature, perhaps given by a friend as a farewell gift. Such was the case with Dickens' pocket edition of Shakespeare.[13]

With the exception of the modern sea cruise, most long journeys by sea are tedious. For most people a cruise lasting longer than 14 days can become a strain despite all of the entertainment laid on. *Great Western*, and its contemporary steamers, had very limited entertainment facilities. One priority, perhaps the only diversion the ship had to offer, was a visit to the engine room. Each crossing, many, including one of Haliburton's letter writers and so, presumably, Haliburton himself, descended into the cavern wherein lived the beast which gave the ship her motion. They will have stared in amazement at the size of the machinery and wondered at its operation. As one visitor observed: 'To a novice, the whole process seemed a mystic operation, and reminded one of the story of an Indian, who, seeing a steam engine, fancied that a spirit lay imprisoned within the boilers, and that by building a fire beneath them, it was excited to fury, and thus put the whole in motion.'[14]

The sea itself offered passengers an infinite variety of moods and events. During the first Atlantic crossing of *Great Western* the passengers were amused by the antics of accompanying porpoise[15] and it is certain that later travellers spent many a happy hour watching the gambolling of these, the friendliest of sea creatures. In northern latitudes the mighty whale would occasionally make its appearance whilst in the warmer southern regions inexperienced voyagers must have gazed in amazement at the aeronautics of the flying fish shoals.

Sea conditions, one day like glass and the next like mountains, will, for most, have been of only passing interest in as much as it affected the individual's comfort; others may have seen poetic magic in every wave. The sea is all things to all men.

Passages through pack ice, during the spring months, presented an arctic sight that must have left unimpressed only the most insensitive. Hoskens relates one such occasion in his autobiography: '. . . we one evening fell in with a similar Field of Ice, and continued our way with the hopes of passing safely as we did the former time; but at 10 pm, finding that the ice was increasing in thickness, we were compelled to turn back and had great difficulty in getting clear; which we did in about two hours. We then coasted the ice keeping southward for the remainder of the night. At sunrise

the following morning we found the Field Ice extending Northward as far as we could see, with four or five ships in it, and around us a great number of Icebergs of various sizes, some very large. It was a splendid sight!'[16] With such a sight to view the passengers were probably oblivious to the danger the ice presented. A danger faced by all who travelled that seaway.

Encounters with other ships relieved the sense of isolation which can afflict any sea voyagers at times. An isolation felt more deeply during periods of severe weather. The rare encounter with wreckage produced a different sensation. Under such circumstances many passengers will have been well aware of their own rather precarious position. On board an insignificant powered island in the midst of an uncompromising ocean. On February 15 1839, during the outward passage of

Fig 52: Commemorative Great Western *jug (Courtesy City of Bristol Museum and Art Gallery).*

voyage No 6, *Great Western* came across some timber and an upturned boat from a wrecked vessel.[17] That day a very subdued atmosphere permeated the living quarters of the ship as those on board pondered the fate of their unknown oceanic companions. Perhaps musing over their own ultimate fate.

In the main, however, life on board was rather light-hearted, possibly even boring at times. No doubt, the number and length of meals helped pass the time for many a traveller. Depending upon the number of passengers making a trip the scope of possible social life will have differed. Certainly the seven passengers carried on the first crossing had plenty of space but social activities must have been restricted. During service on the North Atlantic, and probably in later years, a piano occupied a corner of *Great Western's* mail saloon.[18] In reasonable weather the piano concert must have entertained the assembled travellers nightly, provided that there was a competent pianist on board. In the Victorian drawing room tradition singing around the piano provided relaxation for those taking part and entertainment, or amusement, for those willing to listen. The unmusical, if not engrossed in a book, will have tried their luck at cards, backgammon or chess. Those passengers wishing to retire early can have had little solitude. Retreating to a cabin off the main saloon would be no escape from noise as the partition walls were so thin. Those with main deck cabins must have suffered with any noise from below. Only those with forward saloon cabins had any escape from the joviality of the main saloon. Only the deck allowed sanctuary from the banter of the forward saloon.

Ship noises had to be endured, from these there was no escape. The engines probably made little discernable noise but the rhythmic crashing of the paddle wheels will have affected, at least initially, the sleep of those occupying the amidship cabins. The howling of wind in the rigging and the flapping of sails may be romantic in a book but they have a very disturbing influence upon the ability to fall asleep. As with any other wooden vessel the timbers of *Great Western* creaked as the ship moved causing another disturbance and, perhaps for the first time traveller, a disconcerting one. Most people, however, soon accustom themselves to the normal shipboard sounds and their influence upon usual activity is negligible.

Personal hygiene presented a problem on all of the early steamships because they carried no baths. With space at a premium the luxury of bathrooms could not be allowed. Passengers by *Great Western* may not have found the two week (or three week on the South Atlantic) interval between baths unusual and the use of toilet waters and perfumes will have made the problem less discernable. The absence of water closets within the accommodation, they being all on deck, can only have increased passenger discomfort. Chamber pots will have been placed in each cabin, as in all hotels ashore at that time, but regular emptying was a necessity. In rough weather it would not have been an easy task to perform. Rough weather also brought on seasickness with its associated problems. The result upon the accommodation environment is best left to the imagination of the reader. The smell must have been appalling, particularly as the skylight would be closed due to bad weather.

A characteristic of early wooden ships, including *Great Western*, was the leaking deck. Though not necessarily unhygienic the phenomena had unpleasant and, perhaps, unhealthy aspects. Regular caulking of the decks kept the leakage to a minimum but steady working of the ship resulted in its reappearance. Soaking clothing and bed linen could greet the unfortunate passenger upon his return to his cabin for a night's sleep. Even worse, the steady drip of water might descend during his repose. If no cabins were free a bed might be made up on one of the saloon sofas. Occasionally a bed could be found in the room of an officer on watch. A traveller on the Royal Mail steamer *Forth,* in 1847, had cause to be grateful to one of the officers for giving up his berth in similar circumstances. The passenger had been driven from both his cabin and a made-up bed in the saloon by water leaking through the deck.[19]

Obviously it was the seaman who had to ensure that all decks were, as fas as possible, leak proof. It was the steward's lot to clean up the mess in the cabin and to supply fresh, dry bed linen. They were there, as were the remainder of the crew, to serve the fare paying passengers.

As mentioned earlier, *Great Western* carried a large crew with the number varying according to the number of passengers on board. The actual crew required for ship operations remained fairly constant but the passenger service element varied with passenger numbers.

It is unnecessary to give crew lists for all voyages and space does not allow it. The crew list for voyage No 43, Liverpool/New York/Liverpool, in 1846, is given in appendix No 2. This voyage represented operation in the final period of North Atlantic service and is typical of most periods of operation. During service with the RMSPC *Great Western* also carried an Admiralty agent as she was then a contract mail steamer. Most articles of agreement for *Great Western*, from which the above mentioned list has been compiled, are still extant at the Public Record Office, Kew. They provide a valuable and interesting source of information. During service on both North and South Atlantic, crews tended to remain fairly stable with about 75 per cent undertaking a second trip and some 60 per cent remaining for more than two voyages. For obvious reasons the catering department had the greatest turnover in crew with the non-officer deck side following closely behind. Despite the conditions, engine room hands, generally tended to stay for a number of voyages. Why this should be so is uncertain. A fireman's money was better than that of a sailor. But, perhaps, more importantly there was a lack of alternative jobs elsewhere. The articles of agreement show that well over half of the crew could, at least, write their own names and that the crew were drawn from many parts of Britain not just the local ports.

Crew accommodation was certainly less palatial than that of the fare paying passengers. Master and senior officers — including the Chief Engineer in that category — probably had their own cabins whilst the remainder of the officers and engineers are likely to have shared cabins. Apart from the Master all crew accommodation will have been on the main deck forward, an early modification made to the ship being the removal of the crew from below the forward saloon to a position above it. Whilst officers and engineers slept in bunks, hammocks sufficed for the crew.

Work was hard and all on board certainly earned their money. Fortunately some of *Great Western's* log books survive and so it is possible to obtain a fair idea of the duties carried out. The term 'normal day' cannot be applied as the log books indicate that the days varied quite considerably. The deck logs for voyages Nos 23 and 43 do not illustrate the routine in the engine room but the surviving engine room log for the first voyage provides reasonable detail.

It would appear that, for most people, the working day consisted of twelve hours when watchkeeping. On deck a single officer and half of the sailors kept the watch. The Chief Officer always took the 4.00 am to 8.00 am watch, the other four-hour periods being taken, on a rotating basis, by the Second and Third officers. In the engine room two engineers, Second and Fifth or Third and Fourth had charge of the watch for six-hour periods. The Second and Fifth engineers took the 12 o'clock until 6 o'clock periods morning and afternoon. It is highly likely that one engineer looked after the boilers whilst the other had control of the engines. Tradesmen such as the carpenter, joiner and boilermaker were employed on day work but being called out, as were the off-watch crew, whenever circumstances dictated. At sea, then as now, there is no such thing as actually finishing work for the day. Everyone is permanently on call. The hours of the catering department were determined by the meal times but an early start, 6.00 am or 7.00 am, would have been required in order to prepare for breakfast.

At sea it would be the primary duty of the deck watch to adjust the sails in accordance with the wind conditions. Some watches would pass with little or no sail adjustment whilst others would be spent almost entirely aloft. The 8.00 am to noon watch on May 7 1842 had a rough time: '8 am Took in two reefs in the Main Spencer and set it. At 9 (am) Set the Fore Spencer. 9.30 Let one reef out of the Topsail and one reef out of the Main Spencer. At 10.30 Set the outer Jib and Mizzen Spencer. Noon, let the reef out of the Topsail.'[20] Whenever not required for ship keeping duties the watch would be assigned varied tasks as were most necessary. Three days before the above log insertion the 8.00 am to noon watch were reported about various tasks as there was only one sail adjustment required: 'Watch employed making boat grips, painting fenders, making gaskets, repairing wind sails (air scoops for ventilation), etc.' Without doubt the watch preferred the safety of the deck to the dangers of the rigging. Working high above the heaving deck in a cold North Atlantic gale may have been routine for the sailors but it was hazardous, gruelling work made no easier by the choking clouds of smoke belching from the funnel.

The available log books illustrate the duties assigned to the seamen during periods in harbour at New York. Naturally most tasks were carried as part of day work rather than watchkeeping. There would be, however, one person, at least, acting as a night watchman for security reasons. Apart from a few necessary tasks such as pumping the bilges and washing the decks no work was carried out on a Sunday and the crew were given the time off. The log book for voyage No 23 indicates that the seamen performed the tasks of cargo discharge and loading as well as the loading of coal. Shore labour was employed whenever necessary to assist them. Four years later, during voyage No 43, shore labour appears to have carried out all cargo and coal handling. Why this should be is uncertain, but the seamen were kept busy with many other tasks and it was probably considered better to employ the crew in keeping the ship in its first class condition.

When possible all sails were loosed and draped in order to allow them to dry. Repairs would be carried out as necessary and the sails stowed for use. Rigging also received attention, being given a coating of protective tar if needed. Washing of decks and all paintwork occupied the seamen for many hours. As at sea, the decks were holystoned in order to keep them clean and in good condition. Many passengers did not take kindly to these blocks of holystone being pushed backwards and forwards just above their heads. The noise was harsh and uncomfortable and no hour seemed right for the performance of this necessary task. As one passenger commented, '. . . infliction in the first degree, and suited to an age ere the inquisition became an exquisite. But the moment chosen invariably happens to be that at which you have just fallen into an afternoon nap, or are enjoying the rapture of delicious morning dreams! — and this; but I cannot find a name for the foul torture.'[21]

Having been washed, much of the paintwork required a further coat of paint. *Great Western* was, after all, a passenger steamer and a clean fresh appearance mattered. Hull, lifeboats and deck fittings were painted, the funnel blacked and masts varnished. All brass and exposed copper was cleaned and polished. The weather, naturally had its influence and at times paintwork had to be repaired when the original coat had been washed off by rain.

At times the tradesmen and sailors would be assigned to duties in the engine room. Refelting of the boilers had to be carried out in order to preserve efficiency and during the stay at New York in April 1842 two men found themselves in unfamiliar territory on top of the boilers. Both joiner and carpenter had regular tasks assisting the engineers and making items for use in the engine room. Relining the bunkers and repair work on the paddle wheels were two frequently performed jobs. This work was not without its danger as the log book for voyage No 43 relates: 'Monday 17th August 1846. 11 am W. Pottinger, Carpenter, whilst working on the Larboard Paddle Wheel was injured in the head by one of the Coal Trimmers letting a piece of wood fall on it.' The injury must have been fairly bad for it kept Pottinger away from work for the next six days.

Unfortunately no engine room log book, apart from that for the first voyage, appears to have survived and so it is difficult to obtain a complete picture of engine room events. The available log book does, however, provide some idea of the conditions and the tasks met by the crew 'down below'. Without doubt, all engine room personnel were very much relieved to reach port. Though conditions improved somewhat on later voyages, more stokers and coal trimmers being available, the first voyage illustrates the hardships faced and met. During the early voyages, before fitting of the tubular boilers, coal consumption averaged 24 tons each day. Of the ten firemen carried it is likely that eight tended the boilers whilst two assisted with the engines. Early in the first crossing Pearne found it necessary to organise the men into watches with four firemen and four coal trimmers comprising each watch. Using these simplified figures each man needed to shovel three tons of coal into the boilers during his 12-hour working day. Each trimmer had to supply the boilers with an equivalent amount. Add to this the cleaning of fires and the removal of ashes for disposal overboard and it all results in a very hard day's work. Bad weather aggravated matters, particularly for the coal trimmers who, with their small wheel barrows had to transport tons of coal from the furthest end of the ship to the ever demanding boilers. Engine room hands earned their meagre pittance of £4 per month for firemen and £3 10s per month for coal trimmers.

In comparison, the lot of the engineer may appear to have been an easier one but he also well earned his keep. Boilers and engines required constant attention to ensure that they functioned in the manner desired; for the same reason the stokers and trimmers needed similar attention. Any breakdown or serious malfunction of the machinery necessitated the efforts of all engineers thus requiring more than the accustomed 12-hour day. Though a limited number of spare engine parts would have been carried many components had to be manufactured, or repaired on board. In this task the engineers had the assistance of a blacksmith and, when in the service of the RMSPC, a boilermaker.

In the comparative comfort of a port engine room work became a little easier. Stokers and trimmers no longer sweated shifting their tons of coal whilst the furnaces tried to roast them or the sea endeavoured to dash them against the nearest solid object, moving or stationary. Clambering through the tortuous passages of the boilers or between the frames and linkages of the engine to clean or repair became a treat, a luxury to be enjoyed particularly as, at the end of the day, the many attractions of the port awaited. Such delights obviously awaited all willing and brave enough to avail themselves. Seaports are notoriously rough and the fact that a man belonged to the crew of the premier Atlantic steamship conveyed no privileges in Bristol, Liverpool, New York or anywhere else. The men worked hard and they probably played equally hard. Newspapers of the period do not indicate any serious incident involving a crew member from *Great Western* and it is reasonable to presume that behaviour was no worse than that of other seafarers.

On board *Great Western*, and all early steamers, engineers were the elite. Their wages in comparison to the deck officers illustrate their importance (Appendix 2). It was essential to attract and keep skilled engineers if the ship was to perform in the manner intended. Joseph Williams, Chief Engineer during the final years of North Atlantic service, served the company on board *Great Western* for over six years, commencing as one of the junior engineers. Without doubt engineers received favourable treatment particularly if a dispute arose concerning others on board ship. Woolward, in his autobiography, indicates one such incident during the early years of the RMSPC. Whilst the *Medway* lay at Bermuda she was visited by the engineers from the *Tweed* and both sets of engineers set about enjoying themselves. Not taking kindly to orders for lights to be extinguished at the regulation 10.00 pm the engineers made their displeasure known, forcibly. The deck officers, unable to end the soiree by persuasion, with the assistance of the dockyard guard, resorted to coercion and the

engineers from the *Tweed* spent the night in the guardroom. News of this incident preceeded *Medway* home and led to an enquiry. Woolward was held to be responsible and transferred to another ship. Bitterly he makes the comment; '. . . as engineers in those days were more scarce than they are now, the blame was put on me, . . .'[22]

During the early years of oceanic steamships promotion for navigators and engineers could be very rapid. This was particularly so with the RMSPC with its rapidly expanding fleet. Unfortunately, few deck officers had any experience on steamers and this fact probably contributed to the considerable fleet losses suffered by that company during its early years. Woolward relates one incident when an inexperienced Third Mate managed to get part of the studding sail rigging wrapped around one of the paddle wheels which then proceeded to 'wind down' the studding sail boom resulting in considerable damage and delay.[23] Fortunately *Great Western* appears to have avoided such misfortunes being crewed, at least when in the service of her original owners, by competent men.

Though they fared less well than the passengers crew members had no cause to complain about the victualling standards with four pence per man per day being allowed for provisions during the year 1840.[24] The minimum daily food allowance for each man formed part of the articles of agreement and, for voyage No 43, is given in Appendix 2. What is not known is the quality of the provisions and its presentation. Engineers and mates undoubtedly received the better cuts of meat this being served to them by their own servants; one being provided for each group. Sailors and engine room hands probably had to fetch their food from the galley, consuming it in their mess rooms which also served as their sleeping quarters. Though daily allowances were indicated for food it is highly unlikely that the figures laid down were strictly adhered to but they formed the minimum basis upon which the food order for a particular voyage could be determined. One allowance upon which each man will have insisted was that of one gill of rum daily. Firemen and coal trimmers received an extra gill daily whenever involved in taking night watches. The rum allowance and the minimum provision levels were very similar for ships operated by the RMSPC and such was the case when *Great Western* entered the service of that concern.

Neither the Great Western Steam Ship Company nor the RMSPC permitted any liquor on board their ships apart from that introduced by them. This was not a measure designed at making a profit from selling the alcohol but a means of controlling drunkeness amongst the crew. Apart from the daily rum allowance it is unlikely that crew members were allowed any alcoholic drinks. Certainly the regulations of the RMSPC do not give any indication that crew members were allowed to purchase liquor although they do lay down maximum amounts which might be purchased by the officers and engineers. Such does not mean that engine room hands and seamen could not obtain beverages of the variety denied them. Whilst in port a flowing supply could be procured from one of the many taverns along the dockside. Inevitably quantities were 'spirited' on board to be consumed at a later date. The available log books do not show a high level of drunkeness only the occasional incident being recorded.

With such a large number of people in close proximity for relatively long periods health, or rather the lack of it, could present a problem. *Great Western* carried a surgeon whose primary task was to administer to the needs of the passengers but he was obviously on hand to ensure that medicines and treatment were available to any sick or injured crew member. Standards of catering hygiene during the mid-nineteenth century were not as high as those demanded in later years and food poisoning could easily affect all on board a ship. *Great Western* appears to have avoided epidemics due to this or other causes. Other ships of the period, particularly those carrying large numbers of steerage passengers, were not so lucky. A ship's complement of passengers and crew could be devastated by smallpox or yellow fever brought on board by a single person quite unwittingly. Towards the end of the homeward leg of voyage No 43 a greater than usual number of crew members reported sick. On one day five men were ill with another joining the list two days later. Three of the invalids were from the catering department, the butcher, pantryman and a waiter. Whether this had any affect upon the passengers is unknown but it illustrates how precarious the good health of all on board could be. With respect to accidents a number have already been described in this and previous chapters. It is fortunate for those concerned that a surgeon was available.

Service aboard *Great Western* did present problems for a number of her crew members from a financial point of view. At the time it was common practice for any man who had signed articles to receive an advance on his wages ostensibly for the purchase of clothing and equipment to be used on the forthcoming voyage. This advance, known as the 'dead horse', would be repaid from the earnings during the ensuing months. *Great Western* completed her voyages in about forty days, leaving the seaman with little or no money with which to 'pay off'. Aware of the likely problems the Great Western Steam Ship Company reduced the amount of advance, probably to about two weeks wages. One, seemingly very literate, seaman was commissioned by *The Bristol Magazine* to document his opinions of life on board and offered the following views upon the payment of wages.

'The *Great Western* is a real good ship, and no mistake, and well officer'd too; but there's nothing perfect in this world, and that you'll find out when you've lived as long as I have. It's all very well, no doubt, for passengers who have their business on shore, to be anxious to whip across the Atlantic in twelve or fourteen days, if they can; but I tell you what, sir, it don't answer poor sailors at all; and if the wages were paid on the old plan we would never have a sixpence in our pockets, to spend as we liked, because the vessel gets home again before we've had time to work out the 'dead horse', (month's advance) which, I dare say you know, generally goes to the wife, except a few shillings for a jacket, or a pair of shoes, or some other article o' clothing we may want for the next voyage.'[25]

More often than not, the bulk of the advance never reached the wife or outfitters; owners of dockside bars were, however, well satisfied with the system of paying in advance. Relatively short Atlantic voyages and the absence of a large 'pay off' probably accounted for the fact that sailors tended to remain in service aboard the Bristol ship for no more than a few voyages.

Though the seamen may have had cause to dislike certain aspects of the early steamship operations, one person at least had no reason to complain. A ship's Master has always enjoyed certain privileges not available to his more lowly companions. In this respect Hosken and Matthews were no different. The salary paid to the Master must have exceeded the £20 per month paid to the Chief Engineer and for the period that was good. Very good in fact, for it caused much concern amongst a number of shareholders in the Great Western Steam Ship Company, during financial difficulties in 1842, that the Master of *Great Western* received a higher salary than that enjoyed by any Captain employed by the RMSPC or the Cunard Line.[26] (In 1850 Masters of the RMSPC large steamers received £25 per month whilst those responsible for the smaller vessels were paid £5 less.)[27] Apart from salary there were many additional payments to be obtained. The extent of those available to Hosken and Matthews whilst serving in *Great Western* on the North Atlantic is uncertain but they must have been substantial and no worse than the level of perquisite enjoyed by their counterparts in the RMSPC. Mailships on the West Indies run carried appreciable quantities of bullion and specie for which the Royal Mail Company received 2½ per cent as freight, of which the Master received 2 per cent. Not bad when, as in one case quoted by Woolward, the consignment could be worth three million dollars.[28]

Whilst *Great Western* occupied the North Atlantic run her owners probably took steps to victual her themselves although it must have left scope for her Master to increase his earnings through the purchase of extra provisions considered necessary. West Indies service presented victualling difficulties as the run and ports of call could not be guaranteed and so provisions were purchased when and where possible. This was left in the hands of the Master who was allowed to dray from the ship's funds and, when this was not sufficint, to draw a bill on the company.[29] In January 1854 when Captain Bevis took command of *Great Western* the RMSPC board of managers held a special meeting in order to discuss the matter of provisions for the forthcoming voyage. They concluded, '. . . That he, Captain Bevis, should be guaranteed against any loss on his part of his undertaking and that should the account and vouchers at the end of the voyage show that no profit accrues to the captain the matter will be submitted to the court (board of directors) with an understanding that it will deal liberally with the question of remuneration.'[30] The master, obviously, could not lose; whether, or not, the passengers and crew got value in terms of their food is unknown.

Hosken and Matthews both received presentations of silver plate from satisfied passengers during their years in command of *Great Western* on the North Atlantic. Such silverware must have had considerable value. Hosken, following his appointment to the *Great Britain*, was presented with one hundred guineas by the insurance underwriters in recognition of his 64 Atlantic crossings, accomplished in complete safety, aboard *Great Western*.[31] Masters of vessels on the West Indies run also looked upon the receipt of a silver testimonial as a normal part of the voyage, if not a right. Many no doubt were deserved and given. Woolward recounts the tale of one Captain who, upon finding that his testimonial was only a paper one, addressed the passengers very curtly. 'Ladies and gentlemen, thirty years I have been an officer in HM Service, and have not come here to ask a character from a parcel of "Travelling Tinkers". Take it back waiter.'[32]

Whilst at New York, and to some extent Bristol and Liverpool, there was little work for the Captain to do, thus allowing a considerable amount of free time. Certainly Hosken enjoyed his visits to New York: '. . .I used generally to take a week or ten days on each arrival at New York, to visit various parts of the United States.'[33] No other crew member enjoyed such privilege. It is unlikely that the tight South Atlantic schedules allowed the luxury of impromptu holidays. Certainly not to the same extent.

A number of seafarers did, however, take advantage of the transportation offered by *Great Western* and used the westward crossing as a means of emigrating to America. Surviving articles of agreement illustrate many examples of seamen 'jumping ship' at New York. The simple entry on the sheet, 'deserted at New York', hiding many hopes and expectations of a new American. Crew members were not adverse to a little smuggling whenever the opportunity arose and, no doubt, the authorities were equally keen to prevent the action succeeding. In order to avoid any consequences arising from the discovery of contraband aboard their vessel the Great Western Steam Ship Company had regular searches made during the homeward passage. The log book for voyage No 43 contains two entries reading, 'Searched the ship this day for contraband goods but found none.'[34] Failure of the search does not mean that illicit imports were not on board. Almost certainly they were, but well hidden. Contraband and cheap emigration were, after all, the only 'perks' available to the average seafarer.

Chapter 11

Mailship at last

Throughout the first four decades of the nineteenth century the only mail communication between Britain and its Caribbean colonies was provided by the small 'coffin' brigs, similar to those employed upon the North Atlantic. Based at the packet station of Falmouth the sailing brigs maintained a regular sailing schedule, but arrival dates could, be in no way guaranteed. Inter-island transportation depended upon elderly ten-gun brigs which had been converted to steam power by the provision of 100 horse power engines. Concerned at the inadequacies of the service a Scot, James MacQueen, set about trying to improve matters. MacQueen had been manager of a sugar estate on the West Indian island of Grenada before returning home to pursue a literary career.

In July 1837 MacQueen presented the government with proposals for a steam packet service between Britain and the Caribbean. September of that year saw more detailed proposals for worldwide mail communication, including Australia and China. The plan called for main line steam routes with feeder systems operated by smaller steam or sailing ships. MacQueen also envisaged a canal through the Central American isthmus, his mail routes to take full advantage of such a waterway. Though not acted upon immediately the proposals must have spurred the government of the day to reconsider its mail policies. The resultant mail contracts to P&O, Cunard and the RMSPC testify to the basic soundness of the MacQueen plan.

The West India Committee, a group of West Indies planters and merchants, became very interested in MacQueen's proposals and requested him to prepare a more detailed plan for a mail service to the Caribbean region. This he did and early in 1839 the scheme was laid before the government. MacQueen and a group from the committee founded the Royal Mail Steam Packet Company which was granted a Royal Charter on September 26 1839 to operate a steam mail service to, and within, the Caribbean. Granting of the charter was followed by negotiations with the Admiralty for the carriage of mails. By November of that year negotiations were complete and the contract was signed on March 20 1840. In part, at least, MacQueen's dream was about to be fulfilled.

The first contract called for a number of large steamers to operate a transatlantic service from a British port to Barbados, then calling at Grenada, Santa Cruz, St Thomas, Nicola Mole, Santiago de Cuba, Port Royal, Savannah la Mar and Havana. On the return the vessel would call at most of the ports in the reverse order. A twice monthly service would operate across the Atlantic portion. Connecting with these main line steamers were to be seven smaller steamers and three sailing vessels to provide a feeder service with all principal islands on the Spanish Main and Gulf of Mexico. Such a network required a total annual mileage of 684,816; the subsidy payable being £240,000. The contract set a commencement date of December 1 1841, by which time fourteen steamers and three sailing vessels had to be operational.

A share prospectus, issued in March 1840, was well received and the building of ships could commence. Construction and engining of fourteen steamers in so short a period of time presented problems, particularly as they were amongst the largest vessels built to that date. So as to ensure early delivery the orders were

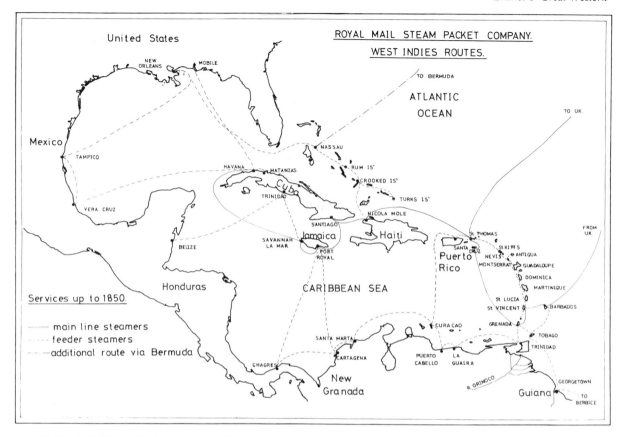

Fig 53: Royal Mail Steam Packet Company's West Indies Routes.

spread around the builders then capable of constructing such ships. In all but two cases, Acraman's of Bristol and Caird's of Greenock, separate engine contracts were made. Due to Acraman's later bankruptcy his two ships, *Avon* and *Severn,* were completed by William Patterson and entered service much later than the other vessels. All steamers had side lever engines driving paddle wheels and were constructed from wood. Apart from two steamers purchased ready built, all of the RMSPC vessels carried the names of British rivers. Before the mail service actually began some minor changes in the routes were made. These included a call at Bermuda homeward for an Atlantic crossing from Nassau. Southampton became the British terminal.

The vessels *Forth, Solway, Clyde* and *Tweed* all departed in late December 1841 to take up stations throughout the West Indies in order to trans-ship the UK mails. On January 3 1842 the steamers *Tay* and *Thames* left Falmouth with the first consignments of mail under the contract. *Thames* headed for Barbados whilst *Tay* steamed south to Berbice in Guiana.

Under the terms of the contract each vessel had to carry an Admiralty agent who was responsible for the mail and its safe delivery. These agents could, and frequently did, over-ride the instructions of the Master on any matter loosely connected with the mails. On such a contract vessel this included practically everything. With the service less than four months old both the *Tay* and *Forth* met at Nassau. Neither agent would agree to the other vessel taking home the mails with the result that both ships returned to England. The *Forth* brought only six passengers and a few bags of mail.

The incident brought only additional headaches for the infant company already concerned at the late delivery of the Bristol ships. Matters worsened the following month when *Medina* became a total loss off Turks Island, fortunately without loss of life.

Elimination of calls at certain ports giving a route mileage reduction of nearly 300,000, whilst the subsidy remained unaltered, was necessary after only six months service otherwise the whole venture would have been jeopardised. A second disaster struck in September of the first year of operations when the steamer *Isis* grounded off Puerto Rico. Refloated and temporarily repaired she sailed for England but sank in heavy weather off Bermuda on October 8. Matters improved with the delivery of the Bristol built ships early in 1843 but April saw the end of the *Solway* with the loss of 35 lives. The fatalities appear to have resulted from an error of judgement by the Master who had no previous steamship experience. *Solway* ran aground on a reef near La Coruna but was quickly refloated by putting the paddles astern. Aiming to beach his ship the Captain ordered full speed ahead but *Solway* was taking water fast. Aware of this the Captain had the boats lowered whilst the ship was moving ahead at speed. Several boats were swamped and *Solway* went down before all could get off safely.

Actaeon, one of the smaller inter-island steamers, became a casualty in October 1844 when she hit a shoal near Cartagena, Columbia. There was no loss of life and the incident was officially ascribed to the inaccuracy of the chart. However, the owners found no further need for the services of the Master and most of the deck officers. The next two years saw a small modification in the mail contract and its extention until 1852, giving the RMSPC greater confidence in its operational survival. A most serious incident in February 1847 shook that faith. The large steamer *Tweed* was about her inter-island calls following a crossing from Southampton when she foundered with considerable loss of life. During heavy overcast weather Captain Parsons, unable to take any sights of the sun, relied upon dead reckoning for his navigation between Havana and Vera Cruz, in Mexico. Unfortunately, on the night of February 11, two days out from Havana, *Tweed* was actually 30 miles north of her estimated position and heading for the Alecranes coral reef off the coast at Yucatan. At 3.30 am on the 12th *Tweed* drove up onto a coral spur.

Severely holed *Tweed* began to list badly and in a very short time broke up. Lifeboats were smashed as they were launched but many people found salvation in the broken timbers of the ship, which provided the essential support for them to reach relative safety higher up on the reef. It took some considerable time before the survivors were rescued. The disaster took the lives of 41 crew members and 31 passengers. *Tweed* became the fifth ship lost by the RMSPC since the service began and a replacement had to be found with the utmost urgency if the mail contract was to be fulfilled. Fortuitously, the solution lay, ready and available, at Bristol.

Consequent upon the stranding of *Great Britain* at Dundrum the Great Western Steam Ship Company moved their paddle steamer, *Great Western*, from Liverpool back to Bristol. In order to meet some of the salvage costs of the iron steamer the small wooden sister had to be sold. At a sparsely attended public auction in Bristol on March 11 1847 the bidding only reached £20,000, some £5,000 below the reserve. Needless to say the vessel was not sold.[1] Shortly after the auction William Patterson, on behalf of himself and some friends — possibly Gibbs, Bright & Co, who subsequently purchased *Great Britain*, offered £22,000 for the ship but this was turned down.[2] Another very interested party, perhaps out of desperation, happened to be Captain Chappel, secretary to the RMSPC. On Wednesday April 14, Chappell, Mills (the superintendent engineer) and a Mr Ashton journeyed to Bristol to view the ship. A very thorough inspection took place the following day.

Though the engines gave no cause for concern Mills considered that the government authorities might object to the tubular boilers as the ship would be operating a mail service. The hull was in excellent condition as were the accommodation spaces. Keen on purchasing the ship, Chappell entered into negotiations with some directors of the Great Western Steam Ship Company. The directors gave him one week in which to conclude or decline the purchase. The briefest of consultation with the Royal Mail board followed and the board gave its approval. One condition imposed by the directors of the Bristol company was that disapproval by the government, following a government surveyor's report, should not be assigned as a reason for the ultimate ending of negotiations.[3] Memories of the abortive P&O sale must have still been bitter.

The Royal Mail Steam Packet Company obtained *Great Western* for the sum of £25,000, less £250 for the replacement of paddle wheels and movement down to Kingroad. Silver plate and the ship's chronometer were not included in the sale. By means of a bill of sale, which became due on June 16, two months after the agreement, *Great Western* passed out of the hands of her once proud, idealistic and imaginative creators to become just another member of a large but undistinguished fleet. She was, however, far from being just another ship, she remained unique and, in her class, unequalled.

In order to avoid being delayed awaiting a tide, *Great Western* moved down to Kingroad on Saturday April 17 and there completed preparations for the short voyage to her new home base, Southampton.[4] Arriving at the Hampshire port in the morning of May 3, the former queen of the Atlantic was placed in dock and examined carefully. Mr Ellsmie, the superintendent shipwright, and William Pitchers, a shipbuilder of Northfleet who carried out much building and repair work for the RMSPC, furnished lists of the minimum work necessary to allow a Caribbean voyage in the near future. A week in drydock allowed much of the work to be completed.[5] A government surveyor inspected the machinery and, as expected, was not over impressed with the tubular boilers. The urgent need for tonnage on the service resulted in a machinery dispensation for a single voyage to the West Indies and back. Mills reported that the boilers and engines could be made ready in three weeks and *Great Western* was fixed to carry out the mails on June 2 1847.

Following the repairs a group of directors visited the ship for sea trials down Southampton water. They left *Great Western* very impressed by her speed and performance and obviously pleased with their bargain buy. Later that day, with 33 passengers and a fair cargo, including 1,650 bottles of mercury for the silver mines, Brunel's first steamer began her new career carrying Her Majesty's mail to the West Indies.[6]

On the outward passage a call was made at Madeira to land and pick up passengers as well as for coal bunkers. Of the seven day voyage from Southampton Captain Abbott expressed great satisfaction. He reported to the directors that his charge performed and steered well, was easy to handle and as fast as any other vessel in the fleet. He also reported no difficulty at all in keeping steam.[7] In view of these facts it is difficult to appreciate the desire of the Admiralty surveyor to have replaced the, still fairly new, tubular boilers. Throughout that first Caribbean voyage and for three years on the North Atlantic the tubular boilers had performed efficiently allowing the ship to maintain a speed as good, if not better, than her contemporaries. However, he who pays the piper calls the tune and as the government provided the subsidy the government decided how the ships were to be built, equipped, manned and operated, even if the system was not as efficient as it might be.

Returning to Southampton on September 5, *Great Western* was two days earlier than anticipated, a further testimony to the abilities of the ship and her machinery. Notwithstanding this, the boilers had to be replaced and the owners set about the task. Unfortunately no real details concerning the new boilers are available but it is known that they were designed by Mills and were, almost certainly of the flue type. Alterations to the fabric of the ship were to be made in order to bring her into keeping with the style formulated for the rest of the fleet. These included replacement of the spar deck, then in two sections, fore and aft, by a complete spar deck over the entire length of the ship. Normally work of the nature envisaged would have been entrusted to William Pitchers at his yard on the Thames, but both of his docks were already occupied and so all alterations took place at Southampton. As during surveys in earlier years sections of planking were removed to expose the main structure which, as usual, was in first class condition.[8]

By October 26 the new boilers were on board. Three weeks later it was reported that the spar deck had been laid and that engine repairs were proceeding well. Early January 1848 saw all of the main tasks complete with the profile of *Great Western* altered somewhat by the new spar deck. She still had her single funnel and four masts. The latter distinguished her from the other large vessels in the fleet which only had three masts. Engine trials in the Solent passed without any trouble, *Great Western* averaging 10½ knots during two runs over the measured mile. The new boilers performed faultlessly as did the engines. An Admiralty survey on January 19 produced the same pleasing result and *Great Western* was again ready to resume her revenue earning role.[9]

Unlike her service on the North Atlantic *Great Western* was now operating a service in conjunction with a number of other steamers and, being part of a large fleet, was subject to regular changes in crew and Master. Under such circumstances no Master or set of officers became accustomed to the ship and its peculiarities. This possibly resulted in a lessening of the operating efficiency and, maybe, contributed to the number of grounding incidents which plagued the Royal Mail fleet. Obviously, a brief encounter with a ship did not allow the Master or crew member to identify with that vessel, causing them to develop a somewhat lax attitude to her performance and condition.

With Captain Chapman in charge *Great Western* sailed on her second West Indies voyage during the morning of February 2 1848. Again going by way of Madeira the refurbished ship headed for Barbados. The performance of ship and machinery exceeded all expectations. Instead of making the usual run between the main islands *Great Western* remained in the West Indies operating as a feeder for the transatlantic vessels. After six months amongst the islands she returned to Southampton in the evening of August 19. Following discharge of mails and cargo the managers ordered a thorough inspection of the hull and machinery. No drydock being available at Southampton this necessitated a trip to Northfleet on the Thames. The two week sojourn in Pitchers' drydock corrected some minor defects but proved *Great Western* to be as secure as ever.[10]

Eighty passengers took passage on the next voyage which was to be via Bermuda. Total receipts for that outward passage amounted to just over £3,800, a figure better than that earned by most running mates and, in fact, in excess of that generally earned by *Great Western* herself in future years.[11] Had it not been for the mail subsidy the RMSPC could not have continued in business. Another prolonged stay in the West Indies had been scheduled but the steamer *Thames* was delayed and failed to make a connection. *Great Western*, being available, brought home the mails no doubt much to the annoyance of the crew of the *Thames*.[12]

During 1849 two round trips to the West Indies were completed; the second actually ended on January 20 1850. *Great Western* evidently settled into her role as a mail steamer but her performance was marred by one incident whilst returning to Southampton in April 1849. A few days before arrival the starboard engine

crankpin fractured completely disabling that engine. Running on the port engine only *Great Western* arrived just a few hours later than expected.[13] Obviously repairs had to be carried out before sailings could be resumed. These, again, took place at Northfleet. Following this incident *Great Western* sailed for Bermuda on June 2 and remained in the West Indies until the end of the year.

The West Indies inter-island service presented many operating difficulties for ships' crew and the managers. All coal had to be shipped in, most of it being imported from Britain. As each steamer consumed over two hundred tons of coal per week a prodigious supply had to be maintained. Sailing colliers, chartered for the purpose, kept the stockpiles high. Delays due to bad weather sometimes meant that a coal depot ran short and this resulted in the curtailment of local steamer services. On such occasions sailing vessels had to be hired in order to transport the mails. A Caribbean cruise may be the ideal holiday for many a person but navigation of that waterway during the mid-nineteenth century presented far greater problems than exist today. Inaccurate charts and unlit reefs contributed to the loss of many lives and ships, though it must be stated that indifferent navigation and careless deck watchkeeping caused the loss of many early Royal Mail steamships. Aware of the chart deficiencies many Masters avoided certain coastal regions preferring to keep far out to sea until actually approaching the required port. Such action was especially important at night due to the inadequacies of the warning lights on reefs and rocks.

For those on board the short passage between some islands could be annoying as there was little time to settle into any routine. At some ports the ship could actually go alongside a berth whilst at others only an anchorage was available. If at anchor passengers, mail and even cargo had to be transported by the ship's boats; a tedious task if the ship lay a number of miles off the port. Certain locations possessed no berths of any kind and the small boats had to be beached in order to land the passengers, a risky business at times. Woolward relates one occasion when a boat in his charge failed to make a good beach landing, all occupants ending up in the boiling surf. No one suffered physical injury but the new bride of one of the army officers at the local garrison lost some of her dignity and at the same time had her trousseau ruined.[14]

In the closely grouped island areas three ports in a single day was not unusual, particularly if there happened to be little business to conduct. Calls at Antigua, Nevis and St Kitts could be accomplished within a normal daylight period. Those who had to row the boats ashore, naturally, were relieved to depart. Where ports were not too far apart and a master was in a hurry to make the second port before night-fall he would sometimes leave the small ship's boat to land the mails and make his way on. Those in the landing party, including the Admiralty agent who would be privy to the arrangements, had to catch up when they could. In his autobiography Woolward also recalls an event of this nature when he sailed the 23 miles from the island of Tortola to rejoin the steamer *Tweed* at St Thomas.

A reliable mail service necessitated a complex arrangement of feeder ships within the Caribbean area. Connections had to be made which meant that good timekeeping had to be adhered to at all times. Failure to arrive at the required port in time resulted in the home-ward bound mails not being taken. Similarly, outward mails might suffer considerable delays before they finally arrived at their destination. Woolward's auto-biography, full of revealing and informative anecdotes, records an incident when the steamer *Avon* gave chase to her sister *Tay*. *Avon*, through an error navigation, failed to connect with *Tay* at St Thomas. In conse-quence the latter ship was ordered to head for England taking her mails with her. *Avon*, due to make the return Atlantic crossing, gave chase and, fortunately, came upon the *Tay* the day after she left St Thomas. Mails and passengers were transferred allowing *Avon* to head for home via Bermuda. *Tay* returned to her inter-island service. What would have transpired had the rendez-vous not taken place is uncertain. Two steamers returning home would leave the feeder service incon-veniently short and, no doubt, a number of people with red faces.[15]

Throughout the years 1850 and 1851 *Great Western* continued on the transatlantic service, the actual round voyage time varying due to the amount of time actually spent running between the islands. During this period her performance was exceedingly creditable consider-ing her age. Both Atlantic crossings on voyage No 50 were made via Bermuda and on both occasions *Great Western* recorded the fastest times by any vessel to that date. The 3,013 miles between Southampton and

Bermuda occupied 12¾ days outwards and 14½ days on the return.[16] Good performances, however, did not make a ship immune to the Royal Mail steamers' disease, that of grounding.

At 7.45 pm on March 26 1851 *Great Western* went aground off Cape Aguiya near Santa Marta. The weather was calm but rather dark and hazy when the ship struck the ground and the blame lay solely in the hands of those responsible for her navigation. For-tunately the ground was soft and no serious damage resulted, the ship freeing herself in a short period of time. Naturally the owners called for an enquiry into the incident and this was convened at the London office on May 15, shortly after the ship's return from the West Indies. Captain Wolfe was called upon to explain his actions in running a course which took his ship so close to the land. His only defence was that the course steered aimed at counteracting the strong current running off the coast. The Chief Officer, a Mr Rogers, also faced reprimand for not advising the Master of the dangers. In the end the enquiry, well aware that such incidents cast serious doubts upon the credibility of the operators, found both men to be at fault and it recommended that they be suspended from the company's service. In giving their verdict the committee of enquiry stated that they felt, 'compelled to give their opinion that Captain Wolfe was guilty of a great error of judgement in steering the course SSW ½ W towards the land after 3.00 pm, and more particularly, in running the full distance to the land in dark hazy weather thereby endangering his ship and the lives of all on board.' Mr Rogers was found to be similarly guilty for approving the actions.[17]

Following the grounding incident *Great Western* was rescheduled to bring the mails home in order that she could undergo a drydock inspection. On that return passage she carried ten distressed British seamen whose vessel the *Caroline*, of Bristol, had burned at sea off the small island of Savo.[18] Most crew members were, no doubt, conscious of the fact that they themselves had so narrowly missed making a similar return home. The drydock inspection, at Pitchers' yard on the Thames, revealed no serious defects and *Great Western* was soon ready to resume her interrupted service.

On the outward leg to the West Indies the trans-atlantic vessels might call at Madeira or Bermuda depending upon the route to be sailed. If coal was

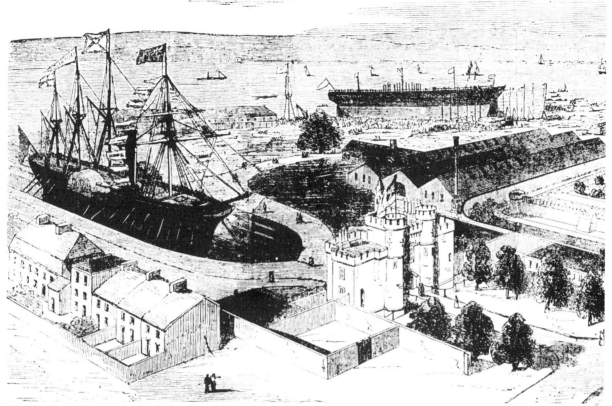

Fig 54: Great Western *in drydock at Northfleet, May 17 1851, with* Orinoco *ready for launching* (Courtesy Liverpool City Library).

required this would be picked up. During a return passage the ports of call could be Bermuda or Fayal, in the Azores. Following her inspection *Great Western* made for St Thomas, this being the main entry port for the mail ships following the new agreement signed on May 4 1850. The next four months of inter-island service were completed without major incident and the return home from St Thomas began on October 19. Strong easterly gales impeded progress for the whole of the passage. No call at Fayal had been planned but a desperate bunker situation necessitated a departure from route. Fortunately the weather abated enough for coal to be shipped aboard, allowing *Great Western* to reach Southampton without further trouble. Some 21 days were required for a crossing which, in fair weather, should have taken no more than 18 or 19 days.[19] At times inclement weather did not allow a ship to take any

bunkers at Fayal and so the voyage had to proceed as best it could. Judicious use of engines and sails to eke out the remaining fuel generally could be relied upon to bring the vessel safely to port in as short a time as possible. One problem, however, could not be overcome so readily. Coal bunker spaces occupied the lower portions of the ship and when full of coal could be relied upon to enhance the stability. Towards the end of a crossing, particularly if the cargo was not large, the ship would become top-heavy and develop a disconcerting tendency to roll badly. Many an early steamer arriving at Southampton showed signs of this 'coal-fever', indicating the inability to bunker en route.

Following a further three-month voyage at the turn of 1851 *Great Western* sailed for St Thomas on April 2 1852 and did not see home waters again for over a year. Woolward sailed as Chief Officer having, fortunately for him, been transferred from the ill-fated *Amazon* shortly before *Great Western* sailed. Some ships did spend long periods in the Caribbean but an epidemic of yellow fever raged throughout the West Indies during 1852 and it was probably considered preferable to keep the ship on station out there, particularly as she was performing well. Many of the mail steamers suffered deaths of crew members whilst others had to be invalided home. Captain Wooley, of *Great Western*, came into the latter group and Woolward found himself in command for the first time. His crew seriously affected by the disease, Woolward kept his remaining fit engineers and Chief Officer but repatriated all other white crew members. These he replaced with locals and suffered no further troubles with yellow fever. Shortly before *Great Western* herself returned to home waters Woolward was transferred to the steamer *Thames* and demoted back to Chief Officer.[20] His former charge was not completely free of the disease as, on her return passage to England, a passenger died from its effects. The girl, a servant from Belize, died on April 10 eight days out from St Thomas. It was thought that she exposed herself to the disease during an imprudent trip ashore.[21] Quarantine regulations, in those days, were not as strict as today but all on board, no doubt, received a thorough inspection, although the nineteen day passage from the West Indies would have been a long enough incubation period for the disease.

Apart from the occasional loss of a steamer the mail service to the West Indies progressed admirably during its first decade. Expansion of the operations became more than a passing fancy. It had, in fact, been part of James MacQueen's original scheme to provide a mail service to South America. Tactfully, early in 1849, the RMSPC approached the government with its own proposals. A few remaining 'coffin' brigs, the sole survivors of the once extensive fleet of Admiralty mail packets, still plied the route between Falmouth and Rio de Janeiro. In the light of the successful, if costly steamer mail contracts, replacement of the small brigs became merely a matter of time.

July 5 1850 saw the signing of a new mail contract which modified the West Indies service and, more importantly, opened up the route to South America. The contract called for a monthly service between Southampton and Rio with intermediate calls being made at Lisbon, Madeira, St Vincent in the Cape Verde Islands, Pernambuco (now Recife) and Bahia (now Salvador). From Rio a small vessel would carry the mails to Buenos Aires. As with the West Indies service, agencies and coal depots had to be organised but the directors expecting the contract to be granted, had their plans well in hand. St Vincent was to become the intermediate coaling station. On November 10 1850 the little steamer *Esk* left Southampton to take up her station at the South American terminal. Of only 232 gross tons and smaller than any other unit in the fleet, *Esk* was significant in being screw propelled. This is rather strange in view of the Admiralty's reluctance to condone the use of screw propelled vessels for the carriage of the mails until a much later date.

Refitted, partially reconstructed and with new machinery *Teviot* had the honour of inaugurating the new service. With 45 passengers and a limited mail she departed Southampton during the afternoon of Thursday January 9 1851. One of the passengers was Admiral Pascoe Grenfell who was proceeding to Rio in order to command the Brazilian fleet which, at that time was preparing for the expected conflict between Brazil and Buenos Aires. Not the ideal time to open up a mail service. *Teviot* reached Pernambuco on February 2 and Rio de Janeiro five days later. An absence of reefs and narrow, rocky channels boded well for the safety of the ships and those on board. So it turned out, at least as far as distant waters were concerned.

With a new mail contract and two services to operate, the existing fleet would be severely stretched and additional tonnage became a matter of urgency. A crash building programme saw vessels delivered throughout 1851. These were *Orinoco*, *Magdalena* and *Parana* of nearly 3,000 tons, together with *Amazon* of 2,256 tons. In 1852 the *La Plata*, Cunard Line's *Arabia*, was purchased whilst building to replaced the ill-fated *Amazon*, lost due to a fire only two days into her maiden voyage in January 1852. Another ship in this series, *Demerara*, had been ordered from William Patterson at Bristol. Machinery was to be built and installed on the Clyde and so, at 7.00 am on Monday, November 10 1851, *Demerara* was towed through the Cumberland Basin into the Avon. Due to a misunderstanding between the Pilot, tug Master and ship's Master and as a consequence of the fast current *Demerara* hit one bank and then swung around until bow and stern rested on opposite banks. The fast ebbing tide left her suspended resulting in serious structural damage which made her totally unsuitable as a mail steamer. Two new ships had been lost in as many months. Fortunately the RMSPC was able to continue with its services despite the losses the new tonnage had to be ordered to replace these ships and some, now ageing ones, of the original fleet. The only available picture of *Great Western* during her service in the Royal Mail fleet is from this period. *The Illustrated London News* depicted the scene at Northfleet on May 17 1851, the day *Orinoco* was launched. *Great Western* is in dry dock and it may be observed that her profile remained, more or less, unaltered compared with her North Atlantic days, apart from the, now continuous, spar deck.

The new larger and faster ships were immediately placed upon the transatlantic route freeing the older vessels for the Caribbean inter-island service and the Brazil line. Following her year in the West Indies *Great Western* was given a thorough overhaul at her owner's Southampton facilities. In order to give more stowage space the lower deck areas were altered. Cabins and saloons received attention to provide more comfortable accommodation. Though the timbers were still sound the hull required re-coppering and some masts had to be replaced due to defective wood.[22] Experiments with feathering paddle wheels had been carried out by the RMSPC and this form of wheel fitted to some vessels during the early years of the 1850s. Whether, or not, such wheels were tried on *Great Western* is unknown. Certainly that form of wheel had advantages, but in rough water they soon became defective and were subsequently removed by the company. The board of managers' minute book, volume 6, with an entry on May 2 1853, indicates that the repairs to be carried out should allow two years of service within the Caribbean or on the Brazil run. In July of that year a decision was made to place the ship on the Brazil line. New waters for *Great Western* and far from those envisaged by Brunel when he conceived his ship.

Under the command of Captain Onslow and with 71 passengers on board *Great Western* left Southampton at 2.30 pm on July 9 to head south for Rio. A further trip was completed that year though not without incident, as two crew members deserted at Rio de Janeiro and another died on the passage out. Two days were lost at Rio on the first trip as the small steamer *Prince* had difficulties in obtaining coal at Monte Video whilst on passage from Buenos Aires with the mails and passengers.[23]

Passenger and cargo figures began to improve by comparison with the initial year of operations and, obviously, the Royal Mail directors were well pleased with their new, subsidised, mail operations. *Great Western* consistently carried large cargoes and passenger numbers kept up well compared with the run to the West Indies. Calls at Lisbon and Madeira produced changes in the passenger lists both outward and on return. This was particularly so for Lisbon as many Portuguese and Spanish expatriates made for or returned from their South American homes. Four round trips to Brazil were made during 1854, all without real incident and within the time allowed by the mail contract. Bad weather could, and did, cause delays though none was ever serious. Apart from the loss of a quarter boat in a gale during the first return no other damage seems to have occurred.[24] The only other incident of note took place at the end of the same trip when *Great Western* caused some damage to the schooner *Loyal* in Southampton water. The nature and extent of the damage is unknown but the repair account was charged to Captain Onslow, the Master at the time.[25]

In spite of being an efficient and valuable vessel, without any obvious major defects, it appears to have been the lot of *Great Western* to be constantly up for sale. Scourged by financial difficulties her original owners had her almost perpetually on the market. By the beginnings of 1854 the Royal Mail company considered themselves secure enough to attempt the disposal of some parts of their fleet. *Medway* and *Trent* were in Admiralty service as troopships, the Crimean war having broken out, but were also available for sale. *Esk, Severn* and *Great Western* appeared on the list of other vessels for which offers would be considered.[26] No offer was forthcoming and the former Bristol favourite continued on the South American line. At least for a short while.

Three well patronised trips to Rio occupied the first nine months of 1855 but *Great Western's* Atlantic wanderings ceased when she returned to Southampton on September 13 of that year. Following cargo discharge she went to an empty berth to await her fate.

Chapter 12

Finished with engines

The Crimean war posed considerable logistical problems for the British government as no garrison was stationed in the region concerned. Troops, horses, armaments and supplies all had to be shipped in and ships were the only means of transport possible for the scale of supply required. Britain's merchant fleet had always played a part in keeping open the supply lines for the forces overseas, but this war was different because steamships were available. Not only could these vessels operate independent of wind and weather, they were also larger and faster than their sail powered sisters. Because of the mail contracts the British government was able to call upon the services of a large number of steamers. Ships of the Royal Mail, Cunard and P&O companies were amongst the first to be requisitioned. Though not particularly happy with the situation the owners gave up their vessels for military duties and tried to maintain the mail services with depleted fleets. This did not prove to be as difficult as it might have been as the British government allowed some mail services to be reduced and, in any case, each of the mail companies was engaged in a new building programme. Vessels, steam and sail, from many companies joined the supply fleet, some for short periods others for the duration of hostilities. Amongst those steamers requisitioned for over a year was *Great Britain*, now rebuilt for the Australian trade.

Early in the Crimean conflict the Royal Mail Company supplied three ships for government service, these being *Orinoco*, *Trent* and *Medway*. During the evening of February 22 1854 *Orinoco* departed from Southampton, having embarked the 1st Battalion Coldstream Guards, for Constantinople. Some weeks later

Trent and *Medway* followed. The 14-day passage to the Bosphorus cannot have been pleasant for the ships were crowded, not only with people but also with horses. On her first trooping voyage *Trent* took 1,180 men of the 23rd Regiment (Royal Welsh Fusiliers). Increasing hostilities resulted in the need for further troop steamers and *Magdalena*, *Thames* and *Tamar* quickly followed their sisters into government service. It was soon discovered that the steam ships could provide valuable towing assistance for the sailing ships in their passages through the Dardanelles and most steamers generally had something in tow whilst in that stretch of water. Vessels were requisitioned to suit the needs of the government at any particular time and could be discharged from duty at any time. In the case of vessels from the Royal Mail fleet this resulted in an overhaul and refit followed by a return to service on the West Indies or South American routes. *Tamar* left government service during the middle of 1855 and following a much needed refit became part of the South American fleet; replacing *Great Western*.[1]

When *Great Western* returned to Southampton in September 1855 more than two years had elapsed since her last major drydock and overhaul. A considerable sum of money would be needed to be expended to equip the vessel for further mail and passenger operations. This the RMSPC were loathe to consider particularly as newer and faster vessels had recently entered service fulfilling all immediate requirements. Despite the calls of the government for troop transports the directors of the Royal Mail felt secure enough to dispense with the services of *Great Western*. Besides which, if another trooper was needed the former Bristol

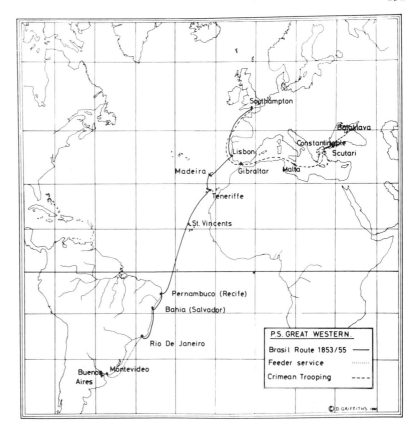

steamer would be readily available and could be easily taken up for war service.

Within a month it looked as though the call had come. In its edition of October 6 1855, *The Times* carried the brief statement that arrangements were being made for *Great Western* to be taken into government service. It further added that expectations were for the ship to convey 300 navvies and their implements to Sevastapol. Times had certainly changed for the premier Atlantic steamship. The thought of some 300 navvies 'gracing' the saloon of *Great Western* would have taken on nightmarish proportions to the enterprising Bristol citizens whose child she was, but for a while, at least, the ship's decks remained free of the boots of those who could never have afforded to purchase a passage in her. Whether another vessel was found or the need for the navvies ceased is not known, but the outcome was that *Great Western's* requisition did not

proceed. She remained at her moorings in Southampton, apparently, unwanted.

That situation changed early in 1856 when the RMSPC received orders from the Admiralty to prepare *Orinoco* and *Great Western* for the transport service.[2] The ships were to be made ready by March 2. This task was easily accomplished and both vessels lay at Southampton, on that date, fully prepared for sea. Officially *Great Western* entered the transport service with the Admiralty on March 1 1856. Her owners being recompensed at the rate if £1 18s per ton per month.[3] Based upon a quoted nett tonnage of 1,154 this represented earnings of almost £2,200 per month. The Royal Mail Steam Packet Company had to provide the crew, and pay them, but the Admiralty found the coal. Even taking account of wages and the victualing bill there must have been a substantial profit from the charter, a charter readily entered into as the vessel was surplus to requirements and actually costing money to keep laid-up in harbour.

Preparation for the transport service entailed, as it did for vessels at later times in history, the removal of normal passenger luxuries, such as carpets and curtains. Saloons and cabins gave way to austere dormitories which contained rather primitive sleeping facilities; the same space probably also served for dining and recreation purposes. It is certain that the massed military did not enjoy food to the same standard as the previous occupants. The catering establishment being altered to suit the changed circumstances. An essential item of military equipment of the period was the horse, no army going anywhere without its cavalry. For ease of shipment and convenience of care the animals would be housed, on the upper deck, in specially built boxes. Exercise for the horses would be impossible and also undesirable as a moving deck is not the safest surface for any animal. Bad weather, coupled with the inexperience of the seamen in handling horses, often took its toll of the poor creatures. Woolward, in his autobiography, relates one incident when, in 1855, *Medway* was acting as a troop and horse transport. In May of that year they had on board some 221 horses, together with officers and men, belonging to X Battery of Royal Artillery. Extremely rough weather in the Bay of Biscay, aggravated by the extra weight on the upper deck due to the horses and their boxes, caused the vessel to roll heavily. Seasick troopers were unable to handle the horses and the task fell to the inexperienced seamen. Next day, after the storm abated, 67 horses were dead and many more lame.[4]

Throughout the day of March 11 1856 Southampton docks echoed to the clatter of horses hooves and raucous orders of command as *Great Western*, now No 6 transport, took on board her new cargo; the type of cargo never imagined by Claxton or Brunel. By the time the ship sailed she provided a temporary home for one officer, 20 men and 45 horses of the Royal Artillery, 13 officers from the Royal Engineers, 300 sappers and miners, together with an assortment of military individuals.[5] The following morning *Great Western* sailed for new waters to the east. Like her Royal Mail sister *Medway* she experienced severe gales in the Bay of Biscay, the storm being at its height during the night of March 15 and 16. So bad was the pounding of the waves that structural damage resulted. Most could be readily

repaired by the ship's crew but the split rudder could not and necessitated a call at Gibraltar where extensive facilities were available. Three of the horses on board died as a result of injuries received during the storm.[6]

Repairs at Gibraltar presented no difficulty but occupied three days from March 20 until the 23rd. Due to this *Great Western* ceased to earn money for her owners, the government deducting £221 15s from the amount due to the RMSPC for the charter. This represented the days lost in repairing the vessel.[7] Following repairs and, no doubt, a much needed run ashore for the troops on board, *Great Western* proceeded on her voyage east. A five-day stop at Malta allowed coal to be taken on and some of the passengers to leave. The final leg of the outward voyage took the former Atlantic liner to Constantinople. Unfortunately the exact movements do not appear to have been recorded but visits to Scutari and Balaklava are highly probably. Returning from the Black Sea *Great Western* called at Malta on April 20 1856 and arrived at Portsmouth on May 4. Although the contemporary media made no reference to passengers taking the homeward passage it is almost certain that some injured servicemen were carried. This was the common practice for the returning transports and *The Times* of May 9 indicated that 250 sick and wounded invalids had recently arrived home.

Following rapid bunkering and victualling *Great Western* left Portsmouth on May 9, for her second voyage to the Black Sea. Again there is no indication of the passengers carried, if any. The recent cessation of hostilities in the Crimea removed the necessity for further troops and so, at most, only a few passengers can have made the trip. With an intermediate stop at Malta, *Great Western* again made for Scutari and Balaklava. She left Malta on May 20 and must have made Constantinople about five or six days later on May 25 or 26. *Great Britain* was in those same waters at the time, arriving at Malta from Constantinople on May 28.[8] The possibility that *Great Western* encountered her younger sister, for the last time, in the warm waters of the Aegean is romantic but not too fanciful. Regretably no records are available. It is unlikely that any on board either vessel would have been aware of the significance of such an encounter as both ships had long since changed owners and, to some extent, appearance. During her passage through the Black Sea *Great Western* made calls at Scutari and Balaklava picking up

21 officers, 411 men, 55 horses and 15 tons of baggage belonging to the 3rd, 8th and 12th Battalions of Royal Artillery. Leaving Balaklava on May 30, following calls at Constantinople, Malta and Gibraltar the returning ship arrived off Spithead on June 23. The next morning *Great Western* went alongside the dockyard jetty to disembark her final passengers. Following this she was paid off from the transport service and made the short trip up Southampton Water to her home port.[9]

After a short period alongside the wharf *Great Western* moved to a mooring out in the stream. She joined the steamer *Severn*, also apparently unwanted. Both ships had been discharged from the transport service in June and both were in poor condition; so poor, in fact, that 'the Directors did not feel justified in giving into such extensive repairs as required to render them efficient for the mail service'.[10] Throughout July the ships lay at their moorings awaiting their fate. It was unlikely that a buyer would be found willing to fit *Great Western* for further service and such was the case. Early in August the RMSPC accepted an offer of £11,550 for both ships as they lay.[11] The purchaser, a Mr I. Marks of Greenwich.[12]

Directories for the Greenwich area indicate that Israel Marks ran an established brass foundry and iron merchants business in Bridge Street. The firm had a yard and wharf at Copperas Ground, later renamed Bridge Wharf, a short distance up the River Ravensbourne from the Thames.[13] In purchasing the two redundant steamers Mr Marks was obviously interested in the considerable quantity of ferrous and non-ferrous metal they contained. The copper sheathing and pipework together with the brass fittings must have been worth a considerable sum.

Severn left Southampton for the Thames during the morning of August 7[14] whilst *Great Western* was prepared for departure a few days later. Her prior owners are likely to have removed any items of further use to themselves, such as the plate and crockery. The sails were almost certainly taken ashore after the final arrival at Southampton as these would represent a considerable investment and could be utilised aboard one of the other ships in the fleet. This presented a problem, how were the vessels to reach the Thames? Engines and boilers must have been in a reasonably fit state and operable but the cost of providing sufficient men to operate the plant for the short trip to Greenwich

would be prohibitive. Towage offered the most reasonable option and, as far as *Great Western* is concerned, was the method employed. Departure from Southampton took place early on August 12,[15] the timing being arranged so as to gain maximum assistance from the tide. It must have been a rather undignified end to a spectacular career and a sad sight to any who witnessed it and was aware of the significance. Such a difference to the sight almost nineteen years previously when, under canvas, *Great Western* had raced up that same stretch of water on her way to London to received her engines.

The Times for August 14 1856 contains the final media reference to *Great Western* during her operational service, at least as far as the author has been able to ascertain. In the shipping column of that day's edition is the simple statement: 'Deal, Thursday; Passed Deal *Great Western*, screw steamer, (in tow) from Southampton for River'. Referring to the ship as a screw steamer the correspondent was certainly in error but his observations may have been confused if the paddle wheels had been removed in order to reduce the drag effect during the towing operation. Assuming that the tides were satisfactory and that the berth was available *Great Western* must have reached Israel Marks' wharf at Greenwich sometime that weekend. This was not, however, to be her final berth.

Throughout the succeeding months the boilers, engines and most metal fittings would be removed. An arduous and time consuming task before the advent of the oxy-acetylene burner. With the vessel lying on the mud at low tide the copper sheathing could be stripped from the hull and all ship's side valves removed. Following the latter task the holes left had to be plugged if the hull was to remain water tight. Having removed all of the metal he could, Israel Marks had no further use for the hulk, indeed, it was probably an embarrassment as it occupied his only wharf. Disposal to a shipbreaker, Henry Castle, solved the problem. Castle's yard was at Millbank, Vauxhall, near the site now occupied by the Tate Gallery, and a number of Thames bridges barred the way to the passage of larger vessels. Such obstacles were not, however, insurmountable as the removal of masts and the upper deck reduced the height sufficiently for a vessel to pass under the bridges at low water; not too low or the ship would ground. There are no references to the hull of *Great Western* undertaking this passage but there are for other, even larger vessels.

The Royal Mail steamer *Orinoco*, 2,901 gross tons compared with 1,775 gross tons for *Great Western*, was found to be badly affected by dry rot and disposed of in 1858. She was broken up at Castle's yard and to allow passage under the Thames bridges had her two upper decks removed at Victoria Dock.[16]

Sometime early in 1857 the hull of *Great Western* was towed up river to its final berth at Vauxhall. That final sad journey took it past the East India Dock, from where it had made its triumphal first voyage as a steam ship, and also past the Isle of Dogs' where Brunel's final engineering project, the monster steamship *Great Eastern*, towered over the River Thames and the surrounding area. Eventually in the hands of the breakers her timbers were pulled apart to be employed again for other purposes; perhaps in the structure of some building ashore or even for a smaller, less significant, ship. Good oak and other timber was in short supply and there is no evidence that the timbers of *Great Western* were in anything but good condition. She had been constructed from the best and well maintained throughout her life. It is inconceivable that she would merely provide firewood for the drawing rooms of London.

Not everyone had forgotten the ship which changed the North Atlantic sea route and maritime history. Brunel remembered and took time from his last great marine project, which was eventually to kill him, to visit her at Vauxhall. In his biography of his father, Brunel's son, Isambard, comments; 'Among those who went there to take a farewell of her before she finally disappeared was Mr Brunel; thus he saw the last of his famous ship'. The thoughts which passed through the head of that engineering genius can only be imagined. Sorrow certainly, to see his original steamer at the end of its existence and now unwanted. However, there must have been some satisfaction too that this, his ship, had done so much to change, for ever, the way in which people moved about the oceans. Finally there will have been regret that the promise of the original project had not been fulfilled. *Great Western* had played her part magnificently but subsequent events in the building and operation of her larger sister, resulted in the demise.

Little has survived of the fabric of *Great Western*, in fact until recently it was thought that nothing had survived. However, amazingly, the ship's bell still exists and is displayed by the Great Britain Project, near the SS Great Britain, at the Great Western Dock, Bristol. This bell was donated to the project by the South Eastern Electricity Board in October 1972.[17] It came into the possession of the Board's predecessor, the London and Home Counties Joint Electricity Authority, when that Authority took over Bursford Lodge, near Dorking, Surrey.[18] Exactly how the bell reached that location is unknown but, fortunately, it did and has survived as the only, known, relic from the ship itself. A number of log books and other documents relating to *Great Western* are still extant and these have been mentioned throughout the text. It is sad that more does not remain of this remarkable vessel but the pace of maritime advancement which *Great Western*, itself, accelerated probably resulted in the achievements and importance of the early steamships being overlooked. Indeed, it is only by the fortuitous hulking of Brunel's *Great Britain* in the Falkland Islands and the dedication and persistence of a few men, that we can still view that ship today.

In retrospect it is relatively easy to appreciate the significance of steam in terms of maritime evolution, particularly on the North Atlantic. Steamships quickly monopolised the lucrative passenger and mail services eventually ousting sail almost completely. Nobody could have foreseen that a parallel situation would exist in the 1960s when the jet airliner forced the passenger ship from the North Atlantic route. Although steam services would have, eventually, replaced those by sailing ship between the old and new worlds, *Great Western* hastened the change. Certainly steamships had operated in coastal waters for a number of years prior to 1838 and, at least two other schemes were instigated at the time that the Great Western Steam Ship Company proposed its own service from Bristol. There had even been earlier, less substantive, propositions. Neglecting the role played by *Sirius* as it was not a serious contender, there were three steamers available for the 'North Atlantic Steamship Trials' held during the years 1838 and 1839. Upon the results of these unofficial trials depended the immediate future of a steamer service across the Atlantic and, more importantly, the possibility of a mail contract on this and other routes.

Great Western, British Queen and *Liverpool* showed their paces and were judged accordingly. The performance of the Bristol ship has been covered in depth whilst brief accounts of the operations of the other vessels have been laid out in a previous chapter. Without going into detailed comparisons again it is obvious that *Great Western* was the better of the three in terms of reliability and performance. Only after the first year of successful operation by *Great Western* was the government prepared to consider the granting of a steamer mail contract. Had the Bristol ship not been so reliable, or had it not existed, a mail contract is unlikely to have been considered at that time. Certainly not on the evidence of the performances turned in by *British Queen, Liverpool* and, later, by *President. Great Western* provided the bench-mark by which all other steamers would be judged and all early contemporaries fell well short of that mark.

It is no accident that the initial vessels ordered by the two oceanic mail contractors, Cunard and the RMSPC, were very similar, in size, power and speed, to *Great Western*. After all, it would have been naive, and not a little stupid, of the contractors to divert from a tried and proven design in order to experiment and, possibly, fail. Those early ships were no improvement on *Great Western* though they were designed and constructed a number of years later. In a variety of respects the mail ships actually fell below the standards set by Brunel and those who collaborated in the design and construction of the Bristol ship. Internal decoration could not be matched, indeed Cunard made no attempt to do so. The smaller Cunard ships were less powerful and, generally, not as fast, whilst the RMSPC vessels of similar size and power could not match *Great Western* for speed, at least when she was new. Structural strength and stability were characteristics in which Brunel's ship was unsurpassed. It is unlikely that many other contemporary vessels would have confronted the storm of September 1846, described earlier, and survived with as little damage as did *Great Western*. It is an unfortunate

fact that due credit is not always given to the designers, builders, owners and operators of *Great Western* whenever maritime history is discussed. The reason probably lies in the fact that all of the early mail contractors survived and prospered whilst the Great Western Steam Ship Company had a relatively short and unsuccessful existence. In the famous Cunard liners, culminating in the *Queen Mary, Queen Elizabeth* and *Queen Elizabeth II,* a legend grew up inculcating superiority. Though these latter day liners were, certainly, better than their contemporaries that is not true of the first ships. However, such is success. It is to be regretted, though, that all due credit is not awarded to those associated with *Great Western* and to the ship itself. In most general history books the section covering shipping or trade refers to Cunard's *Britannia* as the vessel opening the Atlantic steamer service; no mention is made of the contribution from Bristol. Such neglect this book has endeavoured to amend.

For all of its innovation and quality *Great Western* possessed a major weakness and only Brunel, Thomas Guppy and, perhaps, a few other individuals were aware of it. In being so good and successful *Great Western* terminated that branch of steamship evolution. It was the end of a short, but very important, line. There could be no other major improvements in the design of wooden, ocean going paddle steamers. Though larger and faster ships came along they were not stronger, nor were they an advancement in ship design. *Great Western* was, in effect, the first and last of the line; those which followed were merely variations. Brunel recognised that important fact and set about redirecting steamship evolution. His next ship, *Great Britain*, introduced the iron hull and screw propellor to oceanic transportation. The riveted iron hull has only been superseded by better joining techniques, welding, and a better material, steel. The screw propeller has remained in universal use since that time.

Appendix 1

Maudslay's specification for marine steam engines from Mr Field, 1836

'A pair of Marine Steam Engines made from the best materials and workmanship and upon the latest and most approved construction the general dimensions being as follows:

The cylinder to be 70 inches diameter, and the stroke 7 feet every part being in proper proportion, the piston to be metallic.

The whole to be framed very strongly upon Foundation plates or platforms of Iron.

All the Cross-heads, Connecting rods, and side rods throughout to be of wrought Iron.

Also the crank throws, the Crank, and the Paddle Shafts of the same material.

The Barrels of the Air pumps to be lined with Gun Metal, the Buckets, the rods, the foot of the discharge valves to be of the same material, the packing of the air pump bucket to be tightened down by screws.

All the pipes and cocks through the bottom of the Ship under water, to be most securely constructed, and wholly of Gun Metal.

The Steam pipes, feed, bilge, and blowing off pipes to be of strong Copper, and all cocks or valves of Brass.

The boiler to be upon the most improved construction with reference to economy of Coal, and formed of the best Iron.'

The above information is taken from the 'Facts Book' page 5, in the Brunel Collection held at Bristol University. Spelling and punctuation as in the original. Courtesy of the Librarian, University of Bristol.

Appendix 2
Crew lists for steamship *Great Western*

First voyage beginning at Bristol, April 7 1838

Master	J. Hosken	Stokers and trimmers	Thompson
Mate	B. Matthews		Hummerston
Deck Officers	Tollevy		Wheatley
	Berry		Merney
	Phillips		Rowland
Carpenter	J. Brooking		Tillett
Joiner	Stone		Porter
Bos'un	Payne (?)		Smith
Seamen	McCullin		Wacket
	Carr		Bannon
	Henderson (?)		Scully
	plus about 10 others		Raid
Boy	Allan		Crooks
Pilot for Irish coast	(?)		Edwards
Cook	(?)		Grell
Baker	(?)		
Stewardess	(?)		
Stewards	(?)		
Chief Engineer	G. Pearne		
2nd Engineer	W. Roberts		
Assistant Engineers	S. Edwards		
	C. Henderson		
	M. Julyan		

The above list has been compiled through references to:

a *Logs of the First Voyage of the Steamship Great Western* By C. Claxton.

b *The Steamship Great Western* by Grahame Farr, published by the Bristol Historical Association.

c Articles of Agreement for the second voyage held at the PRO, Kew.

Crew list for voyage No 23 (Bristol/New York/Liverpool)
Signing on at Bristol, March 28 1842:

J. Hosken	Master
B. Matthews*	1st Mate
N. Thomas	2nd Mate
T. Guollam	3rd Mate
T. Stafford	4th Mate
G. King	Bos'un
W. Shaffey	Carpenter
R. Hall	Carp' Mate
C. Howell	Seaman

J. Luscombe	Seaman		T. Reardon	Fireman
C. Whilling	Seaman		H. Taylor	Fireman
W. Soper	Seaman		A. Calrat	Fireman
T. Phillips	Seaman		T. Legg	Fireman
G. Howe	Seaman		J. Hellman	Fireman
J. Saland	Seaman		J. Beke	Fireman
N. Nicholas	Seaman		M. Carrol	Trimmer
J. Rees	Seaman		T. Hara	Trimmer
T. Dick	Cook		W. Wiston	Trimmer
H. Bowden§	Cook's Mate		W. Comer	Trimmer
L. Jones	Ordinary Seaman		W. Dunsphy	Trimmer
T. Stayter	Ordinary Seaman		T. Horton	Trimmer
G. Hook	Ordinary Seaman		J. Harral	Trimmer
J. Hallard	Ordinary Seaman		J. Seaborn	Trimmer
J. Dooey	Painter		G. Parry	Apprentice
H. Lewis	Boy		C. Hooper	Apprentice
J. Lewis	Steward		T. Mather	Apprentice
W. Roberts	1st Engineer		T. Gailard	Apprentice
J. Willians	2nd Engineer			
P. Cavanagh	3rd Engineer			
R. Hutchinson	4th Engineer			
H. Egan	5th Engineer			
J. Reid	Blacksmith			
J. Porter	Fireman			
H. Pollock	Fireman			
J. Quish	Fireman			
M. Dee	Fireman			

§H. Bowden, Cook's Mate, deserted whilst at New York

*B. Matthews, 1st Mate, performed the signing off duty at Liverpool on May 11 1842, as the Master, J. Hosken, was confined to his bed.

The above information is derived from the Articles of Agreement for the voyage held at the Public Record Office, Kew.

The crew lists for voyages No 23 and 43 have been selected as examples because the log books for both voyages still exist. That for voyage No 23 at the City of Bristol Museum and that for voyage No 43 at the Central Library, Bristol.

Crew list for voyage No 43 (Liverpool/New York/Liverpool) July-Sept' 1846

Name	Age	Position	Monthly pay		
			£	s	d
B.R. Matthews	43	Master			
Henry Brown	25	Mate	14	0	0
. . . Guilland	27	2nd Mate	7	7	0
James O'Farrel	24	3rd Mate	5	5	0
Christopher Hooper	19	4th Mate	3	0	0
John Courtenay	34	Surgeon			
Henry G. Taylor	27	Purser	6	0	0
George Dring	32	Bos'un	5	0	0
William Pottinger	31	Carpenter	6	0	0
Robert Hall	36	Joiner	5	5	0

George Whitney	30	AB		3	10	0
William Bronham	35	AB		3	10	0
William Hixson	34	AB		3	10	0
George Dans	33	AB		3	10	0
William Dacy	45	AB		3	0	0
Henry Nott	27	AB		3	0	0
George Hook	23	AB		3	0	0
James Shibling	25	AB		3	0	0
John Roberts	41	AB		3	0	0
Robert Alexander	39	AB		3	0	0
William Weare	29	AB		3	0	0
John Gayes	24	AB		3	0	0
Richard Roberts	31	AB		3	0	0
John Landing	26	AB		3	0	0
John Hichins	19	OS		2	0	0
John Williams	18	OS		1	10	0
Peter Roberts	17	OS		1	10	0
Thomas Brown	40	Ship's Cook		3	0	0
John Underhill	17	Cook's Mate		1	10	0
Joseph Williams	28	Chief Engineer		5	0	0	per week
Thomas Hadden	35	2nd Engineer		15	5	0
George P. Griffiths	23	3rd Engineer		13	5	0
William Bastin	35	4th Engineer		10	15	0
John Jones	22	5th Engineer		10	15	0
Samuel Givens	34	Blacksmith		6	0	0
Walter Treat	35	Fireman		4	0	0
Thomas Philips	23	Fireman		4	0	0
Hugh Cameron	37	Fireman		4	0	0
George Keely	22	Fireman		4	0	0
Samuel Hughes	28	Fireman		4	0	0
Alexander Bruce	27	Fireman		4	0	0
Peter Garvey	27	Fireman		4	0	0
Simon Atkins	32	Fireman		4	0	0
George Hogg	23	Fireman		4	0	0
William Morton	32	Coal Trimmer		4	0	0
John Scott	49	Coal Trimmer		3	10	0
Bernard Rice	20	Coal Trimmer		3	10	0
Arthur Hall	33	Coal Trimmer		3	10	0
William Carvel	54	Coal Trimmer		3	10	0
P. . . White	37	Coal Trimmer		3	10	0
Edward Scott	27	Eng's Servant		1	10	0
Augustus Duece	28	Off's Servant		2	0	0
William Crawford	42	Head Steward		2	0	0	(per week?)
George Richards	48	2nd Steward		6	0	0
John Dower	44	Head Pantryman		4	0	0
John Waddle	29	Store Keeper		4	10	0
Frederick Pegler	23	2nd Store Keeper		1	10	0

Charles Josse	40	Waiter	3	10	0
William Crutchly	30	Waiter	3	10	0
James Connel	26	Waiter	3	10	0
William Kerney	38	Waiter	3	10	0
Thomas Franklin (of New York)	29	Waiter		$15-00	
John Lucas	21	Waiter	3	0	0
William Henry Williams	24	Waiter	2	10	0
William Sims	25	Waiter	3	0	0
Robert Sims	19	Waiter	3	0	0
Thomas Richards	22	2nd Porter	2	0	0
William Thomas	26	Head Porter	2	10	0
Jacob Darrel (from USA)	47	Cook		$15-00	
Edward Green	24	Cook	4	10	0
Augustus Gilmore	19	Cook	2	10	0
David Boscombe	36	Dishwasher	3	10	0
William Curtis	27	Butcher	3	0	0
John Jones	34	Pastry Cook		$16-00	
John Philby	21	Baker	2	0	0
Robert Parr	14	Boy		10	0
John Hawkes	27	Waiter	3	0	0
Joseph Dallington	34	Waiter	2	10	0
Thomas Rudd	30	Waiter	3	10	0
Edward Evans	18	Waiter	1	10	0
Morris Gaisley	37	Fireman	4	0	0
John Hamilton	14	Apprentice			
Charles Peters	16	Apprentice			
William O'Braddock	15	Apprentice			
William Evans	14	Apprentice			

William Morton, coal trimmer, was discharged before the ship sailed from Liverpool.
John Underhill, cook's mate, deserted at New York.

Daily allowances for food (minimum)

	Mon	Tues	Wed	Thurs	Fri	Sat	Sun
Beef lbs		1½		1½		1½	1½
Pork lbs	1½		1½		1½		
Flour lbs				1			1
Peas pints	½		½		½		
Potatoes lbs		1				1	

Bread, as much as required. Tea, ¼ oz per day. Sugar, 1½ oz per day. Cocoa, 1 oz per day. Biscuit, 1 lb per day. Vinegar, ½ pint per week. Rum, 1 gill per day. Firemen and coal trimmers to get 1 gill extra for working night watches.

Note The above daily allowances will, of necessity, have varied and been supplemented by other vegetables and fruit.

The above information is derived from the Articles of Agreement for the voyage held at the Public Record Office, Kew.

Appendix 3

The voyages of the paddle steamship
Great Western

Voyage	Sailed	Arrived	From	To	Time	Pass	Crew	Captain	Comments
a	18/8/37	22/8/37	Bristol	London					Under sail
b	31/3/38	2/4/38	London	Bristol	2d 12h			Hosken	
1	8/4/38	23/4/38	Bristol	New York	15d 10h	7	55		
	7/5/38	22/5/38	New York	Bristol	14d 0h	66	59		
2	2/6/38	17/6/38	Bristol	New York	14d 16h	57	50		
	25/6/38	2/7/38	New York	Bristol	12d 14h	91	52		
3	21/7/38	5/8/38	Bristol	New York	14d 18h	131	60		
	16/8/38	30/8/38	New York	Bristol	13d 2h	87	46		
4	8/9/38	24/9/38	Bristol	New York	16d 9h	143	55		
	4/10/38	16/10/38	New York	Bristol	12d 12h	127	48		
5	27/10/38	15/11/38	Bristol	New York	19d 0h	107	48		
	23/11/38	7/12/38	New York	Bristol	13d 6h	80	48		
c	20/12/38	20/12/38	Bristol	Milford Haven					Drydock for check and o/h
d	17/1/39	17/1/39	Mil Hav	Bristol					
6	28/1/39	16/2/39	Bristol	New York	18d 20h	104	48		
	25/2/39	12/3/39	New York	Bristol	14d 12h	36	48		
7	23/3/39	14/4/39	Bristol	New York	22d 6h	104	48		
	22/4/39	7/5/39	New York	Bristol	15d 0h	113	48		
8	18/5/39	31/5/39	Bristol	New York	13d 12h	107	48		
	13/6/39	26/6/39	New York	Bristol	13d 6h	115	48		
9	6/7/39	22/7/39	Bristol	New York	16d 0h	114	48		
	1/8/39	13/8/39	New York	Bristol	12d 10¼h	64	48		
10	24/8/39	10/9/39	Bristol	New York	16d 20h	113	48		
	21/9/39	4/10/39	New York	Bristol	13d 0h	43	49		
11	19/10/39	2/11/39	Bristol	New York	14d 22h	137	48		Drydock Bristol at end of trip
	16/11/39	30/11/39	New York	Bristol	13d 10h	31	48		

Voyage	Sailed	Arrived	From	To	Time	Pass	Crew	Captain	Comments
12	20/2/40	7/3/40	Bristol	New York	15d 7h	77	48	Hosken	
	19/3/40	2/4/40	New York	Bristol	14d 4h	52	48		
13	15/4/40	3/5/40	Bristol	New York	17d 20h	100	48		
	9/5/40	23/5/40	New York	Bristol	14d 2h	137	51		
14	4/6/40	18/6/40	Bristol	New York	14d 18h	85	48		
	1/7/40	14/7/40	New York	Bristol	13d 12h	152	48		
15	25/7/40	9/8/40	Bristol	New York	14d 23h	97	48		
	18/8/50	31/8/40	New York	Bristol	13d 1h	69	48		
16	12/9/40	27/9/40	Bristol	New York	15d 7h	54	48		
	10/10/40	23/10/40	New York	Bristol	13d 6h	97	48		
17	7/11/40	24/11/40	Bristol	New York	16d 12h	40	48		Drydock Bristol
	9/12/40	23/12/40	New York	Bristol	14d 9h	70	48		at end of trip
18	8/4/41	23/4/41	Bristol	New York	15d 12h	44	48		
	1/5/41	14/5/41	New York	Bristol	13d 1h	94	48		
19	27/5/41	10/6/41	Bristol	New York	14d 12h	42	48		
	19/6/41	3/7/41	New York	Bristol	14d 2h	81	48		
20	14/7/41	29/7/41	Bristol	New York	15d 2h	98	48		
	7/8/41	20/8/41	New York	Bristol	12d 10h	68	48		
21	1/9/41	16/9/41	Bristol	New York	15d 10h	111	45		
	25/9/41	8/10/41	New York	Bristol	12d 13h	43	48		
22	23/10/41	8/11/41	Bristol	New York	16d 12h	127	48		Drydock Bristol
	23/11/41	6/12/41	New York	Bristol	13d 5h	30	48		at end of trip
23	2/4/42	17/4/42	Bristol	New York	15d 4h	69	48		To Liverpool
	28/4/42	11/5/42	New York	Liverpool	12d 7½h	77	55		lightship
24	21/5/42	4/6/42	Liverpool	New York	14d 2½h	64	45		
	16/6/42	29/6/42	New York	Bristol	12d 12h	99	48		
25	16/7/42	30/7/42	Bristol	New York	14d 1½h	65	48		
	11/8/42	24/8/42	New York	Liverpool	12d 19h	70	50		
26	3/9/42	17/9/42	Liverpool	New York	14d 10h	97	49	Hosken	
	29/9/42	12/10/42	New York	Bristol	13d 4h	35	48		
27	22/10/42	6/11/42	Bristol	New York	15d 8h	109	48		
	17/11/42	30/11/42	New York	Liverpool	12d 15h	29	46		
e		4/12/42	Liverpool	Bristol					
28	11/2/43	12/3/43	Bristol	New York	29d 1h	52	48		Via Madeira
	16/3/43	1/4/43	New York	Liverpool	15d 11h	24			Touched shoal
									leaving New York
f	4/4/43	6/4/43	Liverpool	Mil. Hav.					Drydock inspection
g	17/4/43	18/4/43	Mil. Hav.	Liverpool					

Voyage	Sailed	Arrived	From	To	Time	Pass	Crew	Captain	Comments
29	29/4/43	11/5/43	Liverpool	New York	12d 18h	60	45		
	25/5/43	8/6/43	New York	Liverpool	13d 8h	126	40		
30	17/6/43	1/7/43	Liverpool	New York	13d 16h	67	49		
	13/7/43	26/7/43	New York	Liverpool	12d 21h	104	40		
31	5/8/43	21/8/43	Liverpool	New York	15d 16h	124	50		
	31/8/43	14/9/43	New York	Liverpool	13d 8h	73	40		
32	23/9/43	7/10/43	Liverpool	New York	14d 4h	136	40		
	19/10/43	1/11/43	New York	Liverpool	12d 17h	99	43		
h	3/11/43	5/11/43	Liverpool	Bristol	30h				Winter o/h
j	12/6/44	14/6/44	Bristol	Liverpool				Matthews	Unsuccessful sale to P&O
33	22/6/44	6/7/44	Liverpool	New York	14d 20h	33	40		
	20/7/44	4/8/44	New York	Liverpool	14d 20h	66	40		
34	17/8/44	31/8/44	Liverpool	New York	14d 5h	135	46		
	14/9/44	29/9/44	New York	Liverpool	15d 8h	30	42		
35	12/10/44	26/10/44	Liverpool	New York	14d 10h	139	42		
	9/11/44	23/11/44	New York	Liverpool	13d 21h	31	42		
k			Liverpool	Bristol					Winter o/h
l	28/3/45		Bristol	Liverpool					
36	29/3/45	16/4/45	Liverpool	New York	17d 18h	90	76	Matthews	
	24/4/45	8/5/45	New York	Liverpool	14d 6h	141	75		
37	17/5/45	1/6/45	Liverpool	New York	14d 18h	64	84		
	12/6/45	27/6/45	New York	Liverpool	14d 22h	96	71		
38	5/7/45	21/7/45	Liverpool	New York	15d 17h	132	74		
	31/7/45	18/8/45	New York	Liverpool	18d 6h	69	74		
39	23/8/45	9/9/45	Liverpool	New York	17d 5h	145	70		
	18/9/45	3/10/45	New York	Liverpool	15d 8h	49	79		
40	11/10/45	27/10/45	Liverpool	New York	16d 15h	130	84		
	6/11/45	21/11/45	New York	Liverpool	14d 11h	50	104		
m	23/11/45	24/11/45	Liverpool	Bristol	33h				Winter o/h
n		10/4/46	Bristol	Liverpool					
41	11/4/46	28/4/46	Liverpool	New York	17d 0h	120	84		
	7/5/46	**21/5/46**	New York	Liverpool	13d 18h	128	83		
42	30/5/46	15/6/46	Liverpool	New York	16d 0h	109	84		
	25/6/45	10/7/46	New York	Liverpool	14d 12h	92	79		
43	25/7/46	10/8/46	Liverpool	**New York**	15d 12h	138	84		
	20/8/46	3/9/46	New York	Liverpool	14d 2h	75	84		
44	12/9/46	30/9/46	Liverpool	New York	18d 0h	126	84		Severe gales
	8/10/46	24/10/46	New York	Liverpool	15d 12h	64	84		

Voyage	Sailed	Arrived	From	To	Time	Pass	Crew	Captain	Comments
45	31/10/46	16/11/46	Liverpool	New York	16d 12h	96	84		
	26/11/46	12/12/46	New York	Liverpool	16d 0h	30	84		
p	19/12/46		Liverpool	Bristol					Laid up

Sold to West Indies Royal Mail Steam Packet Company

Voyage	Sailed	Arrived	From	To	Time	Pass	Crew	Captain	Comments
r	29/4/47	1/5/47	Bristol	S'thampton				Vincent	
46	2/6/47		S'thampton	W.Indies(b)		33		Abbott	Via Madeira
	15/8/47	5/9/47	W.Indies	S'thampton	19d	49	96		Via Bermuda

Drydocked and overhauled at Southampton. Spar deck and new boilers fitted

Voyage	Sailed	Arrived	From	To	Time	Pass	Crew	Captain	Comments
47	2/2/48		S'thampton	W.Indies		47	93	Chapman	Called at New York
		19/8/48	W.Indies	S'thampton		53	86		on way home
s	26/8/48	27/8/48	S'thampton	London				Moss	Drydocked at
t	16/9/48	17/9/48	London	S'thampton					Pitchers yard Northfleet
48	2/10/48		S'thampton	W.Indies(h)		80	96	Moss	Via Bermuda
		22/12/48	W.Indies	S'thampton		23	92	Chapman	Came home instead of Thames
49	17/1/49		S'thampton	W.Indies(b)		96	94	Clark	Via Madeira
		24/4/49	W.Indies	S'thampton		47	97	Wolffe	
u	5/5/49	6/5/49	S'thampton	London				Wolffe	Drydocked at
v	23/5/49	24/5/49	London	S'thampton					Pitchers
50	2/6/49		S'thampton	W.Indies(h)		37		Wolffe	Via Bermuda
	1/1/50	20/1/50	W.Indies	S'thampton	19d	23			

Overhauled at Southampton

Voyage	Sailed	Arrived	From	To	Time	Pass	Crew	Captain	Comments
51	18/2/50		S'thampton	W.Indies(b)		39	94	Wolffe	Largest cargo yet
	15/5/50	2/6/50	W.Indies	S'thampton		74	94		taken by the company's ships
52	2/7/50		S'thampton	W.Indies(b)		26	96	Wolffe	Via Bermuda
		18/9/50	W.Indies	S'thampton		31	96		
53	1/10/50		S'thampton	W.Indies(b)		97		Wolffe	Struck reef near
	19/4/51	8/5/51	London	S'thampton	18d	122			Pt Aguiya (Santa Marta)
w	10/5/51	11/5/51	S'thampton	London				Wolffe	Drydocked at
x	20/5/51	21/5/51	London	S'thampton					Pitchers
54	2/6/51	21/6/51	S'thampton	W.Indies	19d	53		Brown	Called Fayal for
	19/10/51	10/11/51	W.Indies	S'thampton	21d	55		Wooley	coal 3/11/51
55	2/12/51	22/12/51	S'thampton	W.Indies	20d	85	101		
	23/2/52	18/3/52	W.Indies	S'thampton	23d	63	99		
56	2/4/52	23/4/52	S'thampton	W.Indies	21d	71		Wooley	Yellow Fever in

Voyage	Sailed	Arrived	From	To	Time	Pass	Crew	Captain	Comments
	2/4/53	22/4/53	W.Indies	S'thampton	19d	80		Jellicoe	West Indies. One death on board
			Drydocked and repaired at Southampton						
57	9/7/53		S'thampton	Rio		71	95	Onslow	
	15/8/53	14/9/53	Rio	S'thampton		90	94		
58	10/10/53		S'thampton	Rio		107	98	Hast	Two crew deserted, one deceased
	15/11/53	17/12/53	Rio	S'thampton		34	95		
59	9/1/54	7/2/54	S'thampton	Rio		42		Bevis	
	14/2/54	16/3/54	Rio	S'thampton		32			
60	10/4/54		S'thampton	Rio		33	96	Bevis	
	16/5/54	14/6/54	Rio	S'thampton		137	96		
61	10/7/54		S'thampton	Rio		59	94	Bevis	
	15/8/54	12/9/54	Rio	S'thampton		49	96		
62	9/10/54		S'thampton	Rio		117		Bevis	
	14/11/54	16/12/54	Rio	S'thampton		65	96	Bevis	
63	9/1/55		S'thampton	Rio		92	105		
	14/2/55	19/3/55	Rio	S'thampton		92	112		
64	9/4/55		S'thampton	Rio		64		Bevis	
	15/5/55	15/6/55	Rio	S'thampton		176	112		
65	9/7/55		S'thampton	Rio		81		Bevis	
	14/8/55	13/9/55	Rio	S'thampton		98	96		

W.Indies (b) — West Indies entry port at Barbados
W.Indies (h) — West Indies entry port at Havana

Note On South America run the ships called at Lisbon, Madeira, Teneriffe, St Vincents, Permambuco and Bahia on the way to Rio. These ports were visited in the reverse order on the return passage.

The *Great Western* was now laid up at Southampton before being taken into government service as *Transport No 6.*

Trooping voyages under the command of Captain Baynton

Voyage	Sailed	Arrived	From	To	Comments
66	12/3/56	20/3/56	Southampton	Gibraltar	Bad Storm
	24/3/56	28/3/56	Gibraltar	Malta	
			Malta	Constantinople	
				Balaklava	
				Scutari	
				Constantinople	
		21/4/56		Malta	
	21/4/56	4/5/56	Malta	Portsmouth	

Voyage	Sailed	Arrived	From	To	Time	Pass	Crew	Captain	Comments
67		20/5/56		Portsmouth	Malta				
	20/5/56	Malta		Constantinople					
				Balaklava					
				Scutari					
				Constantinople					
		6/6/56			Malta				
	7/6/56	24/6/56		Malta	Portsmouth				
y	24/6/54	24/6/56		Portsmouth	Malta				
		Laid up at Southampton awaiting sale							
z	12/8/56	14/8/56 (off Deal)		Southampton	London (Greenwich)			Under tow	

Appendix 4

Particulars of *Great Western*

Length overall	236 ft
Length between perpendiculars	212 ft
Length of keel	205 ft
Breadth in clear of paddle wheels	35 ft 4 in
Breadth over paddle-boxes	59 ft 8 in
Depth of hold	23 ft 2 in
Measured tonnage	1,340 ft
Length of after saloon deck	75 ft
Length of lower deck (aft)	73 ft
Length of fore cabin deck	59 ft
Length of engine-room	72 ft

Displacement

	Ft	in		Tons	cwt	qrs	lbs
At	6	8	Draught of	694	8	0	12
At	10	0	water at	1202	9	3	18
At	13	4	launching	1750	6	0	25
At	16	8		2305	4	0	23

Details from registry certificates

Date	2/9/1837	1/6/1847	5/1/1848	21/9/1848	28/5/1849
Certificate Number	33/1837	201/1847	7/1848	342/1848	166/1849
Registered Number					13981
Length in feet	207 1/10	207 1/10	210	207 1/10	210
Breadth in feet	31 8/10	31 8/10	32 2/10	32 6/10	32 2/10
Depth of hold in feet	23 1/10	23 1/10	29 6/10	23 1/10	30 6/10
Tonnage	11				
Rule of 1773	705 11/94				
Act of 1835	679 1414/3500	798 1414/3500	1155 1795/3500	898 1/10	1153 7/10
Length of ER in feet	80 4/10	65 7/10	58 5/10	58 3/10	58 3/10

Tonnage of ER	641 175/924	522 3/10	623 260/924	475 1/10	621 5/10
Place	Bristol	London	London	London	London

Note Length is from inner part of main stem to fore part of stern post aloft. The final certificate, 166/1849, is endorsed: 'Said to be broken up, Registry closed. Certificate being delivered up by owner for this purpose 8/2/1858.'

Materials

	Tons	cwt	qrs	lbs
Oak 16,592 ft³ at 58 lb/ft³	429	12	1	4
Elm 3,340 ft³ at 37½ lb/ft³	74	11	0	8
Hard pine 12,431 ft³ at 40 lb/ft³	221	19	2	16
Yellow pine 4,339 ft³ at 34½ lb/ft³	71	5	3	0
Oakum, pitch, tar, paint, etc,	6	10	0	0
Iron-work, copper and composition, to hull	60	0	0	0
Carvings at bows and stern	0	12	0	0
Water closets, lead work, pumps, etc,	2	10	0	0
Cooking apparatus	1	15	0	0
Cabins and furniture	24	0	0	0
Anchors and chain cables, etc,	23	0	0	0
Rigging, masts and spars	15	0	0	0
Boats	4	0	0	0
Sundries for crew and their chests	10	0	0	0
Weight of hull, masts, rigging, etc,	944	15	3	0
Water, provisions and stores for crew and 120 passengers	41	0	0	0
Passengers and luggage	16	0	0	0
Iron ballast	40	0	0	0
Coals and cargo	850	4	1	0
Engines and boilers	400	0	0	0
Water in boilers	80	0	0	0
TOTAL	2,372	0	0	0

These figures are for the ship as she appeared in April 1838

The information given is derived from *The Logs of the First Voyage between England and America by the Great Western* compiled by Christopher Claxton, and from the certificates of registry as indicated.

Appendix 5

Financial aspects of the *Great Western* steamship

	£	s	d
Cost as at Dec 31 1839	58,491	8	8
Known costs of individual items and approx costs where actual costs are not known			
Shipbuilding costs	21,373	13	10
Rigging, sails, anchors, cables etc	1,452	16	5
Machinery; boilers, engines, etc (approx)	22,500	—	—
Furniture, etc*	5,399	—	—
Kyan Process, pumps, wc's, etc	2,009	0	8
Decorations, initial stores, etc	3,758	—	—
New cabins in July 1838	2,000	—	—
New deck, accommodation for crew, repairs made in early 1840	3,155	6	4
*Furniture; cabin furniture	3,372		
bedding/table linen	1,130		
glass	434		
plate	463		
Total cost of *Great Western* as at December 31 1840	61,671	15	10

	£	s	d
Repairs and additions; known costs			
1838	2,000		
1839	367		
1840	3,155		
1841			
1842	535		
1843 (includes part cost of new boilers)	1,492		
1844 (new boilers, paddle wheels and general repairs)	9,768		
1845			
1846			
1847 sold to West India Royal Mail Steam Packet Company	25,000	0	0
Less £250 for removal to Kingroad and replacement of paddle wheels			
Cost of setting up moorings at Pill, 1838	360		

Appendix 6

Receipts, running expenses and profits

Year	No of voyages	Receipts			Expenses			Profits		
		£	s	d	£	s	d	£	s	d
1838	5	37,286	19	3	29,607	8	0	7,679	11	3
1839	6	52,338	3	4	38,883	5	5	13,454	18	11
1840	6	50,537	4	8	37,905	9	9	12,631	14	11
1841	5	33,763	5	10	28,155	15	2	5,607	10	8
1842	5	30,830	8	2	26,620	7	1	4,210	1	1
1843	5	33,406	0	4	24,054	9	3	9,351	11	1
1844	3	17,952	9	7	12,128	8	9	5,824	0	10
1845	5	35,914	10	3	23,482	10	6	12,431	19	9
1846	5	36,601	1	0	24,700	5	11	11,900	15	1

Receipts are passage money, postage and freight. Expenses include running costs, repairs, agencies, etc but not new boilers, cabins, etc.

Whilst in the service of the West India Royal Mail Steam Packet Company costs, earnings, expenses, etc, were not itemised, as the *Great Western* was just part of a large fleet. The costs attributable to the *Great Western* are, therefore, not directly available except for the following.

	£	s	d
New boilers, fixings, etc, for *Great Western* and *Severn*	12,780	18	10
Hull repairs to *Great Western* (including a new spar deck), *Trent, Clyde* and *Tay*	24,516	16	4

The *Great Western* was sold for demolition, with the *Severn*, in August 1856 to Mr Marks of Greenwich. The price was £11,550 the pair.

Appendix 7

Great Western steamship

Details of main engines, boilers and paddles

Main engine

Type: one pair of side lever engines
Maker: Maudslay, Sons & Field, London
Diameter of cylinder: 73½ inches
Length of stroke: 7 feet
Diameter of air pump cylinders: 40 inches
Stroke of air pump: 42 inches
Indicated power (approx): 750 horse power
Nominal power (approx): 450 horse power
Steam cut off: variable in ten steps from 1/6th stroke to almost full stroke
Expansion valve: double-beat or equilibrium
Revolutions per minute: 15 to 16
Length, centre of shaft to centre of cylinders: 19 feet 6 inches
Width, centre to centre of engines: 13 feet
Crankshaft diameter: 17½ inches
Width of bearings: 15 inches
Height to centre of shaft: 18 feet 6 inches
Weight of engines: 245 tons

Paddles

Type: cycloidal, fitted 1838
Diameter of paddle wheels: 28 feet 9 inches
Diameter of paddle shafts: 18¾ inches
Weight of paddle shafts: 6½ tons
Number of arms on wheels: 20
Number of floats per arm: 4
Length of floats: 10 feet

Depth of floats: No 1 (iron) 4½ inches
No 2 (wood) 12 inches
No 3 (wood) 10 inches
No 4 (wood) 8 inches
Float type: plain, fitted 1844
Number of arms on wheels: 28
Number of floats per arm: 1

Boilers

Boilers 1, fitted March 1838
Type: Flue, pressure 5 psi
Maker: Maudslay, Sons & Field, London
Number: 4
Number of furnaces on each boiler: 3
Dimensions of each boiler
Height: 16 feet 9 inches
Length: 11 feet 6 inches
Width: 9 feet 6 inches
Heating surface: 9.6 square feet per hp
Fire-grate area: 0.5 square feet per hp
Steam volume: 2.875 cubic feet per hp
(calculated on horse power of 400)
Weight: 22.5 tons
Weight of water: 20 tons
Coal consumption per horse power: 6.25 lbs (approx)

Boilers 2, fitted June 1844
Type: Tubular, pressure 12 psi
Maker: Great Western Steam Ship Company, Bristol
Number: 3 (coupled as a single unit)

Number of furnaces: 3 on each outer boiler
                    2 on the centre boiler
Overall dimensions of the combined boiler
Height: 18 feet 6 inches
Length: 24 feet
Width 12 feet 9 inches
Heating surface: 17,875 square feet per hp
Fire-grate area: 0.3625 square feet per hp
Steam volume: 3.3 cubic feet per hp
(calculated on horse power of 400)
Weight of combined boiler: 56 tons
Total weight of water: 52 tons
Coal consumption per horse power: 5.6 lbs (approx)
Iron tubes length: 8 feet
Iron tubes internal diameter: 3 inches

Boilers 3, fitted January 1848
Details of these boilers are not available, but it is possible to obtain some information from the Daily Record Book of the Royal Mail Steam Packet Company. The boilers were built by Smith & Ashby of Southampton to the drawings of Mr Mills, the Engineer of The Royal Mail Steam Packet Company. Boilers fitted in the *Trent,* a similar ship to the *Great Western*, at the same time were of the flue type and as these were made by the same company with the same designer, it is likely that the boilers of the *Great Western* were also of the flue type. The boilers in the *Great Western* operated at a pressure of 5 psi. There was a single stokehole between the boilers and as with the *Trent* it is likely that there were four boilers.

References

Chapter 1

1 H.P. Spratt, *Marine Engineering* Part II, Science Museum, p14.
2 R. Armstrong, *Powered Ships* E. Benn 1975, p47.
3 *Marine Engineer & Naval Architect* May 1950, p187.
4 ibid Armstrong, p51.
5 *United Service Magazine* Jan 1843, p7.
6 J.M. Brinnin, *The Sway of the Grand Saloon* Macmillan 1971, p10.
7 C.R.V. Gibbs, *Passenger Liners of the Western Ocean* Staples Press 1952, p25.
8 ibid Brinnin, p50.
9 ibid Brinnin, p38.
10 *Liverpool Albion* March 7 1836.
11 *Liverpool Albion* Dec 14 1835.
12 *The Times* Aug 27 1836.
13 *Civil Eng & Arch Journal* 1838, p167.

Chapter 2

1 I. Brunel, *Life of Isambard Kingdom Brunel* Longman 1870, p233.
2 R.A. Buchanan, *I.K. Brunel & Port of Bristol, Newcomen Soc Trans* vol 42, 1969, p44.
3 *Bristol Mirror* March 5 1836.
4 C. Claxton, *Logs of the First Voyage of Steamship Great Western* 1838, p60.
5 ibid Claxton, p55.
6 ibid Brunel, p233.
7 ibid Claxton, p55.
8 *Bristol Mirror,* March 5 1836.
9 Brunel Manuscript about *Great Western*, Bristol Univ. Lib. Brunel Coll.

10 ibid Claxton, p11.
11 ibid Brunel Manuscript about *Great Western*.
12 Brunel Letter Book No 1, p121, Bristol Univ Lib.
13 *Bristol Mirror* July 30, 1836.
14 Brunel Letter Book No 2, p83, Bristol Univ Lib.
15 *Bristol Mirror* July 22 1837.
16 *Bristol Mirror* July 29, 1837.
17 *Bristol Mirror* July 22 1837.
18 E. Corlett *The Iron Ship* Moonraker Press 1975, p15.
19 ibid Claxton, p57.

Chapter 3

1 G. Pattison *Shipping & the East India Docks, Mariner's Mirror* 1952, p212.
2 ibid Pattison.
3 *Civil Eng & Arch Journal* 1838, p167.
4 Private corres, Librarian of Royal Academy of Arts, Jan 29 1979.
5 Private corres, Victoria & Albert Museum, August 22 1979.
6 *Bristol Mirror* March 31 1838.
7 Berth Plan for Voyage No 7, Rail Collection, PRO Kew.
8 *The Sun* March 28 1838.
9 C. Claxton, *Logs of the First Voyage of the Steamship Great Western* p61.
10 ibid Claxton, p61.
11 *Shipping Gazette & Comm Advertiser* Jan 25 1838.
12 C. Penrose, *Cent of Atl Steam Nav, Newcomen Soc Trans,* vol 17, p169.
13 ibid Claxton, p1.

14 Brunel, *Life of I.K. Brunel* Longman 1870, p243.
15 *Mechanics Magazine* April 7 1838, vol 29, p6.
16 *Bristol Mirror* April 7 1838.
17 *Bristol Mirror* April 14 1838.
18 Directors' Report March 7 1839, Rail Collection PRO Kew.
19 R.A. Buchanan, *I.K. Brunel & Port of Bristol, Newcomen Soc Trans* vol 42, p41.

Chapter 4
1 C. Claxton *Logs of the First Voyage of the Steamship Great Western* p3.
2 I. Town, *Atlantic Steamships* Wiley 1838, p19.
3 ibid Claxton, p12.
4 ibid Claxton, p16.
5 ibid Claxton, p25.
6 Official Engineers' Log Book, Bristol Ref Lib.
7 ibid Claxton, p18.
8 ibid Claxton, p2.
9 ibid Claxton, p66.
10 ibid Claxton, p71.
11 ibid Town, p17.
12 ibid Claxton, p iv.
13 ibid Claxton, p33.
14 New York Coroner's Report June 4 1838, New York City Archives.
15 ibid Claxton, p iv.
16 ibid New York Coroner's Report.
17 *Bristol Mercury* May 26 1838.
18 *Bristol Presentements* April 9 and May 24 1838, Bristol Ref Lib.
19 *Bristol Mercury* May 26 1838.
20 ibid Town, p27.
21 *Bristol Mercury* May 26 1838.
22 J.M. Brinnin, *The Sway of the Grand Saloon* Macmillan 1971, p68.
23 ibid Town, p30.
24 ibid Town, p33.
25 ibid Town, p34.
26 ibid Claxton, p36.
27 ibid Claxton, p38.
28 ibid Claxton, p47.
29 ibid Claxton, p vi.
30 *Bristol Mirror* March 16 1839.

Chapter 5
1 *Bristol Mirror* June 9 1838.
2 *Bristol Mirror* July 14 1838.

3 *Bristol Mirror* July 28 1838.
4 *Parliamentary Papers* 1846, vol 563, p32.
5 *Bristol Mirror* March 9 1839.
6 *Bristol Mercury* March 9 1839 and *Bristol Mirror* March 9 1839.
7 *The Times* Nov 30 1838, Advert.
8 *Bristol Mirror* Sept 22 1838.
9 *Bristol Mirror* Jan 26 1839 and *The Times* Jan 30 1839.
10 Private Corres Lloyds Register of Shipping May 1 1979.
11 Directors' Report March 26 1840, Rail Collection PRO Kew.
12 *Bristol Mirror* Jan 25 1840.
13 *Bristol Mirror* Feb 4 1843.
14 *Bristol Mirror* March 16 1839.
15 Log Book for Voyage No 23, Bristol Museum.
16 J. Hosken, *Autobiographical Sketch of the Life of Admiral J. Hosken* Rodda, 1887, p17.
17 Directors' Report March 7 1839, Rail Collection PRO Kew.
18 *Mechanics Magazine* Nov 24 1838, vol 30, p114.
19 ibid ref 17.
20 *The Times* Oct 29 1838.
21 *The Times* Nov 29 1838.
22 Directors' Report March 11 1841, Rail Collection PRO Kew.
23 Directors' Report March 26 1840, Rail Collection PRO Kew.
24 ibid ref 22.
25 *Parl Papers* 1846, Vol 563, p16.
26 *The Times* Feb 22 1840.
27 *The Times* Aug 23 1841, Advert.
28 *Herapath's Railway Journal* April 15 1843, p385.
29 GWSSC Secretary's Letter Book June 22 1843, Rail Coll PRO Kew.
30 *Parl Papers* 1846, Vol 464, p5.
31 *Parl Papers* 1846, Vol 563, p9.
32 *Parl Papers* 1846, Vol 464, p21.
33 *Herapath's Railway Journal* April 1 1843.
34 *Parl Papers* 1846, Vol 563, p19.
35 ibid ref 29, but date April 10 1840.
36 ibid ref 34.

Chapter 6
1 Sir R. Seppings, *A New Principle of Constructing Ships in the Mercantile Service, Phil Trans Royal Soc* March 9 1820.

2 C. Claxton, *Logs of the First Voyage of the Steamship Great Western* p60.
3 ibid Claxton, p61.
4 Great Western SS, Engine Room Layout Drawing, Science Museum Library.
5 ibid Claxton, p61.
6 *Bristol Mirror* March 31 1838.
7 Log Books for Voyage 1 and 43 (Bristol Ref Lib) and Voyages 23 (Bristol Museum).
8 Directors' Report March 11 1841, Rail Coll PRO Kew.
9 Directors' Report March 3 1842, Rail Coll PRO Kew.
10 Directors' Report Feb 28 1843, Rail Coll PRO Kew.
11 ibid Claxton, p59.
12 ibid Claxton, p61.
13 *Mechanics Magazine* Sept 23 1837, Vol 27, p414.
14 ibid Claxton, p59.
15 ibid ref 9.
16 ibid Claxton, p II.
17 Document No Rail 1014/8, PRO Kew.
18 *Bristol Mirror* Jan 26 1839.
19 Directors' Report March 26 1840, Rail Coll PRO Kew.
20 ibid ref 8.
21 *New York Tribune* October 1 1846.
22 RMSPC Special Reports Book, p73-74, University College Library, London.
23 J. Hosken, *The Life of Adm' J. Hosken* Rodda 1887, p17.
24 ibid Claxton, p16.
25 ibid ref 22, p73.
26 ibid ref 22, p73.
27 E. Corlett, *The Iron Ship* Moonraker press 1975, p82.
28 *Bristol Presentements* June 7 1838, Bristol Ref Library.
29 Log Book for Voyage 43 Aug 12 1846, Bristol Ref Library.
30 RMSPC Managers' Daily Minute Book, Sept 8 and Oct 1 1847. University College Library, London.
31 ibid ref 30, Feb 16 1850.

General Reference:
Murray *Theory & Practice of Shipbuilding* Black 1861.

Chapter 7

1 *Civil Eng & Arch Journal* vol 5, 1842, p17.
2 RMSPC Special Reports Book, p72, Univ Col Library, London.
3 Field Papers, Science Museum Library.
4 C. Claxton, *Logs of the First Voyage of the Steamship Great Western* p11.
5 ibid ref 2, p71.
6 *United Services Magazine* June 1843, No 170, p5.
7 ibid Claxton, various pages.
8 Murray, *The Marine Engine* p19.
9 *Civil Eng & Arch Journal* vol 1, 1838, p13.
10 *The Atheneum* 1838, p234.
11 *Liverpool Mercury* April 7 1843.
12 *The Artisan* Jan 1844, p10.
13 *The Times* April 25 1849.
14 Brunel Letter Book No 1, p273, Bristol Univ Library.
15 ibid ref 14, p270.
16 *Bristol Mirror* March 28 1840.
17 Bourne, *A Treatise on the Steam Engine* Longmans 1876, p212.
18 Drawings of Boiler of Great Western, Science Museum Library.
19 Bourne, *A Treatise on the Steam Engine* Artisan Club 1846, p63-64.
20 *Pract Mech & Eng Magazine* vol 2, Nov 1842, p65.
21 Directors' Report March 14 1844, Rail Coll PRO Kew.
22 ibid ref 19.
23 ibid ref 19.
24 Directors' Report Nov 20 1840, Rail Coll PRO Kew.
25 Brunel Letter Book No 4, p171, Bristol Univ Library.
26 RMSPC Managers' Daily Minute Book, Jan 11 1848, Univ Col Lib, London.
27 Private Corres District Librarian, Southampton Lib Dec 26 1978.
28 Tredgold, *The Steam Engine* 1856, p140.
29 ibid ref 21.
30 Brunel Letter Book 2B, p13, Bristol Univ Library.

General references:
Bourne, *A Treatise on the Steam Engine*. 1846 and 1876 editions.

Robinson, *The Nautical Steam Engine Explained*
Saunders & Otley 1839.

Chapter 8

1 Liverpool Dock Co Minutes for July 12 and 19 1838, Liverpool Ref Lib.
2 *Bristol Gazette* March 10 1842.
3 Directors' Report Feb 26 1843, Rail Coll PRO Kew.
4 *The Albion* (Liverpool) May 16 1842.
5 *The Albion* (Liverpool) Aug 27 1842.
6 *The Times* Oct 24 1842.
7 *Bristol Mirror* Nov 12 1842.
8 *Bristol Mercury* Oct 22 1842.
9 GWSSC Secretary's Letter Book Jan 1843, Rail Coll PRO Kew.
10 ibid ref 3.
11 *Bristol Mirror* April 8 1843.
12 *Liverpool Mercury* April 7 1843.
13 *Herapath's Railway & Comm Journal* April 15 1843.
14 Directors' Report March 14 1844, Rail Coll PRO Kew.
15 *Parl Papers* 1846, Vol 563, p24, Question 186.
16 ibid ref 15, p31, Quest' 301-303.
17 *Parl Papers* 1846, Vol 464, p28.
18 *The Times* Oct 21 1842.
19 *Bristol Mirror* Aug 20 1842.
20 *Bristol Mirror* Nov 12 1842, July 4 1843, March 16 1844, March 8 1845 and March 7 1846.
21 *Herapath's Journal & Railway Mag* April 6 1844, p383.
22 *Herapath's Journal & Railway Mag* June 8 1844, p677.
23 *The Times* June 15 1844.
24 *Herapath's Journal & Railway Mag* June 22 1844, p736.
25 *Herapath's Journal & Railway Mag* June 22 1844, p736.
26 *Parl Papers* 1846, Vol 563, p26, Q205, and p31 Q306.
27 *Liverpool Mercury* June 21 1844.
28 Brunswick Dockmaster's Record Book 1842-46, Mersey Dock & Harbour Co.
29 ibid ref 28.
30 *Bristol Mirror* March 7 1846.

31 *Herapath's Railway & Comm Journal* Dec 2 1843, p1252.
32 ibid ref 31. Nov 18 1843, p1202-1203.
33 ibid ref 32.
34 Log Book for Voyage No 43, Bristol Ref Lib.
35 Log Books for Voyages No 23 and 43.
36 E. Corlett, *The Iron Ship* Moonraker Press 1975. p242.
37 *New York Tribune* Oct 1 1846.
38 Directors' Report March 4 1847, Rail Coll PRO Kew.

Chapter 9

1 C. Dickens, *American Notes,* Quoted in *Port Out Starboard Home* by A. Spoule, Blandford 1978.
2 Tyler, *Steam Conquers the Atlantic* p46.
3 *Parl Papers* 1846, Vol 464, p5.
4 ibid Tyler, p71.
5 ibid Tyler, p71.
6 ibid Tyler, p67.
7 ibid Tyler, p67.
8 *Mechanics Magazine* July 13 1839, p271.
9 Bourne, *A Treatise on the Steam Engine* Longmans 1876, p221.
10 *Mechanics Magazine* May 2 1840, p684.
11 *Mechanics Magazine* Jan 9 1841, p26.
12 *Mechanics Magazine* July 13 1839, p270.
13 Fincham, *A History of Naval Architecture* p316.
14 *Mechanics Magazine* Dec 11 1841.
15 *The Albion* (Liverpool) April 4 1842.
16 Gibbs, *Pass Liners of the Western Ocean* Staples Press 1952, p33.
17 *Herapath's Railway & Comm Journal* Dec 14 1839.
18 ibid Gibbs, p33.
19 ibid Tyler, p109.
20 ibid Gibbs, p39.
21 ibid Fincham, p316.
22 ibid Gibbs, p40.
23 ibid ref 3, p24 and p28.
24 ibid ref 1.

General references:
Corlett, *The Iron Ship.*
Tyler, *Steam Conquers the Atlantic.*
Gibbs, *Passenger Liners of the Western Ocean.*

Chapter 10

1 Directors' Report March 1 1849, Rail Coll PRO Kew.
2 Quoted, Brinnin, *The Sway of the Grand Saloon* p155.
3 J. Hosken, *Autobiography of Admiral J. Hosken* Rodda 1887, p19.
4 T.A. Bushell, *Royal Mail* Trade & Travel Publications 1940, p33.
5 Woolward, *Nigh on Sixty Years at Sea* p47.
6 Log Book for Voyage 23 April 27 1842, Bristol Museum.
7 ibid Woolward, p84.
8 RMSPC Regulations 1850, Nat Maritime Museum.
9 *Bristol Mirror* Dec 8 1838.
10 ibid ref 9.
11 Articles of Agreement Voyage no 43, PRO Kew.
12 RMSPC Managers' Daily Minute Book Vol 8, Feb 18 1850, Univ Col Lib, London.
13 J.M. Brinning, *The Sway of the Grand Saloon* Macmillan 1971, p156.
14 C. Claxton, *Log of the First Voyage of Steamship Great Western* p67.
15 ibid Claxton, p69.
16 ibid Hosken, p16.
17 *Bristol Mirror* March 16 1839.
18 RMSPC Special Reports Book April 1 1847, p74, Univ Col Lib, London.
19 Greenhill & Gifford, *Travel by Sea in the 19th Century* A&C Black 1972.
20 Log of Voyage No 23, May 7 1842, Bristol Museum.
21 ibid Claxton, p67.
22 ibid Woolward, p88-80.
23 ibid Woolward, p49.
24 *Bristol Mirror* Oct 22 1840.
25 *The Bristol Magazine* No 35, Aug 28 1841.
26 *Bristol Mercury* Nov 12 1842.
27 ibid ref 8.
28 ibid Woolward, p85.
29 ibid ref 8.
30 ibid ref 12, Vol 6, p205, Jan 9 1854.
31 ibid Hosken, p20.
32 ibid Woolward, p50.
33 ibid Hosken, p21.
34 Log Book Voyage No 43, Aug 28 1846 and Sept 1 1846, Bristol Ref Lib.

Chapter 11

1 *Bristol Mirror* March 13 1847.
2 RMSPC Special Reports Book April 1 1847, p72, Univ Coll Lib, London.
3 ibid ref 2, p75.
4 RMSPC Managers' Daily Minute Book Vol 7, April 17 1847.
5 ibid ref 4, May 3 1847
6 ibid ref 4, June 2 1847.
7 ibid ref 4, June 20 1847.
8 ibid ref 4, Oct 1 1847.
9 ibid ref 4, Jan 11 and 19 1848.
10 ibid ref 4, Feb 2, Aug 19 and Sept 17 1848.
11 ibid ref 4, Oct 2 1848.
12 *The Times* Dec 23 1848.
13 *The Times* April 25 1849.
14 ibid Woolward, p59.
15 ibid Woolward, p91.
16 *The Times* Jan 21 1850.
17 ibid ref 2, May 15 1851, p252-254.
18 *The Times* May 9 1851.
19 *The Times* Nov 11 1851.
20 ibid Woolward, p96.
21 *Hampshire Independent* April 30 1853.
22 ibid ref 4, May 18 1853.
23 *The Times* Sept 15 1853.
24 *The Times* Dec 19 1853.
25 ibid ref 4, Oct 31 1853.
26 RMSPC Directors' Report April 1854, Univ Col Lib, London.

General references:
RMSPC Managers' Daily Minute Books.
T.A. Bushell, *Royal Mail* Trade & Travel Publications 1940.

Chapter 12

1 *The Times* Sept 14 1855.
2 *The Times* Feb 19 1856.
3 *Return of Steam Vessels Engaged in the Transport Services, Parl Papers* 1856, Vol 345, XLI, p341.
4 Woolward, *Nigh on Sixty Years at Sea* p106.
5 *The Times* March 12 1856.
6 *The Times* April 2 1856.
7 ibid ref 3.
8 E. Corlett, *The Iron Ship* Moonraker Press 1975, p243.

9 *The Times* June 24 1856 and *Hampshire Independent* June 28 1856.

10 RMSPC Directors' Report Oct 16 1856, Univ Coll Lib, London.

11 ibid ref 10.

12 *Hampshire Independent* Aug 9 1856.

13 Private Corres Local History Librarian, London Borough of Greenwich, May 10 1979 and Aug 24 1979.

14 ibid ref 12.

15 *Hampshire Independent* Aug 16 1856.

16 T.A. Bushell, *Royal Mail* Trade & Travel Publications 1940, p99.

17 Private Corres from T. Webb, GB Project, Aug 9 1979.

18 *The Ship's Bell* (manuscript unpublished) GB Project, Bristol.

General references:

T.A. Bushell, *Royal Mail* Trade & Travel Pub 1940
Lloyds lists, various issues.

Index

Index of ships